Frommer's

PORTABLE

London
from $90 a Day

2nd Edition

by Donald Olson

W9-CFN-447

Here's what critics say about Frommer's:

"Amazingly easy to use. Very portable, very complete."

—*Booklist*

"Detailed, accurate, and easy-to-read information for all price ranges."

—*Glamour Magazine*

Wiley Publishing, Inc.

Published by:

WILEY PUBLISHING, INC.
111 River St.
Hoboken, NJ 07030-5744

ISBN 0-7645-4109-9

Editor: Christine Ryan
Production Editor: Blair J. Pottenger
Photo Editor: Richard Fox
Cartographer: Elizabeth Puhl
Production by Wiley Indianapolis Composition Services

For information on our other products and services or to obtain technical
support, please contact our Customer Care Department within the U.S. at
800-762-2974, outside the U.S. at 317/572-3993 or fax 317/572-4002.

Wiley also publishes its books in a variety of electronic formats. Some content that appears in print may not be available in electronic formats.

Manufactured in the United States of America

5 4 3 2 1

Contents

List of Maps

ABOUT THE AUTHOR

Donald Olson is a novelist, playwright, and travel writer. His sixth novel, *My Three Husbands* (written under the nom de plume Swan Adamson), was published in 2003. *Oregon Ghosts,* his play based on Oregon's legendary spirits, premiered in Portland in 2003. His plays have also been produced in London, New York, Amsterdam, and Rotterdam. Donald Olson's travel stories have appeared in the *New York Times, Travel & Leisure, Sunset, National Geographic* guides, and many other national publications. He is the author of *London For Dummies, Germany For Dummies,* and *England For Dummies,* which won the 2002 Lowell Thomas Travel Writing Award for "Best Guidebook".

AN INVITATION TO THE READER

In researching this book, we discovered many wonderful places—hotels, restaurants, shops, and more. We're sure you'll find others. Please tell us about them, so we can share the information with your fellow travelers in upcoming editions. If you were disappointed with a recommendation, we'd love to know that, too. Please write to:

Frommer's Portable London from $90 a Day, 2nd Edition
Wiley Publishing, Inc. • 111 River St. • Hoboken, NJ 07030-5744

AN ADDITIONAL NOTE

Please be advised that travel information is subject to change at any time—and this is especially true of prices. We therefore suggest that you write or call ahead for confirmation when making your travel plans. The authors, editors, and publisher cannot be held responsible for the experiences of readers while traveling. Your safety is important to us, however, so we encourage you to stay alert and be aware of your surroundings. Keep a close eye on cameras, purses, and wallets, all favorite targets of thieves and pickpockets.

FROMMER'S STAR RATINGS, ICONS & ABBREVIATIONS

Every hotel, restaurant, and attraction listing in this guide has been ranked for quality, value, service, amenities, and special features using a **star-rating system.** In country, state, and regional guides, we also rate towns and regions to help you narrow down your choices and budget your time accordingly. Hotels and restaurants are rated on a scale of zero (recommended) to three stars (exceptional). Attractions, shopping, nightlife, towns, and regions are rated according to the following scale: zero stars (recommended), one star (highly recommended), two stars (very highly recommended), and three stars (must-see).

In addition to the star-rating system, we also use **seven feature icons** that point you to the great deals, in-the-know advice, and unique experiences that separate travelers from tourists. Throughout the book, look for:

Finds	Special finds—those places only insiders know about
Fun Fact	Fun facts—details that make travelers more informed and their trips more fun
Kids	Best bets for kids and advice for the whole family
Moments	Special moments—those experiences that memories are made of
Overrated	Places or experiences not worth your time or money
Tips	Insider tips—great ways to save time and money
Value	Great values—where to get the best deals

The following **abbreviations** are used for credit cards:

AE	American Express	DISC	Discover	V	Visa
DC	Diners Club	MC	MasterCard		

FROMMERS.COM

Now that you have the guidebook to a great trip, visit our website at **www.frommers.com** for travel information on more than 3,000 destinations. With features updated regularly, we give you instant access to the most current trip-planning information available. At Frommers.com, you'll also find the best prices on airfares, accommodations, and car rentals—and you can even book travel online through our travel booking partners. At Frommers.com, you'll also find the following:

- Online updates to our most popular guidebooks
- Vacation sweepstakes and contest giveaways
- Newsletter highlighting the hottest travel trends
- Online travel message boards with featured travel discussions

Planning an Affordable Trip to London

Planning an affordable trip to one of the most expensive cities in the world is a challenge, but it's certainly not impossible, especially if you make arrangements in advance. Your trip will be much more fun—and certainly a lot smoother—if you plan it properly. This chapter is designed to help you do that, step by step.

1 The $90-a-Day Premise

Our premise is that two people traveling together can have a great time in London for only $90 a day per person. That will cover the price of a decent double room, a lunchtime refueling stop at a pub or cafe, and a fine feast at an ethnic restaurant in the evening. It's likely that you'll get a free, full breakfast at your hotel. You can do it for less than $90 if you want to, and you can definitely do it for a lot more. Included in the book are recommendations on how to do both.

2 Thirty Money-Saving Tips

PRETRIP PLANNING AND TRANSPORTATION SAVINGS

1. Information pays. Read as much as you can about London before you go. Talk to people who've been there recently. Check in with the **VisitBritain** offices in New York (see "Visitor Information," later in this chapter) for a wealth of free information.
2. Travel off-season. Airfares, hotels, and B&Bs are cheaper if you travel from late fall through early spring.
3. Shop around for your airfare. Surfing the Internet will turn up some great bargains, especially at sites like www.expedia.com, www.orbitz.com, and www.travelocity.com. **Cheap Tickets** (© **800/377-1000** or 212/570-1179; www.cheaptickets.com) sells airline seats at a substantial discount; see "Getting There," later in this chapter.

Central London

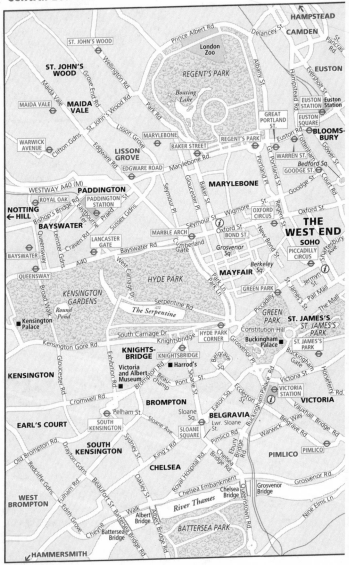

HAMPSTEAD
CAMDEN
Delancey St.
Prince Albert Rd
London Zoo
ST. JOHN'S WOOD
St. Pancras Rd
EUSTON
ST. JOHN'S WOOD
Wellington Rd
Grove End Rd
REGENT'S PARK
Albany St.
Hampstead Rd
Eversholt St.
EUSTON STATION Euston Station
MAIDA VALE
Maida Vale
St. John's Wood Rd
Boating Lake
Park Rd
GREAT PORTLAND ST.
EUSTON SQUARE
EUSTON
BLOOMS-BURY
WARWICK AVENUE
Clifton Gdns.
Edgware Rd
Lisson Grove
MARYLEBONE
REGENT'S PARK
WARREN ST.
Gt. Portland St.
Gower St.
Bedford Sq.
GOODGE ST.
Court Rd
LISSON GROVE
BAKER STREET
Gt. Titchfield St.
Portland Pl.
Tottenham Ct. Rd
Goodge St.
NOTTING HILL
WESTWAY A40 (M)
ROYAL OAK
EDGWARE ROAD
Marylebone Rd
MARYLEBONE
OXFORD CIRCUS
Oxford St.
THE WEST END
PADDINGTON
PADDINGTON STATION
Bishop's Bridge Rd
Eastbourne
Praed St.
Sussex Gdns.
Seymour Pl.
Baker St.
Wigmore
New Bond St.
Regent St.
SOHO
PICCADILLY CIRCUS
Shaftesbury Ave.
BAYSWATER
Leinster Gdns.
Craven Rd
LANCASTER GATE
MARBLE ARCH
Seymour St.
OXFORD ST.
BOND ST.
BAYSWATER
A40
West Carriage Dr.
Bayswater Rd.
Cumberland Gate
Grosvenor Sq.
Berkeley Sq.
MAYFAIR
Jermyn
QUEENSWAY
Queensway
Broad Walk
HYDE PARK
Park Ln.
GREEN PARK
St. James's St.
Pall Mall
The Mall
KENSINGTON GARDENS
Round Pond
The Serpentine
Serpentine Rd
Piccadilly
GREEN PARK
ST. JAMES'S
ST. JAMES'S PARK
Kensington Palace
South Carriage Dr.
Knightsbridge
HYDE PARK CORNER
Constitution Hill
Buckingham Palace
ST. JAMES'S PARK
Kensington Gore Rd
Grosvenor Pl.
Buckingham Gate
Horseferry Rd
KENSINGTON
Gloucester Rd
Exhibition Rd
KNIGHTS-BRIDGE
KNIGHTSBRIDGE
Victoria and Albert Museum
Harrod's
Brompton Rd
Beauchamp
Belgrave Sq.
Belgrave Pl.
Eccleston St.
Buckingham Palace Rd
VICTORIA STATION
Victoria St.
VICTORIA
Cromwell Rd
Pont St.
Sloane St.
Eaton Sq.
EARL'S COURT
Pelham St.
BROMPTON
Sloane Sq.
BELGRAVIA
Lwr. Sloane St.
Belgrave Rd
SOUTH KENSINGTON
Sloane Ave.
SLOANE SQUARE
Ebury Bridge Rd
Warwick Way
PIMLICO
Old Brompton Rd
Drayton Gdns
Sydney St.
SOUTH KENSINGTON
King's Rd
Pimlico Rd
Ebury Bridge Rd
PIMLICO
WEST BROMPTON
Redcliffe Gdns.
Beaufort St.
CHELSEA
Royal Hospital Rd
Chelsea Bridge Rd
Grosvenor Rd
Fulham Rd
Oakley St.
Edith Grove
Cheyne Walk
Chelsea Embankment
River Thames
Chelsea Bridge
Queenstown Rd
Grosvenor Bridge
Nine Elms Ln.
Albert Bridge
Battersea Bridge
Albert Bridge Rd
BATTERSEA PARK
HAMMERSMITH

2

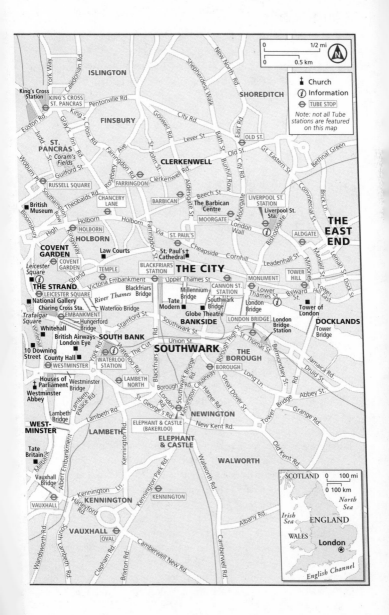

ISLINGTON

SHOREDITCH

King's Cross Station
KING'S CROSS ST. PANCRAS
Pentonville Rd.
York Way
Caledonian Rd.
Shepherdess Walk
New North Rd.
East Rd.

FINSBURY
City Rd.
Goswell Rd.
Lever St.
Bath St.
Bunhill Row
Gt. Eastern St.
OLD ST.
Commercial St.
Brick Ln.

Euston Rd.
King's Cross Rd.
Grey's Inn Rd.
St. John St.
Farringdon Rd.
Old St.
City Rd.
Bethnal Green

ST. PANCRAS
Coram's Fields
Guilford St.
Woburn Pl.
Southampton Row
RUSSELL SQUARE
Theobalds Rd.
CHANCERY LANE
Rosebery Ave.
CLERKENWELL
Clerkenwell Rd.
FARRINGDON
Beech St.
Aldersgate St.
BARBICAN
The Barbican Centre
Moorgate
MOORGATE
LIVERPOOL ST. STATION
Liverpool St. Sta.
Bishopsgate
Commercial St.
Mansell St.

British Museum
Bloomsbury
HOLBORN
Holborn
Holborn
High Holborn
HOLBORN
Kingsway
Farringdon
Via. St. PAUL'S
St. Paul's Cathedral
Cheapside
Cornhill
London Wall
ALDGATE
Leadenhall St.
THE EAST END
Minories
Lemar St.

COVENT GARDEN
Leicester Square
COVENT GARDEN
TEMPLE
Law Courts
BLACKFRIARS STATION
THE CITY
Cornhill
Leadenhall St.
TOWER HILL
Byward St.
Minories
Tower Hill East
Tower Dock St.

THE STRAND
LEICESTER SQUARE
National Gallery
Charing Cross Sta.
Strand
Victoria Embankment
River Thames
Blackfriars Bridge
Upper Thames St.
Millennium Bridge
Tate Modern
CANNON ST. STATION
Southwark Bridge
Globe Theatre
MONUMENT
Lower Thames St.
London Bridge
LONDON BRIDGE
London Bridge Station
Tower of London
DOCKLANDS
Tower Bridge

Trafalgar Square
Whitehall
EMBANKMENT
Hungerford Bridge
Waterloo Bridge
Stamford St.
BANKSIDE
Southwark St.
Union St.
SOUTHWARK
Borough High St.
St. Thomas St.

British Airways London Eye
10 Downing Street
County Hall
WESTMINSTER
SOUTH BANK
The Cut
WATERLOO STATION
Blackfriars Rd.
Southwark Bridge Rd.
THE BOROUGH
BOROUGH
Long Ln.
Bermondsey St.
Jamaica Rd.
Druid St.

Houses of Parliament
Westminster Abbey
Westminster Bridge
LAMBETH NORTH
Borough Rd.
London Rd.
St. George's Rd.
Kennington Rd.
Great Dover St.
Tower Bridge Rd.
Grange Rd.
Abbey St.

WEST-MINSTER
Lambeth Bridge
Lambeth Palace Rd.
Lambeth Rd.
ELEPHANT & CASTLE (BAKERLOO)
NEWINGTON
New Kent Rd.
Old Kent Rd.

Tate Britain
Millbank
Albert Embankment
ELEPHANT & CASTLE
WALWORTH
Walworth Rd.

Vauxhall Bridge
Kennington Ln.
Kennington Park Rd.
VAUXHALL
Harleyford Rd.
KENNINGTON
KENNINGTON
Albany Rd.
Camberwell New Rd.

Wandsworth Rd.
South Lambeth Rd.
VAUXHALL
OVAL
Clapham Rd.
Brixton Rd.
Camberwell Rd.

0   1/2 mi
0   0.5 km
N

✝ Church
ⓘ Information
⊖ TUBE STOP
Note: not all Tube stations are featured on this map

SCOTLAND
0   100 mi
0   100 km
North Sea
Irish Sea
ENGLAND
WALES
London
English Channel

4. Reserve and pay in advance, especially if you plan to rent a car. If you book with an agency like **Europe by Car,** (© **800/223-1516** in the U.S., or 212/581-3040 in New York; www.europebycar.com), the broker **Kemwel** (© **800/576-1590** in the U.S.; www.kemwel.com), or Holiday Autos (© 0870/400-4447 in the U.K.; www.holidayautos.com), you'll pay much less than with a local hire company. Car-rental rates fluctuate according to demand at the online-only **www.easyRentacar.com.**

5. Fly during the week and early in the morning and save big money. Shop around for your airfare. This will be the most expensive part of your trip, so it pays to do some legwork. Surfing the Internet will turn up some great bargains. Alternatively, scour the newspaper for consolidators like **Cheap Tickets** (© **212/570-1179,** 800/377-1000; www.cheaptickets.com), which sells airline seats at a substantial—as much as 60%—discount. Certainly consult your travel agent, who will often be privy to special deals and package rates. Air carriers want to fill every seat on every flight, so they're constantly adjusting the pricing. Also investigate charter flights on scheduled airlines offered by reliable operators see "Getting There," later in this chapter.

6. Consider buying a **vacation package:** one low price that includes airfare, transfers, accommodations. Most of the major airlines and travel Web sites offer package deals.

7. The **Great British Heritage Pass** is great if you're planning any day-trips because it provides entry into almost 600 historic properties. In the U.S. call **RailEurope** © **888/BRITRAIL** (www.raileurope.com). In London, take your passport to the Britain Visitor Centre, 1 Regent St., SW1.

8. Before you leave, get a 3-, 4-, or 7-day **London Visitor Travelcard,** which offers unlimited travel on public transport and is not available in the United Kingdom. Contact your travel agent or **BritRail** (© **866/BRITRAIL** (www.britrail.net). Passes good in the Central zone cost $21 for 3 days, $27 for 4, and $33 for 7; child equivalents cost $9, $11, and $13. See "Getting Around" in chapter 2 for more information.

9. Although using a calling card overseas usually carries a surcharge, it's worth checking it out before leaving home: American Express cardholders should ask about the charges using the company's "Connections" plan. Also see what AT&T, MCI, and Sprint have to offer.

ONCE YOU ARRIVE

10. Take public transportation from the airport into the city. The Piccadilly Line on the Underground runs directly from Heathrow to Central London and costs only £3.70 ($6).

11. Use an ATM to withdraw money from your account at home. You'll get a much better deal on the exchange rate than you would at a bureau de change cashing traveler's checks.

ACCOMMODATIONS

12. When you're looking for a hotel, try a university area like Bloomsbury first. Other London neighborhoods worth investigating for a good supply of budget hotels are Paddington, Bayswater, Victoria, and Earl's Court.

13. If a private bathroom isn't crucial to you, you can save anywhere from £10 to £20 ($16–$32) a night.

14. Negotiate the price. Ask for a discount if you're staying 3 nights or more. Suggest trade-offs—a lower price for a smaller room, and so on.

15. Consider staying at a youth hostel, or at one of the dozens of university dorms. **High Holborn Residence** charges £58 to £68 ($93–$109) for a twin.

16. Don't call home from a hotel phone unless you can access USA Direct or a similar company, and even then, check to see if there's a charge for the connection. Similarly, don't call directly from a pay phone, which may connect to high-priced carriers.

DINING

17. Stay at a hotel providing a full breakfast, not the continental one that some hotels are switching to. I've noted which still serve the "full English breakfast" (cereals, bread, fruit, bacon, eggs, sausage, mushrooms, tomatoes) that would cost you at least £6 ($10) outside the hotel.

18. Check out the ever-expanding range of budget eating options, such as the Soup Opera branches around Soho and Covent Garden, where prices start at £2.95 ($4.75) a cup and include bread and fruit.

19. At many a London restaurant, you'll find fixed-price and pre-theater menus, making a two-course meal available for as little as £6 ($10).

GETTING AROUND TOWN

20. Take advantage of any discounts on public transport. **Travel-cards** (see tip 8, above, and "Getting Around," in chapter 2) allow you to ride the buses and Underground for £4.10 ($7) a day or £19.60 ($31) a week.

21. For London's cheapest tour, ride the no. 11 bus from Liverpool Street to Fulham Broadway, or the new **R1 Riverbus** service from Covent Garden to the British Airways London Eye, Tate Modern, the Globe, and over Tower Bridge to the Tower of London. With a Travelcard, you can go wherever you please inside the zones to which it applies.

SIGHTSEEING & ENTERTAINMENT

22. All the national museums have now ditched their admission charges, so plan to visit them and marvel at some truly great collections.

23. Enjoy London's feast of festivals and ceremonial events: the Changing of the Guard at Buckingham Palace, St. James's Palace, and Whitehall; the Lord Mayor's Show; the Notting Hill Carnival; and a year-long list of many more (see "Calendar of Events," for details).

24. London is a walking city par excellence. Stroll through the different neighborhoods and enjoy the architecture, historic homes (marked with blue plaques), and leafy squares.

NIGHTLIFE

25. Go to nightclubs early or very late to get a discount. For instance, **Bar Rumba** has a happy hour Monday to Thursday, 5 to 9pm, and there's no cover charge then.

26. Queue at the **tkts** kiosk in Leicester Square for half-price West End theater tickets.

27. An hour before the performance you can pick up bargain-rate unsold seats to hear the London Symphony Orchestra at the Barbican or the Royal Philharmonic at Royal Festival Hall. Specially priced same-day tickets are also sold for the Royal Opera and the English National Opera.

SHOPPING

28. Come to London in January and shop the sales. Virtually every store of every description knocks down its prices, and Londoners indulge in a frenzy of post-Christmas spending.

29. Check out Debenhams department store (p. 149), as well as high street fashion chains like Top Shop (p. 152): They've

invited big name designers to create exclusive collections for them, at nonexclusive prices.

30. Get your VAT refund—a whopping 17.5%. Fill out the appropriate forms in the shop, get the form and your receipt stamped at customs, and mail them back to the retailer.

3 Visitor Information

Information about London and traveling elsewhere in the country can be obtained from the office of **VisitBritain** (formerly called the British Tourist Authority). VisitBritain has a New York office open to the public and a toll-free number in the United States that you can call for information and brochures. Their office at 551 Fifth Ave. (at 45th St), 7th floor, New York, NY 10176 (© **800/462-2748** or 212/986-2266), is open for walk-in customers Monday to Friday from 9am to 6pm. The VisitBritain website has sections tailored to each visitor nationality, plus special deals on airfare and hotels, so surf **www.visitbritain.com**.

VisitBritain also has walk-in offices in **Australia,** at Level 2, 15 Blue St., North Sydney, NSW 2060 (© **02/9021-4400**); in **Ireland,** at 18–19 College Green, Dublin 2 (© **01/670-8000**); and in **New Zealand,** at Level 17, NZI House, 151 Queen St., Auckland 1 (© **09/303-1446**). At press time, the Canadian office, 5915 Airport Rd., Suite 120, Missauga, Ontario L4V 1T1 (© **888/VISITUK**), was in the process of closing.

In London, visit the main VisitBritain office in the **Britain Visitor Centre,** 1 Regent St., SW1 (no phone). It's open Monday to Friday 9:30am to 6:30pm, Saturday and Sunday 10am to 4pm (Saturday 9am to 5pm, June to October). It has a Globaltickets booking service for theater, sightseeing, and events; a bureau de change; and a Thomas Cook hotel and travel reservations office.

4 Entry Requirements & Customs
DOCUMENTS
Citizens of the United States, Canada, Australia, and New Zealand need only a valid passport to enter Great Britain.

CUSTOMS
WHAT YOU CAN BRING INTO THE U.K.
Overseas visitors are allowed to import duty-free either 200 cigarettes, or 100 cigarillos, or 50 cigars, or 250 grams of tobacco; 2 liters of still table wine plus 1 liter of alcoholic drinks over 22% volume, or 2 liters

Tips Passport Savvy

Allow plenty of time before your trip to apply for a passport; processing normally takes 3 weeks but can take longer during busy periods (especially spring). And keep in mind that if you need a passport in a hurry, you'll pay a higher processing fee. When traveling, safeguard your passport in an inconspicuous, inaccessible place like a money belt and keep a copy of the critical pages with your passport number in a separate place. If you lose your passport, visit the nearest consulate of your native country as soon as possible for a replacement.

of alcoholic drinks under 22%; 60cc of perfume and 250cc of eau de cologne. Other items can be imported free of tax, provided they're for personal use or, in the case of gifts, do not exceed £145 ($232) in value. Live animals, plants, and produce are forbidden. So are counterfeit and copied goods, and anything made from an endangered species: Leave your fake Rolex and your ivory jewelry at home.

WHAT YOU CAN BRING HOME FROM THE U.K.

Returning **U.S. citizens** who have been away for at least 48 hours are allowed to bring back, once every 30 days, $800 worth of merchandise duty-free. You'll be charged a flat rate of 4% duty on the next $1,000 worth of purchases. Be sure to have your receipts handy. On mailed gifts, the duty-free limit is $200. With some exceptions, you cannot bring fresh fruits and vegetables into the United States. For specifics on what you can bring back, download the invaluable free pamphlet *Know Before You Go* online at **www.customs.gov**.

For a clear summary of **Canadian** rules, write for the booklet *I Declare,* issued by the **Canada Customs and Revenue Agency** (© **800/461-9999** in Canada, or 204/983-3500; www.ccra-adrc. gc.ca). Canada allows its citizens a C$750 exemption, and you're allowed to bring back duty-free 1 carton of cigarettes, 1 can of tobacco, 40 imperial ounces of liquor, and 50 cigars. In addition, you're allowed to mail gifts to Canada valued at less than C$60 a day, provided they're unsolicited and don't contain alcohol or tobacco (write on the package "Unsolicited gift, under $60 value"). All valuables should be declared on the Y-38 form before departure from Canada, including serial numbers of valuables you already own, such as expensive foreign cameras. *Note:* The $750 exemption can only be used once a year and only after an absence of 7 days.

The duty-free allowance in **Australia** is A$400 or, for those under 18, A$200. Citizens can bring in 250 cigarettes or 250 grams of loose tobacco, and 1,125 milliliters of alcohol. If you're returning with valuables you already own, such as foreign-made cameras, you should file form B263. A helpful brochure available from Australian consulates or Customs offices is *Know Before You Go.* For more information, call the **Australian Customs Service** at © **1300/363-263,** or log on to www.customs.gov.au.

The duty-free allowance for **New Zealand** is NZ$700. Citizens over 17 can bring in 200 cigarettes, 50 cigars, or 250 grams of tobacco (or a mixture of all three if their combined weight doesn't exceed 250g); plus 4.5 liters of wine and beer, or 1.125 liters of liquor. New Zealand currency does not carry import or export restrictions. Fill out a certificate of export, listing the valuables you are taking out of the country; that way, you can bring them back without paying duty. Most questions are answered in a free pamphlet available at New Zealand consulates and Customs offices: *New Zealand Customs Guide for Travellers, Notice no. 4.* For more information, contact **New Zealand Customs,** The Customhouse, 17–21 Whitmore St., Box 2218, Wellington (© **04/473-6099** or 0800/428-786; www.customs.govt.nz).

5 Money

CURRENCY

POUNDS & PENCE   The British **pound** (£), a small, thick, pale-yellow coin, is divided into 100 pence (pennies). These come in 1p and 2p copper coins, and silvery 5p, 10p, 20p and 50p coins. There are also large £2 coins. Notes are issued in £5, £10, £20, and £50 denominations.

CREDIT CARDS/ATMS

All major credit cards are widely accepted in London, but be aware some budget B&Bs and restaurants do not accept any credit cards at all (this is one way they keep their costs down). Also be aware that many budget hotels and restaurants refuse American Express and Diners Club because of the merchant charges. In England, Master Card is also called Access. Using plastic is certainly convenient, but it's not as economical as it once was because credit-card companies and the banks that issue the cards now routinely tack on a 3% "conversion fee" for transactions made in foreign countries.

You'll save money if you use an ATM rather than convert your home currency at a traditional bureau de change. The fees are generally lower

The British Pound & the U.S. Dollar

At the time of writing, $1 = approximately 70p (or $1.60 =
£1), and this was the rate used to calculate the dollar values in
this book (rounded to the nearest nickel if the amount is under
$5, rounded to the nearest dollar if the amount is over $5). If
you have access to the Web, you can get the current equivalents
at **www.xe.net/currency**.

and the exchange rate is the "wholesale" rate, which is better. Check
with your bank before you leave about any charges, daily withdrawal
limit, and whether you need a new pin number. Your bank or its
website can also supply a list of overseas ATMs. To find out which
overseas banks belong to the **CIRRUS** network, call ✆ **800/424-7787**
(www.mastercard.com). For **Visa Plus,** call ✆ **800/843-7587**
(www.visa.com).

6 When to Go

Spring and fall are the best seasons for avoiding the hordes that
descend on the major sights in summer. In winter, the weather in
London can be pretty dreary, but the cultural calendar is packed.

THE CLIMATE

A typical weather forecast any time of year predicts "scattered clouds
with sunny periods and showers, possibly heavy at times." Temper-
atures are mild and rarely go below freezing in winter or above 75°F
(24°C) in summer—although the temperature topped 100°F
(38°C) in the summer of 2003.

PUBLIC HOLIDAYS

Businesses are closed on Christmas Day, Boxing Day (December
26), and on New Year's Day. Good Friday is a public holiday as is
Easter Monday. There are also three bank holidays, on the first and
(usually) last Mondays in May, and the last Monday in August.

LONDON CALENDAR OF EVENTS
Please note that the dates for many of these events vary from year to year. Call
or check the event website to verify the exact date.

January
New Year's Day Parade. Starting at noon, 10,000 musicians,
dancers, acrobats, cheerleaders, clowns, and carnival floats set off
from Parliament Square. January 1.

February

Chinese New Year Parade. Chinatown, at Gerrard and Lisle streets. Festive crowds line the streets of Soho to watch the famous Lion Dancers and browse stalls crammed with crafts and delicacies. Mid-February.

April

Flora London Marathon. Almost 30,000 serious athletes run 26 miles, from Greenwich to The Mall, SW1. The start is staggered from 9am (© **020/7620-4117;** www.london-marathon.co.uk). Mid-April.

May

Chelsea Flower Show. This international spectacular features the best of British gardening, with displays of plants and flowers for all seasons, set in the beautiful grounds of the Chelsea Royal Hospital. For ticket information, write Shows Department, Royal Horticultural Society, Vincent Square, London SW1P 2PE (© **0870/906-3781;** www.rhs.org.uk). Tickets go on sale in late November. Late May.

June

Royal Academy Summer Exhibition. This is the world's largest open art exhibition and a great time to hear the critics at their bitchy best. Call © **020/7300-8000** for info (www.royalacademy. org.uk). June through July.

Trooping the Colour. Horse Guards Parade, Whitehall. On a Saturday in June, Elizabeth II inspects her regiments from an open carriage and receives the salute as they parade their colors before her in an official celebration of her birthday. It's quintessential English pageantry that still draws big crowds—many of them waiting to see a wretched young soldier faint in the heat under his ridiculous bearskin hat. Tickets are free and are allocated by ballot. Apply in writing between January and the end of February, enclosing an International Reply Coupon (available at most post offices) to: The Ticket Office, HQ Household Division, Chelsea Barracks, London SW1H 8RF. Canadians should apply to Royal Events Secretary, Canada House, Trafalgar Square, London SW1Y 5BJ. Mid-June.

City of London Festival. A 3-week extravaganza of over 100 events, covering the whole musical spectrum, at venues from St. Paul's Cathedral to City livery company halls not normally open to the public (© **020/7377-0540;** www.colf.org). Usually from the third week of June.

Wimbledon Lawn Tennis Championships. This is a thrilling event where the posh and the people rub shoulders, and you can get right up close to the world's top tennis players. For more information, visit the official website of the championships at www.wimbledon.org. Late June to early July.

July

Henry Wood Promenade Concerts. Famous summer musical season at Royal Albert Hall. Dating back to 1895, it runs the gamut from ancient to modern classics, and jazz, too. It's only £3 ($4.35) to rough it with the promenaders on the floor of the hall (℗ **020/7589-8212;** www.royalalberthall.com or www.bbc.co.uk/proms). Mid-July to mid-September.

Pride in the Park. A huge gay and lesbian costumed march and parade from Hyde Park to Parliament Square is followed by live music, dancing, and fun. (℗ **020/7494-2225;** www.londonmardigras.com). Last Saturday of July.

August

The Notting Hill Carnival. One of the largest street festivals in the world, this carnival attracts more than half a million people. Expect live reggae, steel bands, and soul music, great Caribbean food, and a charged atmosphere—sometimes overcharged because it is much too big a crowd crammed into too small a space. Check the listings magazines for details. Late August.

September

London Open House Weekend. This event showcases centuries of British architecture, as over 400 London buildings usually closed to visitors throw open their doors for the weekend, for free! Call ℗ **09001/600061** (www.londonopenhouse.org). Usually third weekend in September.

November

State Opening of Parliament, Whitehall and Parliament Square. Although the ceremony itself is not open to the public, crowds pack the parade route to see the queen make her way to Parliament in a gilded coach (℗ **020/7291-4272;** www.parliament.uk). Late October or early November.

Guy Fawkes Fireworks Night. Hyde Park, Battersea Park, and other public spaces in London. Commemorates the "Gunpowder Plot," a Roman Catholic conspiracy to blow up King James I and his parliament in 1605. Huge bonfires are lit to burn effigies of the most famous conspirator, Guy Fawkes. Free. November 5 and closest Saturday.

London Film Festival. This 2-week festival features movies from all over the world, including big name premieres, at the National Film Theatre on South Bank and in West End cinemas (② 020/7928-3232; www.lff.org.uk). From early November.

The Lord Mayor's Procession and Show. Over 100 floats follow the new Lord Mayor in his gilded coach from Guildhall, in the City, to his inauguration at the Royal Courts of Justice in the Strand (② 020/7332-1456; www.lordmayorsshow.org). Early November.

December

Tree Lighting Ceremony. Every year a giant Norwegian spruce, a gift from Norway, is lit in Trafalgar Square to signal the start of the Christmas holiday season. First Thursday in December.

New Year's Eve. Drunken lemmings party at Trafalgar Square, where the fountains are switched off to prevent drowning and hypothermia. And there's lots more fun across the city. To find the hottest hotspots, contact the London Tourist Board (② 09068/663344; www.londontown.com) or VisitBritain (see "Visitor Information," earlier in this chapter). December 31.

7 Specialized Travel Resources

FOR TRAVELERS WITH DISABILITIES

London's major museums and tourist attractions are fitted with wheelchair ramps, but call **Artsline** (② 020/7388-2227; www.artsline.org.uk) for free advice on accessibility to theaters, galleries, and events around the city—including youth-oriented info. The phone line is open Monday to Friday from 9:30am to 5:30pm. It's common for theaters, nightclubs, and attractions to offer discounts, called "concessions," to people with disabilities. Ask for these before paying full price.

Organizations that offer assistance to disabled travelers include the **Moss Rehab Hospital** (www.mossresourcenet.org), which provides a library of accessible-travel resources online; and the **Society for Accessible Travel and Hospitality** (② 212/447-7284; www.sath.org; annual membership fees: $45 adults, $30 seniors and students), which offers a wealth of travel resources for all types of disabilities and informed recommendations on destinations, access guides, travel agents, tour operators, vehicle rentals, and companion services.

FOR GAY & LESBIAN TRAVELERS

VisitBritain, the official U.K. tourism agency, has a gay and lesbian section on its website, **www.visitbritain.com.**

When you get to London, head for Old Compton Street in Soho and look for the free *Pink Paper* at gay bars, bookstores, and cafes. *Boyz* and *QX* are excellent for city listings, gossip, and scenes. *Time Out* (www.timeout.com) has a good gay listings section. And lastly, for advice on pretty much anything, including accommodations, call the 24-hour **Lesbian & Gay Switchboard** (℗ **020/7837-7324;** www.llgs.org.uk).

Frommer's Gay & Lesbian Europe (Wiley Publishing), an excellent travel resource with a chapter on London, is available at bookstores.

See also the review of the gay Philbeach Hotel (p. 51) and the "Gay & Lesbian London" section in chapter 7.

FOR SENIORS

In Britain, "senior citizen" usually means a woman at least 60 years old and a man at least 65. Seniors often receive the same discounts as students (both are categorized as "concessions" or "concs" for short). Some discounts are restricted to British citizens only, but check at all attractions, theaters, and other venues.

Membership to **AARP** is open to anyone over 50. It costs $10 a year and gives you access to a purchase privilege discount program on hotels, car rentals, tours, and other travel facilities. For information, contact the AARP, 601 E St. NW, Washington, DC 20049 (℗ **800/424-3410;** www.aarp.org). If you're 55 or older, check out the educational programs sponsored by **Elderhostel,** 11 Ave. de Lafayette, Boston, MA 02111 (℗ **877/426-8056;** www.elderhostel. org). It has classes and programs galore in London and throughout Europe.

FOR STUDENTS

The **International Student Identity Card** (**ISIC**) is the only officially acceptable form of student identification, good for discounts on rail passes, plane tickets, theaters, museums, and so on. If you're no longer a student but are still under 26, you can buy an **International Youth Travel Card,** which will get you the insurance and some of the discounts (but not student admission prices in museums). Both passes cost $22 and are available from CIEE's travel arm, **Council Travel** (℗ **800/2COUNCIL;** www.counciltravel.com), the biggest specialist agency in the world. Ask for a list of offices in major cities so that you can keep the discounts flowing (and aid lines open) as you travel.

London's youth hostels are not only some of the cheapest sleeps, they're also great spots to meet other student travelers and pick up discounts to local attractions. You have to be a member of **Hostelling International (International Youth Hostel Federation)**, which you can join at any hostel for $28 adults, $18 for seniors (55-plus), or free if you're under 18. To apply in the United States and make advance international bookings, contact **Hostelling International (AYH)**, 8401 Colesville Rd., Silver Spring, MD 20910 (© **301/495-1240;** www.hiayh.org). You can also book dorm-beds online and e-mail hostels about other options through the English website (www.yha.org.uk).

8 Planning Your Trip Online

SURFING FOR AIRFARES

The "big three" online travel agencies, **Expedia.com, Travelocity. com,** and **Orbitz.com,** sell most of the air tickets bought on the Internet. (Canadian travelers should try expedia.ca and Travelocity.ca.).

Also remember to check **airline websites**. Even with major airlines, you can often shave a few bucks from a fare by booking directly through the airline and avoiding a travel agency's transaction fee. But you'll get these discounts only by **booking online:** Most airlines now offer online-only fares that even their phone agents know nothing about.

Great **last-minute deals** are available through free weekly e-mail services provided directly by the airlines. Sign up for weekly e-mail alerts at airline websites or check mega-sites that compile comprehensive lists of last-minute specials, such as **Smarter Living** (smarterliving.com).

If you're willing to give up some control over your flight details, use an **opaque fare service** like **Priceline** (www.priceline.com) or **Hotwire** (www.hotwire.com). Both offer rock-bottom prices in exchange for travel on a "mystery airline" at a mysterious time of day, often with a mysterious change of planes en route.

For much more about airfares and savvy air-travel tips and advice, pick up a copy of *Frommer's Fly Safe, Fly Smart* (Wiley Publishing, Inc.).

SURFING FOR HOTELS

Of the "big three" sites, **Expedia** may be the best choice, thanks to its long list of special deals. **Travelocity** runs a close second. Hotel specialist sites **hotels.com** and **hoteldiscounts.com** are also reliable. **Priceline** and **Hotwire** are even better for hotels than for airfares; with both, you're allowed to pick the neighborhood and quality level of your hotel before offering up your money. *Note:* Hotwire overrates its hotels by one star—what Hotwire calls a four-star is a three-star anywhere else.

SURFING FOR RENTAL CARS

For booking rental cars online, the best deals are usually found at rental-car company websites, although all the major online travel agencies also offer rental-car reservations services. Priceline and Hotwire work well for rental cars, too.

9 Getting There

BY PLANE

More than 90 scheduled airlines serve London, more if you count Gatwick as well as Heathrow. They include these major North American carriers: **American Airlines** (℡ 800/433-7300; www.aa.com), **Continental** (℡ 800/231-0856; www.continental.com), **Delta** (℡ 800/241-4141; www.delta.com), **Northwest Airlines** (℡ 800/447-4747; www.nwa.com), **United Airlines** (℡ 800/538-2929; www.ual.com), and **Air Canada** (℡ 888/247-2262; www.air canada.com).

British Airways (℡ **800/AIRWAYS** in North America, 300/134011 in Australia, 800/BRITISH in New Zealand; www.britishairways.com) is the largest U.K. airline and flies to London from the U.S., Australia, and New Zealand. **Virgin Atlantic Airways** (℡ **800/862-8621;** www.virgin-atlantic.com) flies from New York and Newark, New Jersey, as well as from Chicago, Boston, Las Vegas, Los Angeles, San Francisco, Orlando, Miami, and Washington, D.C. **Qantas** (℡ **1300/131313** in Australia; www.qantas.com) is the national Australian carrier, also serving New Zealand, and it code-shares with many foreign carriers. **Air New Zealand** (℡ **0800/737000** in New Zealand; www.airnz.com) flies daily to Heathrow.

FINDING THE BEST AIRFARE

London's popularity and the number of airlines flying there mean heavy competition for customers. So check local and national newspapers for special promotions and always shop around to find the cheapest seat.

The lowest-priced standard economy-class fare usually carries some restrictions like advance-purchase, minimum stay, or a Saturday stopover, as well as penalties for altering dates and itineraries.

> ## *Tips* Make the Airline Pricing System Work for You
>
> Increasingly sophisticated reservations software allows the airlines to practice yield management. They juggle twin priorities: filling the plane and making as much profit as possible from each flight. So, airlines constantly adjust the pricing of each seat on a particular flight according to the immediate demand. Save big money either by trawling the Internet, or by talking to a reliable travel agent or one of the companies that specialize in searching out low airfares: **Air for Less** (© 800/238-8371); **Fly 4 Less** (© 800/359-4537; www.fly4less.com); **Fare Busters International** (© 800/618-0571; www.smartbusinessfares.com); and **1-800 Fly Cheap** (© 800/359-2432; www.flycheap.com).
>
> For more information, consult "Planning Your Trip Online," earlier in this chapter.

Note, too, that weekday flights are slightly cheaper than weekends, and early mornings are cheapest of all.

Make sure to check alternative ticket sources before buying direct from the airline. For instance, consolidators buy blocks of seats and sell them at a discount. Tickets are restrictive, valid only for a particular date or flight, nontransferable, and nonrefundable except directly from the consolidator, and they may also not earn frequent flier miles. Advance-purchase requirements are rare; if space is available, you can buy just before you fly. Always pay with a credit card, though, to protect yourself in case the consolidator goes belly up.

The lowest-priced bucket shops are usually local backroom operations with low profiles and overheads. Look for their tiny ads jam-packed with cities and prices in the travel or classified section of your local newspaper. Those that advertise nationally are rarely as competitive, but they often have toll-free telephone numbers and may be more reliable. Some to try are **Arrow Travel** (© 212/889-2550); **Cheap Tickets** (© 800/377-1000 or 212/570-1179; www.cheaptickets.com); **TFI Tours International** (© 800/745-8000 or 212/736-1140 in New York state; www.lowestairprice.com); **Travel Land International Inc.** (© 212/268-6464); and **Up & Away Travel** (© 212/889-2345).

CHARTERS Another cheap way to cross the Atlantic is on a charter flight. Most operators advertise and sell their seats through travel agents, making them your best source of current information on the deals available.

FLYING INTO HEATHROW

VISITOR INFORMATION   The **Airport Information** desks are located at: **Terminal 3 Arrivals,** open daily from 5:30am to 10:30pm; **Terminal 3 Departures,** open daily from 7am to 9:30pm; and **Terminal 4 Arrivals,** open daily from 5:30am to 10:30pm. The **London Tourist Board** has an information center in the Tube station concourse that connects with **Terminals 1, 2, and 3,** open daily from 8am to 6pm (to 7pm, Mon–Sat, June–Sept).

HOTEL RESERVATIONS   There are **British Hotel Reservation Centre** desks in the arrivals area of every terminal, open daily from 6am to midnight. BHRC will book you into any accommodation anywhere, usually scoring big discounts. The nationwide 24-hour number is ℂ **020/7340-1616** (www.bhrc.co.uk).

CURRENCY EXCHANGE   **American Express,** Terminal 4, Tube station concourse (ℂ **020/8754-7057**), is open daily from 7am to 7pm. At all other bureaux de change, **British Airports Authority,** which runs Heathrow, guarantees charges will match or beat at least one of Britain's big-four high street banks. These companies have numerous branches, open daily at both terminals: **Thomas Cook** (ℂ **020/8272-8073** T3 or 020/8272-8100 T4) is open in Terminal 3 Arrivals from 5am to 10:30pm, and from 5:30am in Terminal 4; and in Terminals 3 and 4 Departures from 5:30am to 10pm; **Travelex** (ℂ **020/8897-3501,** Terminals 3 and 4) never closes in Arrivals, and is open from 5:30am to 10pm in Departures. There are ATMs throughout the airport.

CAR RENTALS   Airport pick-ups are very convenient. The big rental agencies all have branches at Heathrow: **Avis** (ℂ **020/8899-1000**); **Budget Rent-a-Car** (ℂ **020/8750-2511**); **Europcar** (ℂ **020/8897-0811**); and **Hertz** (ℂ **020/8897-2072**).

GETTING FROM THE AIRPORT TO TOWN   The **Underground** is the best value. There are two airport Tube stations on the Piccadilly Line: one for Terminals 1, 2, and 3, and one for Terminal 4. The journey into Central London takes 40 to 50 minutes. Trains leave the airport from 5:08am to 11:49pm and arrive there from 6:29am to 1:07am (shorter hours on Sun). One-way fares to or from zone 1, or Central London (see "Getting Around," in Chapter 2), are £3.70 ($6) for adults and £1.50 ($2.40) for children aged 5 to 15. If you miss the last Tube, the **N97 night bus** leaves at 20 minutes past the hour and 10 to, from the Central Bus Station, and costs £1.50 ($2.40) for adults and children. Call **London Transport Travel Hotline** (© 020/7222-1234; www.londontransport.co.uk) for more information.

Heathrow Express (© 0845/600-1515; www.heathrowexpress. co.uk), the luxury nonstop rail service to Paddington Station, takes 15 minutes from Terminals 1, 2, and 3, and 20 to 25 minutes from Terminal 4. Trains leave Heathrow from 5:07am to 12:08am and arrive there from 5:30am to midnight. All major airlines offer full check-in at Paddington—get there at least 2 hours before your flight, 1 hour if you only have carry-on luggage. Standard-class one-way tickets cost £11.70 ($19) for adults and £5.40 ($9) for children aged 5 to 15, with discounts for online booking.

National Express (© 08705/747777 info, 08705/808080 bookings; www.gobycoach.com) runs two airport bus services and accepts online bookings. The **Airbus** leaves twice an hour from just outside every Heathrow terminal and goes to 23 stops in Central London. The service runs from Heathrow between 5:30am and 10:08pm, and from King's Cross (the last, or first, stop at the London end) between 4am and 8pm. One-way tickets cost £8 ($12) for adults and £4 ($6) for children ages 5 to 15.

Black taxis (see "Getting Around," in Chapter 2) are always available at Heathrow. The approximate fare to London is £45 ($72), which is a good value, door-to-door cost if you can fill the cab with the maximum five passengers and still have room for luggage. The taxi desk numbers are: **Terminal 3** (© 020/8745-4655); **Terminal 4** (© 020/8745-7302).

FLYING INTO GATWICK

There are four ways of making the 25-mile trek into London from **Gatwick Airport** (© 08700/002468; www.baa.co.uk). The most popular is the **Gatwick Express** train, which takes around 30 minutes to reach Victoria, and costs £11 ($18) one-way. The station is below the airport, and trains depart every 15 minutes from 6:50am to 10:50pm. The slightly cheaper option is **South Central Trains,** which charges £8.20 ($13) one-way and takes 35 to 45 minutes. For information on both, call **National Rail Enquiries** (© 08457/ 484950), or pre-book through **www.thetrainline.com**.

Hotelink (© 01293/552251; www.hotelink.co.uk) charges £20 ($32) to take you directly to your hotel. **Checker Cars** (© 01923/ 502808 from South Terminal, or 01923/569790 from North

Tips Smaller Airports

If you're flying to London on a no-frills flight, you may land at **Stansted** (② 08700/000303; www.baa.co.uk). The quickest way to get into London is the 42-minute train trip on the **Stansted Express** direct from the airport to Liverpool Street station. It runs from 5am to 11pm, every 15 minutes at peak times, otherwise half-hourly, and costs £13 ($21) one way (② **08457/444422**; www.stanstedexpress.com). The National Express **Airbus** (see above) makes the journey to Victoria Station in about 1 hour and 40 minutes and costs £8 ($13) one-way.

Charters and cheapie airlines also fly into **Luton Airport** (② 01582/405100; www.london-luton.com). The Greenline 757 bus leaves for London once an hour, takes 70 minutes, and charges £8 ($12) one-way (② **08706/087261**; www.greenline.co.uk). The **Thameslink CityFlier** takes about half an hour from the new Luton Airport Parkway station to King's Cross. There are eight trains an hour from 7am to 6pm Monday to Saturday, then four until 10pm. On Sundays trains run every 10 minutes from 9am to 5pm, then every 15 minutes until 8pm. One-way tickets cost £9.50 ($15). Call **National Rail Enquiries** for further information (② **08457/484950**).

Terminal) provides 24-hour taxi service between Gatwick and Central London; expect to pay about £65 ($104) for the 90-minute journey.

BY TRAIN

Each of London's train stations is connected to a vast bus and Underground network, and there are phones, restaurants, pubs, luggage-storage areas, shops, and London Transport Information Centres at all of them.

If you're **arriving from France,** the fastest way to get to London is by taking the hoverspeed connection between Calais and Dover (see "By Ferry & Hovercraft," below), where you can pick up a train into the city. If you prefer the ease of one-stop travel, you can take the Eurostar train (see below) directly from Paris—or go there and back in a day for a very swanky excursion.

VIA THE CHUNNEL The **Eurostar** direct train service runs from Paris Gare Du Nord and Brussels Central Station to Waterloo International in London. Contact Eurostar in the U.K. at © 08705/186186 (www.eurostar.com); in Paris, at © 08/36353535 or 01/53607000; in Brussels, at © 02/525-9292 (bookings only, no inquiries).

FROM ELSEWHERE IN THE U.K. If you're traveling to London from elsewhere in the United Kingdom, consider buying a **BritRail Classic Pass.** This allows unlimited rail travel anywhere during a set time period (**Eurailpasses** aren't accepted in Britain, although they are in Ireland). A second-class pass costs $189 for 4 days, $269 for 8 days, $405 for 15 days, $515 for 22 days, and $609 for 1 month. Travelers between 16 and 25 can purchase a **BritRail Classic Youth Pass,** which allows unlimited second-class travel: $155 for 4 days, $219 for 8 days, $285 for 15 days, $359 for 22 days, or $429 for 1 month. For those over 60, the **BritRail Classic Senior Pass** costs $245, $345, $519, $659, or $779. There are also passes for three or four people traveling in a group, or for people who are only going to roam close to London.

You must purchase all special passes before you leave home: in the United States, at the **British Travel Shop** next to the Manhattan VisitBritain office, or those in Australia and New Zealand (see "Visitor Information," above). You can also purchase passes on the phone or online directly from **BritRail** (© 888/BRITRAIL; www.britrail.net).

BY BUS

Whether you're coming from the Continent or from another part of the country, London-bound buses almost always go to (and leave

---

Onward! Short Hops Around Britain & Across the Channel

If you want to fly to Europe, or even up to Scotland or across to Ireland, check out the no-frills **easyJet** (© 0870/600-0000; www.easyjet.com), which flies from Stansted and Gatwick; and **Ryanair** (© 08701/569569; www.ryanair.com), which files from Stansted, Luton, and Gatwick. **Virgin Express** (© 020/7744-0004; www.virgin-express.com) only flies from Heathrow. In 2003 KLM sold its low-cost subsidiary, **Buzz,** to Ryanair and **GO** was sold to easyJet. Keep an eye out for promotional deals in newspaper ads as lower prices are posted practically every day.

from) **Victoria Coach Station,** Buckingham Palace Road, 1 block from Victoria train station.

The **Tourist Trail Pass** is ideal for serious day-trippers and round-Britain tourers. This allows unlimited travel on a set number of days, not necessarily consecutive but falling within a fixed time period: either 2 days to be used within a 3-day period, for £49 ($78); 5 days travel, valid for 10, for £85 ($136); 8 days, valid for 30, for £135 ($216); or 15 days, valid for 30, for £190 ($304), or valid for 60 days, £205 ($328). Under-25s and over-50s can buy a discount card for £9 ($14), which cuts pass and individual ticket prices by 20% to 30%. You can buy all passes with a credit card, online, or by phone, direct from **National Express** (✆ **08705/ 808080;** www.gobycoach.com); or, in person, at the Heathrow Central Bus Station and Victoria Coach Station, at National Express offices in St. Pancras station and Earl's Court Tube station, or at any travel agent displaying the National Express logo. The U.S. agent for National Express is **British Travel International** (✆ **800/ 327-6097;** www.britishtravel.com).

Bus connections to Britain from the Continent are not so much uncomfortable as time-consuming, but it is very cheap compared to the train and plane, except for the no-frills carriers (see above). National Express is part of the **Eurolines** network of 31 companies in 25 countries. Buses leave Victoria for more than 460 destinations in Ireland and mainland Europe. For a serious pilgrimage around Europe, check out the 15-, 30-, and 60-day Eurolines Passes, which link you to 46 cities. A 30-day pass during the low season costs £136 ($218) for over-60s and under-26s, £167 ($271) for adults; high-season prices are £186 ($298) and £224 ($358).

BY FERRY & HOVERCRAFT

The shortest ferry crossings are also the closest to London: Dover to Calais, and Folkestone to Boulogne. Note that here, too, you pay less traveling out of season, on weekdays, and at unsociable hours, and if you pre-buy tickets rather than just turn up. To have any hope of squeezing on board in the summer and during public holidays, you must book ahead anyway.

Check with VisitBritain (see "Visitor Information," earlier in this chapter) for a full listing of ferries to the Channel Islands, Ireland, the Isle of Man, and around the Scottish islands. All the companies below put together stopover packages if you fancy a continental break from your London holiday. You can also get day-trip deals. And there are discounts for booking online.

CAR & PASSENGER FERRIES   P&O Stena Line (© **0870/600-0600,** or 01304/864003 from outside the U.K.; www.posl.com) operates car and passenger ferries between Dover and Calais, 35 departures a day, with a journey time of 1 hour 25 minutes. Summer one-way tickets cost £116 ($186) for car and driver, or £28 ($45) for an adult foot passenger. **Sea France** (© **08705/711711;** www.seafrance.com) runs 15 departures a day, with a journey time of 1½ hours. In 2003, round-trip peak-season tickets cost from £69 ($110) for an advance purchase APEX fare to £188 ($301) for standard fare car and up to 9 passengers, £17.50 ($28) for an adult foot passenger.

HOVERCRAFT & SEACATS   Traveling by Hovercraft or SeaCat takes about half the time that a ferry does. For example, a hovercraft crossing from Calais to Dover with **hoverspeed** (© **08702/408070;** www.hoverspeed.co.uk) takes 35 minutes; they have 6 to 12 crossings per day. Their SeaCat crossings take a little longer, about 50 minutes, and there are 5 departures a day.

BY CAR

If you plan to take a rented car across or under the Channel, check with the rental company about license and insurance requirements before you leave. Hertz runs a scheme called **Le Swap** for passengers taking **Le Shuttle** (© **08705/353535;** www.eurotunnel.com), the Channel Tunnel drive-on train service, which allows you to switch cars at Calais and change to the local steering-wheel position (right side in U.K., left side in Europe).

Getting to Know London

London is one of the most exciting cities in the world, and arriving there can be a bit of a shock for bleary-eyed and jet-lagged visitors. Everything will probably seem too noisy, too fast, or too crowded. But despite the bustle, the city is very visitor-friendly: It's laid out in distinct, manageable areas, and traveling between them is easy on public transport.

This chapter will help you get your bearings. It provides a brief orientation and a preview of the city's most important neighborhoods. It also answers questions about how to use those double-decker buses, as well as the Tube. The "Fast Facts" section covers all the essentials.

1 Orientation

VISITOR INFORMATION

The **Britain Visitor Centre,** 1 Regent St., SW1 (no phone), is open Monday 9:30am to 6:30pm, Tuesday to Friday 9am to 6:30pm, Saturday and Sunday 10am to 4pm (Sat 9am–5pm, June to Oct). It brings together the English, Welsh, Scottish, and Irish Tourist Boards. There's a **Globaltickets** booking service for theater, sightseeing, and events; a bureau de change; and a **Thomas Cook** hotel and travel-reservations office.

The **London Tourist Board** has several **Tourist Information Centres** that offer similar services. The main one at **Victoria Station forecourt,** SW1, is open Monday to Saturday, from 8am to 8pm Easter through May, and to 9pm June through September. Sundays and every day during the winter, it is open from 8am to 6pm.

CITY LAYOUT

Central London is like the jam in a doughnut, an amorphous blob rather than an official definition. Ask a local, and they'd probably tell you it means anything falling within the Circle Line on the Underground: the **City,** the **West End,** and **West London** about as far as Earl's Court. Zone 2 of the Tube map loosely conforms to the broader definition of **Inner London. Greater London** includes the vast sprawling mass of suburbs.

The City is the oldest part of London. It covers the original 1-square-mile of the Roman settlement of Londinium. "Square Mile" and "The City" (always capitalized) are shorthand terms for London's financial district, akin to New York's Wall Street. The villages that sprang up around the original square-mile settlement—**Bloomsbury, Holborn, Kensington,** and so on—gradually melded together and became absorbed into the city proper. But each one still has its own heart and character.

The West End is harder to pin down because it's so much more than a geographical term. Locals use it as shorthand meaning razzle-dazzle—the special streets where they shop by day and play by night. **Marble Arch** and **Hyde Park Corner,** with **Park Lane** running between them, mark the westernmost points of the West End. **Westminster** and **Victoria** stand by themselves, outside any catchall description, except that Westminster, where the Houses of Parliament are located, is the center of government. Then, west of the West End, where homes finally outnumber offices, you come to **Bayswater, Notting Hill, Knightsbridge, Kensington, South Kensington,** and **Chelsea.**

This is the prime stomping ground for visitors. If you add on the best bits of Inner London—the cultural highlights close to the Thames at **South Bank, Bankside,** and **Southwark,** stretching as far east as **Greenwich,** as well as the markets of **Islington** and **Camden,** and pretty **Hampstead** village, to the north—that makes an area of around 65km sq. (25 sq. miles).

NEIGHBORHOODS IN BRIEF

Knightsbridge   Posh Knightsbridge is the first area you come to west of the West End and south of Hyde Park. It's very wealthy and very fashionable in a way that is both solid establishment and gossip-column glitz. At **Harrods,** the main attraction in Knights-bridge, green-liveried doormen turn people away for having grubby clothing, ripped jeans, high-cut or cycling shorts, and bare midriffs or feet. The chic Harvey Nichols is 100 yards up the road toward Hyde Park Corner.

Belgravia   Located south of Knightsbridge, Belgravia reached the peak of its prestige in the reign of Queen Victoria, but for the *nouveau riche* and for those aristocrats whose forebears didn't blow all the family heirlooms, it's still a very fashionable address.

Where the Neighborhoods Are

Flip to the map "Central London" on p. 2 for a clear picture of how all the neighborhoods described here fit together.

The Duke of Westminster, who owns vast tracts of Belgravia and Chelsea, lives at Eaton Square. Architecture buffs will love the town houses, especially in the area's centerpiece, Belgrave Square. Budget travelers can hover on the verge of a smart address at the B&Bs in Ebury Street, though that is really Victoria.

Chelsea   One end of this stylish district is defined by the north bank of the Thames, west of Victoria. The action really starts at Sloane Square and moves east down that dangerously captivating shopping heaven, the King's Road. Some large chain stores moved in a few years ago, but it's still more chic than cheap, and retains a funky fashionable feel begun in the 1960s. Chelsea has always been a favorite of writers and artists, including Oscar Wilde, Henry James, and Thomas Carlyle, whose home you can visit. Residents today include aging rock stars (Mick Jagger), aging politicians (Margaret Thatcher), wealthy young Euromigrant families, and former "Sloane Rangers" of the 1980s. Temporary residents won't find many cheap places to stay, but there are a handful of good values and a mix of cheap pop-in eats and restaurants with excellent set meals.

Kensington   This is the heart of the Royal Borough of Kensington & Chelsea. The asthmatic William III started the royal thing in 1689 when he fled Whitehall in search of cleaner air (long gone). Queen Victoria was born in Kensington Palace, which the royals now call "KP." The late Princess Diana lived there, and it's still home to a gang of family members. You can visit the palace (but not the royals, who inhabit their own wing). Kensington lies between Notting Hill, to the north, and South Kensington. There are a couple of great bathless budget sleeps just off Kensington Church Street, which is lined with by-appointment-only antiques shops. Kensington High Street is a good mix of mainstream brands and bargains.

South Kensington is best known as the home of London's major museums, which stand along Cromwell Road: the Natural History Museum, Victoria & Albert Museum, and the Science Museum. They're all built on land bought with the proceeds of Prince Albert's Great Exhibition of 1851. He gave his name to two spectacular landmarks here: the Royal Albert Hall, where the famous promenade concerts are held every year, and the Albert Memorial, commissioned by his grief-stricken wife Queen Victoria and completed with garish Victorian splendor in 1872. South Ken, as it's often called, is stuffed to the gunwales with surprisingly good-value B&Bs and self-catering accommodations.

Earl's Court   This neighborhood west of South Kensington has gone through many incarnations. There are whole streets of budget hotels that really are dives, and whole streets of lovely Victorian terraces. Things are changing overall, and an upmarket sensibility is creeping in. You can see it on the main street, Earl's Court Road, where the smarter cafe chains are starting to join the late-night fast-food joints. The huge Earl's Court Exhibition Centre brings in a lot of convention-size business. Some hotels are upgrading to cater for it, providing good value budget sleeps. London's first gay enclave, Earl's Court, has gay bars, pubs, and a gay hotel.

Notting Hill   Notting Hill is in the process of becoming a victim of its own hype. When house prices began to rise in the mid-1990s, the press climbed on the bandwagon and hip media, music, and fashion types moved in to what had been a sometimes grotty neighborhood. The popular film *Notting Hill,* with Hugh Grant and Julia Roberts, provided a final rocket-blast to the real-estate boom. Bye-bye boho scruffiness, hello Starbucks. Visitors flock here in hordes to visit the great Portobello Market, as you'll see if you stay at any of the good value sleeps I've found for you in this area. **Holland Park,** the next stop west, is a chi-chi residential neighborhood for fat wallets only. Richard Branson runs his Virgin empire from here. Budget travelers can get a fantastic cheap sleep at the youth hostel located in the middle of the park itself.

Paddington & Bayswater   Since 1836, Paddington has been the terminus for trains coming into London from the west and southwest. The presence of the station eventually transformed the area's once-genteel Georgian and Victorian terraces into scruffy sleeps for people just passing through. The area is about to enjoy a massive redevelopment around the canal basin, north of the station—11 acres of offices, overpriced apartments, shops, and eateries. But there are still good B&B deals to be had here, just west of the West End.

Bayswater is a generalization rather than a definable area, arising from Bayswater Road, the main road running across the top of Hyde Park. Walk 5 minutes from Paddington, and you'll come to it. The buzziest bit is **Queensway,** a street of cheap ethnic restaurants, often tacky shops, and an ice-skating rink, with the old Whiteleys department store, now a shopping mall, at the northern end. That is also where Westbourne Grove starts, an increasingly funky street that links up with Notting Hill.

Mayfair   Bounded by Piccadilly, Hyde Park, Oxford Street, and Regent Street, Mayfair is filled with luxury hotels and grand shops. The Georgian townhouses are beautiful, but many of them are offices now—real people can't afford to live in Mayfair anymore. Grosvenor (*Grove*-nur) Square is nicknamed "Little America" because it's home to the U.S. Embassy and a statue of Franklin D. Roosevelt. You must visit **Shepherd Market,** a tiny, rather raffish village of pubs and popular eateries.

Marylebone   Most visitors head to Marylebone (*Mar*-lee-bone) to explore Madame Tussaud's waxworks or trudge up Baker Street in the fantasy footsteps of Sherlock Holmes. Generally, this is an anonymous area, with most of the action in a strip running just north of Oxford Street. Robert Adam finished Portland Place, a very typical square, in 1780. The one must-visit attraction is in Manchester Square: the mini–French chateau called Hertford House, which houses the Wallace Collection, one of London's loveliest free attractions. St. Christopher's Place is a pretty pedestrian street with some reasonable restaurants and unreasonable boutiques close to Bond Street Tube. Marylebone High Street now has a gaggle of posh shops. While budget hotels are as rare as hen's teeth here, you will find good value, big-roomed splurges in Gloucester Place.

St. James's   Often called "Royal London," St. James's basks in its associations with everybody from the "merrie monarch" Charles II to Elizabeth II, who lives at its most famous address, Buckingham Palace. English gentlemen retreat to their St. James's clubs, those traditional bastions of male-only social superiority. St. James's starts at Piccadilly Circus and moves southwest, incorporating Pall Mall, The Mall, St. James's Park, and Green Park. Budget travelers must day-trip here to sample the lingering pomp and pompousness. Cheap eats are hard to find, except close to Piccadilly Circus, but the parks are prime picnic territory. You can get the necessities, or stop for tea, at the world's most luxurious grocery store, **Fortnum & Mason.** It has kept royals, explorers, empire-builders, and the warrior classes supplied with food parcels for over 200 years.

Soho   Soho is a wedge-shaped neighborhood. Its boundaries are Regent Street, Oxford Street (a mecca for mass-market shopping), Charing Cross Road, which is stuffed with bookshops, and the theater-lined Shaftesbury Avenue. Urban streetwear stores are finally starting to push back the tide of tourist schlock on Carnaby Street, where the 1960s swung the hardest. In the middle of Soho, Old Compton Street is the heart of gay London, with scores of gay bars, pubs, and cafes. Cross Shaftesbury Avenue and you come to Chinatown, which is small, yet authentic, and packed with excellent restaurants.

London's best-located youth hostel is on Noel Street in Soho, and there are good deals at the Regent Palace near Piccadilly Circus. But that's it.

Piccadilly Circus & Leicester Square   Piccadilly Circus, named after the "picadil," a ruffled collar created by a 17th-century tailor, is packed with crowds morning, noon, and way past midnight, grazing on fast food, gawking at the bright lights, and shopping at the mega-stores. Though there's a fast-food flavor to the area, you'll find great set menus at Marco Pierre White's Criterion restaurant on Piccadilly Circus. Teeny-bopper delights abound at the Trocadero, where floor after floor is filled with video games and noisy attractions kids love. Its huge signs are part of a whole gallery of neon that illuminates the statue of Eros in the center of Piccadilly Circus. **Leicester** (*Les*-ter) **Square** is wall-to-wall neon, too. At one end you'll find the tkts half-price tickets booth, an essential stop for theatre-lovers. Crowds mill about the square until the early morning. Keep a tight hold on your wallet, as pickpockets cruise for careless tourists. Both Piccadilly Circus and Leicester Square are hubs for London's West End theatre scene.

Bloomsbury   Northeast of Piccadilly Circus, beyond Soho, is Bloomsbury, the academic heart of London. Much of the University of London, as well as several other colleges, are based here. It's quite a staid neighborhood, even boring, but writers such as Virginia Woolf, who lived here, have fanned its reputation. Virginia and her husband Leonard Woolf were the unofficial leaders of a bohemian clique of artists and writers known as "the Bloomsbury Group." Russell Square is the area's main hub, and the streets around it are crammed with excellent value B&Bs. Most visitors come to see the treasures in the British Museum, and there are a few really good and good-value restaurants in the area.

Nearby is **Fitzrovia,** bounded by Great Portland Street, Oxford Street, and Gower Streets (lots of B&Bs there). Goodge

Street is the main Tube stop and the village-like heart, with many shops and restaurants.

Holborn This is the heart of legal London, where the ancient Inns of Court and Royal Courts of Justice lie. Dickens was a solicitor's clerk here when he was 14 and used the experience to good effect in *Little Dorrit*. Once you're off the traffic-laden High Holborn, time rolls back. The Viaduct Tavern, 126 Newgate St., was built over the notorious Newgate Prison. Holborn Viaduct was the world's first overpass. This is too business-like to be a hotel zone, stuck between the West End and the City, and northeast of Covent Garden. But you'll get a great cheap sleep at the Holborn Residence student dorm.

Covent Garden & The Strand This is a very fashion-oriented neighborhood, with more shopping and general razzle-dazzle than Soho, and certainly more tourists. It's quite pricey, too. The restored fruit and flower market hall in the middle of a big pedestrian piazza is filled with boutiques. The character of Covent Garden owes a lot to its long theatrical history, which is why there are so many great pre-theater deals at the restaurants. The Theatre Royal Drury Lane was where Charles II's mistress Nell Gwynne made her debut in 1665. And the actors' church designed by Inigo Jones, St. Paul's Covent Garden, holds memorials to many famous names from Ellen Terry to Boris Karloff to Vivien Leigh. The revamped Royal Opera House is a glorious place to stop for coffee—or a performance, if you like opera and ballet. Stay with visiting performers and fans at the eccentric Fielding hotel, just around the corner.

The **Strand** is a windy thoroughfare lined with theaters and hotels, including the Savoy, where the art of cocktail mixology was born and still flourishes in the American Bar. For a cheaper concoction, go next door to the newly restored Somerset House. The riverside Palladian mansion has three galleries and a 50-jet courtyard fountain. The Strand runs northeast out of Trafalgar Square toward the City, and marks the southern border of Covent Garden. **Trafalgar Square** is a visitor must-see all by itself. Nelson's Column—the triumphal memorial to England's victory over Napoleon in 1805—stands in the center, and the National Gallery, with the National Portrait Gallery just behind it, demarcates the northern side. Recent redevelopment connected the famous square to the National Gallery.

Westminster Dominated by the Houses of Parliament and gothic Westminster Abbey, Westminster runs along the Thames east of St. James's Park. Whitehall, which has long been synonymous with the armies of civil servants who really wield the power, is the main thoroughfare from Trafalgar Square to Parliament Square. Visit Churchill's Cabinet War Rooms, then peer through the gates guarding Downing Street.

Westminster also takes in **Victoria,** a strange area that is both businessy and, because it's dominated by the station, full of cheap (and sometimes nasty) hotels. The classiest ones are in Ebury Street on the fringes of Belgravia. Art lovers come here to visit Tate Britain.

The City The City is where London began. Now it's one of the world's leading financial centers. The Bank of England, the London Stock Exchange, and Lloyds of London are all located here. Much of the City was destroyed in the Great Fire of London, the Blitz, and later in the 1990s with some help from the IRA. Nowadays, it's a patchwork of the ancient and the very modern. You'll see some of the most godawful modern architecture here, alongside such treasures as St. Paul's Cathedral. The Museum of London is a fascinating place to contemplate the centuries of London life, and St. Paul's Cathedral draws plenty of tourists, but the biggest draw in this neck of the woods is the Tower of London, which should be at the top of every visitor's must-see list.

Clerkenwell London's first hospital was here, and then Clerkenwell evolved into a muck-filled 18th-century cattle yard, home to cheap gin distilleries. In the 1870s, it became the center of the new socialist movement: John Stuart Mill's London Patriotic Club was in Clerkenwell, as was William Morris's socialist press later in the 1890s. Lenin lived here while he edited *Iskra.* Neither West End nor City proper, its fortunes then dwindled, but they're on the up and up again today as old commercial buildings turn into chic lofts and new restaurants open. Art galleries and shops run by small designers line Clerkenwell Green. Gritty working life goes on as meat lorries rumble into Smithfield Market. London's oldest church is here, too, the Norman St. Bartholomew-the-Great.

Docklands Since the London Docklands Development Corporation was set up in 1981, billions of pounds have gone into the most ambitious regeneration scheme of its kind in Europe. **Canary Wharf** is the focal point of this new river city, which runs east from Tower Bridge. Canary Wharf's 800-foot tower, designed by Cesar Pelli, is in the center of a covered piazza filled with shops. New skyscrapers are sprouting up around it now, and guesstimates say 60,000 new workers will be needed over the next few years.

South Bank   This is a loose definition, devised by Londoners on the north bank of the Thames, to define the only bit south of the river they're really interested in. As more and more redevelopment takes place, the definition widens. The core is the **South Bank Centre,** the largest cultural complex in Europe and now planning a big expansion and redevelopment. It houses the National Theatre, Royal Festival Hall, Hayward Gallery, the National Film Theatre, and several eateries. Upriver, facing the Houses of Parliament, is the landmark observation wheel, the British Airways London Eye. Beside it is County Hall, once home to the Greater London Council, now part upscale Marriott hotel and part budget Travel Inn, with the London Aquarium in the basement and the new Saatchi Gallery and Dali Universe upstairs. Go downriver (east), and you come to Tate Modern and the new Millennium Bridge, linking **Bankside** with St. Paul's and the City. With Shakespeare's Globe Theatre only a stone's throw away, this is a really exciting neighborhood. The London School of Economics student dorm, Bankside House, offers good quality, cheap accommodations.

Still farther east, you come to London Bridge and **Southwark.** Known as the outlaw borough, it was the city's medieval hotspot for prostitutes, theaters, drinking dens, and crime. Pilgrims rested here, too, on their way to Thomas à Becket's shrine, as recorded in Chaucer's *Canterbury Tales.* There's a feast of history to revisit in this once-run-down area that is now starting to revive in a big way. Next to Tower Bridge is the brand-new (opened in 2002) glass-walled London City Hall, HQ for the London Mayor and the Assembly.

2 Getting Around

BY PUBLIC TRANSPORTATION

The London Underground operates on a system of six fare zones. These radiate out in concentric rings from the central zone 1, which is where visitors spend most of their time. Zone 1 covers an area from the Tower in the east to Notting Hill in the west, and from Waterloo in the south to Baker Street, Euston, and King's Cross in the north. **London Transport (LT)** recently simplified the bus system, so now, for ticket-buying purposes, there's just zone 1, and then the rest of London; there are four fare zones for bus passes, though.

Tube, bus, and river service maps are available at all Underground stations, or you can download them from the excellent website, **www.londontransport.co.uk**. You can also call the 24-hour **travel hotline** ✆ **020/7222-1234.** There are **LT Information Centres** at several major Tube stations: Euston, King's Cross, Liverpool Street, Piccadilly Circus, Victoria, St. James's Park, and Oxford Circus. They're all open daily—except for the last two, which close on Sundays—from at least 9am to 5pm.

FARES   Kids up to age 4 travel free on the Tube and buses. From 5 to 15, they qualify for children's fares, generally around 40% less than adults (children must pay full rates after 10pm on buses). Parents should bring recent pictures of their offspring, plus proof of their age, to the nearest Tube station (just in case, most have photo booths) and get a Child Photocard. It costs nothing, but kids must carry one. Adults will also need passport-size photographs if buying travel passes for 7 days or longer (see below), except the bus-only passes.

London Transport puts up its fares once a year in early January, usually adding 10p to every one-way ticket. At press time, prices were as follows:

Single (one-way) tickets within zone 1 on the Underground cost £1.60 ($2.60) for adults and 60p ($1) for children. Simply double that for a return (round-trip) fare. The price of a book of 10 single tickets, a **Carnet,** is £11.50 ($18), two-thirds that of the same number bought individually. Adult bus fares are £1 ($1.60) within Central London zone 1, 70p ($1.10) outside zone 1, £1.50 ($2.40) on night buses. The flat daytime rate for children is 40p (60¢); they pay adult fares on night buses. A **Saver 6** gives you six journeys for the price of five on zone 1 adult fares.

TRANSPORTATION DISCOUNTS   Anyone planning to use public transport should check out the range of money-saving passes that are available for all public transportation: the Underground, buses, and the Docklands Light Railway.

One-Day Travelcards can be used for unlimited trips before 9:30am (peak) or after 9:30am (off-peak) Monday to Friday, and all day on Saturday, Sunday, and holidays, and on N-prefixed night buses. Adults traveling within zones 1 and 2 pay £4.10 ($7) off-peak and £5.10 ($8) peak. Children pay £2 ($3.20). The **One-Day LT Card** is available for all zones at peak travel times for £8 ($13) per adult, and £3.50 ($6) per child.

Weekend Travelcards are valid for one weekend, or any two consecutive days if Monday is a national holiday, and on night buses.

These cost £6.10 ($10) for adults in zone 1 and 2, and £3 ($4.80) for children.

One-Week Travelcards are good for any number of trips, any hour of the day, and on night buses. The card for zone 1 costs adults £16.50 ($26) and £6.80 ($11) for a child.

Family Travelcards are available to groups that include up to two adults, plus up to four children, and it is only valid when they travel together. These, too, can be used only after 9:30am during the week. They cost £2.70 ($4.30) per adult in the group, and 80p ($1.30) per child, for zones 1 and 2.

Bus passes, valid for travel only on London Transport buses, are available for all zones for 1 day at £2 ($3.20) per adult and £1 ($1.60) per child, and for 1 week at £8.50 and £4 ($14 and $6).

You can buy all these, as well as monthly and yearly passes, at Tube stations, tobacconists, and newsagents with a **Pass Agent** sticker in their window.

THE UNDERGROUND

The Tube map is very easy to use. Every line has a different color: navy blue for the Piccadilly Line (the one that runs in from Heathrow), red for the Central Line, and so on. Station signs in the subway tunnels and on the different platforms clearly direct you to eastbound and westbound, or northbound and southbound trains. A sign at the front of the train and electronic notice boards on the platforms tell you the final destination of that line, so get to know the names of stations at the ends of the lines you use most often. The **Docklands Light Railway** is an extension to the main Tube system. Its driverless trains run east on elevated tracks from Bank Tube station and Tower Gateway, close to Tower Hill. It operates daily at similar hours.

Except for Christmas Day, Tube trains run every few minutes from about 5:30am Monday to Saturday and 7am or so on Sunday. The Underground winds down between 11:30pm and 1am, as trains head back to home base, with stations closing behind them.

There are two ways to buy tickets: at the station ticket window or using one of the push-button machines. Queuing at the window can be phenomenally time-consuming, particularly at West End stations during the summer. Elsewhere, the rush hour clogs things up, especially on a Monday when lots of people renew weekly travel passes. You will have to go to the window, though, if you want to buy a pass valid for longer than 2 days.

There are two kinds of machines: The first takes only coins, and has buttons marked with little more than the price. (There should be a poster next to it that lists fares to every station.) The other machine has a button for each station and type of ticket, and will tell you the price of your choice. It accepts credit and debit cards, coins, and notes up to £10. The machines make change until they run out of spare coins, which tends to happen at busy times.

Hold onto your ticket throughout your ride because you'll need it to exit and London Transport inspectors make random checks. No excuse, however imaginative or heartrending, will get you out of the rigidly imposed £10 ($16) penalty fare.

LONDON BUSES

London's comprehensive bus system makes for a very bewildering map. Most locals know only 2 of the 500-plus routes: from home to work and to the West End, and often that's the same thing. If you find the map completely incomprehensible, call the LT Travel Line (see above), and they'll tell you how to get from A to B. And ask the driver or conductor to let you know when the bus has reached your destination.

To stop a bus when you're on it, press the bell (or tug the wire running the length of the ceiling in an old bus). Without any signal, the driver won't stop unless passengers are waiting to get on the bus. If you're the one waiting, make sure to note whether it is a compulsory (white background on the sign) or a request stop (red background). At the latter, give a big wave or the bus won't stop.

Traveling by bus is a great way to see London, but it can be frustratingly slow, particularly in rush hour and along Oxford Street and King's Road. Normal buses run until around midnight when night buses, with an N in front of the number, take over for the next 6 hours. On most routes, there's one every half-hour or hour, and those to, from, and through the West End all go via Trafalgar Square, so if in doubt, head there. Some travel passes are *not* valid on night buses.

You buy single-trip bus tickets on the bus itself. On older buses, a conductor comes around, but most new buses are now driver-only, so you pay when you board. In either case, proffering a note bigger than £5, unless you're only expecting small change, is likely to produce some very fruity language, particularly from the notoriously eccentric conductors. If inspectors find you without a ticket, the on-the-spot fine is £5 ($8).

BY TAXI

Black cabs carry up to five people and can make sound economic sense for group jaunts. All the drivers are licensed and have to pass

Telephone Dialing Info at a Glance

• To call London from home, dial the international access code: ℂ **011** from the **United States** and **Canada**, ℂ **0011** from **Australia**, and ℂ **00** from **New Zealand**. Follow that with **44**, and then the area code minus its initial zero, and finally the number.

• To call home from London, the international codes are ℂ **001** for the **United States** and **Canada**, ℂ **0061** for **Australia**, and ℂ **0064** for **New Zealand**. Then add the area code minus any initial zero, and the number. Or, you can use these **long-distance access codes:** AT&T USA Direct (ℂ **0800/890011**), MCI Worldphone (ℂ **800/ 890222**), USA Sprint Global (ℂ **0800/890877**), Canada Direct (ℂ **0800/890016**), Telstra Direct for Australia (ℂ **0800/890061**), and New Zealand Direct (ℂ **0800/ 890064**).

• When you're in London, dial ℂ **100** for the U.K. national operator, ℂ **155** for the international operator, ℂ **192** for Directory Enquiries to find out a U.K. telephone number, and ℂ **153** for International Directory Enquiries.

• Free dial-a-directory **Scoot** (ℂ **0800/192192**) can give you the name, address, and phone number of any service you might need in London.

a test called The Knowledge first, so they know London very well. Look for the yellow "For Hire" sign lit up on the roof and wave wildly. Before you get in, tell the driver where you want to go. Except in the West End, many drivers go home at midnight. You can order a black cab but you'll have to pay an extra charge for the time it takes the taxi to get to you—up to £3.80 ($6). These two companies dispatch cabs around the clock: **Dial a Cab** (ℂ **020/ 7253-5000**) and **Radio Taxis** (ℂ **020/7272-0272**).

The average cost of a taxi ride is said to be £8 ($13)—but that means daytime, within central London, and with no unusual traffic jams. The minimum charge is £1.40 ($2.20), and the meter goes up in increments of 20p (32¢). You'll pay an extra 60p to 90p ($1 to $1.40) depending on the time of day (generally after 8pm and between midnight and 6am on weekdays, and slightly different times at weekends, or public holidays). Other extras on the basic fare include 40p (60¢) for every passenger after the first one and 10p (16¢) for every piece of luggage over 2 feet long or that has to go in front with the driver. If you have any complaints, call the **Public Carriage Office** (© 020/7230-1631).

Minicabs are generally cheaper than black cabs, but drivers don't have to have a special license, and some won't know their way around any better than you do. Technically, they must operate from a side-walk office or through phone bookings, and are not allowed to cruise for fares. But some do, of course, particularly at main railway stations and late night in the West End. With minicabs there are none of the guarantees you get with a black cab. Minicabs don't have meters. Always negotiate the fare with the office, and confirm it with the driver. Most firms are open round the clock, and you can pre-book for later, or for the next morning if you've got an early start. They tend to be locally based, so ask your hotel or B&B to recommend a reputable one. **Addison Lee** (© 020/7387-8888) operates citywide.

FAST FACTS: London

Airport See "Getting There," in chapter 1.

American Express American Express has over a dozen city center offices. The main branch is at 30–31 Haymarket, SW1 (© 020/7484-9610; www.americanexpress.com; Tube: Piccadilly Circus). The company has a 24-hour toll-free lines to report lost or stolen cards (© 0800/550011) and traveler's checks (© 0800/521313).

Business Hours Bank opening hours are Monday to Friday 9:30am to 3:30 or 4:30pm. Business offices are generally open Monday to Friday from 9am until 5 or 5:30pm. Stores are generally open Monday to Saturday from 10am to 6pm. Many stay open for at least 1 extra hour on a Wednesday or Thursday, depending on the neighborhood (see chapter 8). Some shops around touristy Covent Garden don't close until 7 or 8pm nightly. Supermarkets and many of the stores in busy shopping areas are also open on Sundays, usually starting at 11am.

Climate See "When to Go," in chapter 1.

Currency See "Money," in chapter 1.

Dentists Try the **Dental Emergency Care Service,** Guy's Hospital, St. Thomas's St., SE1 (© 020/7955-5000), a first-come, first-served clinic on the 23rd floor, Monday to Friday 8:45am to 3pm. On Saturday and Sunday, emergency dental service is available from 9am to 4pm at **Kings College,** Denmark Hill, Camberwell SE5 (*©* **020/7345-3591**).

Doctors **Medcall,** 2 Harley St., W1 (*©* **0800/136106**), operates a late-night practice and 24-hour call-out. **Medical Express,** 117A Harley St., W1 (*©* **020/7499-1991**), is a private clinic with walk-in medical service (no appointment necessary) Monday through Friday 9am to 6pm and Saturday 9:30am to 2:30pm.

Drugstores The Brits call them chemists. **Bliss Chemist,** 5 Marble Arch, W1 (*©* **020/7723-6116**), is open daily 9am to midnight. **Zarfash Pharmacy,** 233–235 Old Brompton Rd., SW5 (*©* **020/ 7373-2798**), never closes. In daytime hours, there are branches of **Boots** and **Superdrug** everywhere.

Electricity British appliances operate on the EU standard of 240 volts. If you're bringing a hair dryer, travel iron, shaver, and so on, you need a transformer. British sockets take different three-pronged plugs than those in the U.S. London department stores and most branches of **Boots** sell adapters. Hotels and B&Bs sometimes have one you can borrow.

Embassies & High Commissions This list will help you out if you lose your passport or have some other emergency:

- **Australia** The **High Commission** is at Australia House, Strand, WC2 (*©* **020/7379-4334**; www.australia.org.uk), and is open Monday to Friday from 9am to 5pm. Tube: Holborn, Temple.
- **Canada** The **High Commission** is at 38 Grosvenor St., W1 (*©* **020/7258-6600**; www.dfait-maeci.gc.ca), and is open Monday to Friday from 8am to 11am. Tube: Bond St.
- **New Zealand** The **High Commission** is at **New Zealand House,** Haymarket, SW1 (*©* **020/7930-8422**; www.new zealandhc.org.uk), and is open Monday to Friday from 10am to noon, and 2 to 4pm. Tube: Piccadilly Circus.
- **The United States** The embassy is at 24 Grosvenor Sq., W1 (*©* **020/7499-9000**; www.usembassy.org.uk), is open for walk-in enquiries 8:30am to 12:30pm, 2 to 5pm (to 5:30pm for phone calls). Tube: Marble Arch, Bond Street.

Emergencies Dial *©* **999** free from any phone for police, fire, and ambulance.

Hospitals Around a dozen city hospitals offer 24-hour walk-in emergency care. The most central is **University College**

Hospital, Grafton Way, WC1 (© **020/7387-9300**). The two best alternatives are **Chelsea & Westminster Hospital,** 369 Fulham Rd., SW10 (© **020/8746-8000**), on the Chelsea/Fulham border; and **St. Mary's Hospital,** Praed St., W2 (© **020/7886-6666**), in Paddington.

Internet Access Britain has got the surfing bug. There are **easyEverything** cyber cafes all over London.

Mail Stamps for postcards to anywhere outside Europe cost 42p (67¢); sending an airmail letter up to 10 grams costs 47p (75¢). See "Post Office," below.

Newspapers/Magazines The *Guardian, Independent,* the *Times,* and *Daily Telegraph* are the so-called quality national daily newspapers, listed here from left to right across the political spectrum. The *Daily Mail* and *Express* are right-wing tabloids. All have Sunday editions. (The *Guardian* has a sister paper, *The Observer.*) The *Evening Standard* is the only paid-for citywide local paper—it has a freebie sister, *Metro,* carried on Tube trains in the morning—and publishes updated editions from 10am to around 5pm. On Thursdays, it has a what's-on supplement, *Hot Tickets.* Most Sunday broadsheets produce entertainment guides, too. But the listings bible is the weekly *Time Out* magazine (www.timeout.com).

Post Office The **Trafalgar Square Post Office,** 24-28 William IV St., Trafalgar Square, WC2, is open Monday to Friday from 8am to 8pm, 9am on Saturday. Most other post offices are open Monday to Friday from 9am to 5:30pm, and Saturday 9am to noon. Look for the red Royal Mail signs. To contact the Trafalgar Square Post office or find the nearest local one, call the **Post Office Counters Helpline** (© **08457/223344;** www. postoffice.co.uk).

Restrooms The Brits have four printable words for restrooms: WC (water closet), toilet, lavatory (the lav), and loo. Some "Public Toilets" are free but keep a few 20p coins handy for the many paid-for ones.

Safety Violent crime is no more common in Central London than in any other big city, and less common than in many. But don't take risks—keep wallets and purses hidden, bags held tight to your side, backpacks zipped, and never leave possessions unattended, even on the floor between your feet. And don't flash your cash, credit cards, or jewelry.

Smoking You can't light up anywhere on the Underground or on buses. Many restaurants have nonsmoking sections, and some ban it completely. Things are also starting to change in budget hotels and B&Bs. A few don't allow smoking at all. More are now keeping some rooms as nonsmoking.

Taxes The national 17.5% value-added tax (VAT) is levied on most goods and services, and is included in the price. Except for the luxury ones, hotels usually include VAT in quoted prices (all rates in this book include tax). Foreign visitors can reclaim the VAT on goods they're taking out of the U.K. Ask for a form from the sales clerk at those stores participating in the Tax-Free Shopping scheme. Then show it and the goods at the VAT desk at the airport for an immediate refund. For more information, see chapter 7.

Taxis See "By Taxi," earlier in this chapter.

Telephones Several companies operate London phone boxes, each branded differently, but BT (British Telecom) is still the largest. There are also pay phones in most large public buildings. Most accept any coin upward of 10p. Others take credit cards and pre-paid BT phonecards, which are available in post offices and newsagents. Look for the green sign.

Pay-phone **call rates** are the same every day, all day. The minimum cost is 20p (32¢) for the first 67 seconds of a local call and 43 seconds of all other calls. The pro-rata cost works out, respectively, at 9p (14¢) and 15p (24¢) per minute. Pay phones accept up to four coins at a time. They don't make change so, unless you're calling long-distance, use small denominations.

Time Zone London's clocks are set on Greenwich Mean Time—5 hours ahead of U.S. Eastern Standard Time, 10 hours behind much of Australia, and 12 hours behind New Zealand. To find out the time, dial **Timeline** (📞 **123**). Daylight saving time is used in Britain, too. The clocks move 1 hour back, to British Summer Time, on the last weekend of March, and forward to GMT again on the last weekend of October.

Tipping The more expensive restaurants tend to add a service charge of 12½% to the bill. Cheaper ones sometimes do, too, but more often only if you're a big group. The tipping policy should be written on the menu. If in doubt, ask. And make sure to check the bill before filling in the gap for a gratuity. In Britain, it is usual practice to tip cab drivers, staff in restaurants, hairdressers, some bars with table service, and hotels, but never pubs. Budget hotels and B&Bs will rarely add a percentage to the bill, so it's up to you. The usual amount on any occasion is 10%.

Weather Surf **www.bbc.co.uk/weather** for 5-day forecasts. Weathercall charges 60p (90¢) a minute for 7-day forecasts (© **09068/505301**).

3

Accommodations You Can Afford

Spend the night in a cupboard. Wash in a cup, then dry yourself with a handkerchief. Practice climbing and build your endurance on the Stairmaster. Whatever it is, do something to prepare yourself for the budget accommodations you'll find in London. It's unlikely that you'll be staying in a new hotel with an elevator (called a "lift" in England) and spacious rooms with marble bathrooms. Instead, if you opt for a B&B, you'll more likely be in an historic building, either Georgian or Victorian, with a certain amount of charm (hopefully) but few luxuries. Bedrooms are small and private bathrooms (called "en suite facilities") are mainly an afterthought and as tiny as the toilet in an airplane. In many budget B&Bs the bathrooms are prefab shower/sink/toilet units that have been fit into the rooms.

I don't mean to paint too bleak a picture because there are plenty of good, small, even charming B&Bs where you'll be perfectly comfortable. I just want you to be prepared.

Truth to tell, every London hotel I visited in 2003 was begging for business and rates have never been lower. Hotels need to fill their beds, so prices drop when tourism dips. Every hotel with a website told me that readers should check the hotel's website for special offers. Using the Web, you might find a lower rate than the non-discounted rack rates listed below.

Tips A Tip for the Bedless

If you arrive in London without a bed for the night, you can call the **London Tourist Board's** new accommodation reservation hotline (© **020/7932-2020**; www.londontown.com/stay). There is a £5 ($8) booking fee. Alternatively, staff at tourist information offices can book hotels and B&Bs—just walk in (see "Visitor Information," in chapter 2).

---

1 How to Save on Sleeping

If you know where to look and what to ask for, you can find bargains in London. Just read on.

- **Play the supply-and-demand game.** Avoid high season. Most hotels make their annual rate increase in April and drop down again in October.

- **Go native.** Many Londoners offer bed-and-breakfast in their homes. The Bed & Breakfast and Hosts Association sets quality standards and the following three members are all well established. Rates are per night and for two people sharing a room: **At Home in London** (© **020/8748-1943;** www. athomeinlondon.co.uk) from £75 ($120) in West London; **Host and Guest Service** (© **020/7385-9922;** www.host-guest.co.uk) from £80 ($128) in Central London; and **Uptown Reservations** (© **020/7351-3445;** www.uptown res.co.uk) from £95 ($144) in Central London.

- **Consider apartment hotels or rooms with kitchens.** Staying in self-catering accommodation can cut down on expensive restaurant bills. Agencies to try include **Emperors Gate Short Stay Apartments,** SW5 (© **020/7244-8409;** www.apartment-hotels.com); **The Independent Traveller** (© **01392/860807;** www.gowithIT.co.uk), run by the very friendly and experienced Mary and Simon Ette; **Residence Apartments** (© **020/7727-0352;** www.residence-apartments.com); and the super-budget **Acorn Management Services** (© **020/8202-3311;** www. acorn-london.co.uk).

- **Go back to school.** During the summer and sometimes at Easter, you can find accommodations starting at around £22 ($35) per person at the dozens of university dorms in London. I've reviewed a handful of the top options. For fuller details of what's on offer, try **Venuemasters** (© **0114/249-3090;** www.venuemasters.co.uk) or contact the three central London universities directly: **University of London** (© **020/7862-8880;** www.lon.ac.uk/accom); **University of Westminster** (© **020/7911-5796;** www.westminster.ac.uk/comserv/halls. htm); or **City University** (© **020/7477-8037;** www.city.ac.uk/ems/accomm1.htm).

- **Sleep super-cheap.** Hostel dorm beds cost from £14 to £24 ($22–$38) per night, and many of them have cheap twin

---

> ⌒*Tips* **Net Savings**
>
> The **British Hotel Reservation Centre** (✆ 020/7828-0601; www.bhrc.co.uk) site is simple to navigate, with the BHRC price next to the rack rate for more than 120 hotels and B&Bs all over London. There are big savings to be had through **www.laterooms.com,** which publishes comparable prices, for bookings up to 3 weeks in advance. It does self-catering accommodation, too. If you can bear the tension, wait until a few days before you fly and then scan **www.lastminute.com**.

---

rooms, too. There are also seven **Youth Hostel Association** sites (✆ **020/7373-3400;** www.yha.org.uk), the best of which are reviewed below.

2 Kensington & Chelsea

In addition to the Trafalgar Square location (see later in this chapter), **Citadines** (✆ **0800/376-3898;** www.citadines.com) also has an apartment hotel in South Kensington near the Gloucester Road Tube station, and another in Holborn near Covent Garden. Special-offer studios start as low as £83 ($133) a night off-season if you stay 1 week. Meanwhile, you'll get an even better deal at **Nell Gwynn House** ⚐, Sloane Ave., SW3 3AX (✆ **020/7589-1105;** fax 020/7589-9433; www.nghapartments.co.uk), where rates start at £470 ($752) per week for a small two-person studio. The downside is that reservations are only taken for whole weeks, the upside that the longer you stay the lower the price.

Abbey House ⚐   There are no private bathrooms at Abbey House, which is why it can charge these rates in such a posh part of town. It's only a short walk up to Notting Hill, or downhill to Kensington High Street. Abbey House, owned by Albert and Carol Nayach, is a gem set in a gracious Victorian square. The bright hallway has a checkerboard floor and wrought-iron staircase lined with lithographs of glum-faced royals. The bedrooms are simple, attractive, and big for London. The second-floor room at the front gets the balcony above the front door. The bathrooms are Laura Ashley style and impeccable; there's one for every three bedrooms. And there's a kitchenette, where you can make tea and coffee for free. The staff treat you terribly well here, whether you need a hair dryer, babysitting, or restaurant advice.

11 Vicarage Gate, London W8 4AG. © **020/7727-2594**. Fax 020/7727-1873. www. abbeyhousekensington.com. 16 units, none with bathroom. £45 ($72) single; £74 ($118) double/twin; £90 ($144) triple; £100 ($160) quad. Rates include full English breakfast. Discount available off-season. No credit cards. Tube: High St. Kensington, Notting Hill Gate. **Amenities:** Babysitting arranged. *In room:* TV, no phone.

Prince's Gardens Halls, Imperial College ☞   Prince's Gardens is like a holiday camp. The maze of rooms is decorated in the usual student style, and most are singles, so book early if you want a twin. There are no private bathrooms, but only four rooms share each public facility. Because Prince's Gardens is part of the campus at Imperial College, you get to use all the on-site amenities. There's a bank as well as a bureau de change, a tourist information desk and travel agency, even a medical center. Guests also get a discount rate at the sports center. The Basics restaurant does pizza for half the price you'll pay anywhere else, and you can do a bar crawl without even leaving the complex. You'll want to leave, though, because this is a fantastic location. Harrods, the Victoria & Albert Museum, the Natural History Museum, Kensington Gardens, Hyde Park, and the Royal Albert Hall are all within a short walk.

Accommodation Link, Watts Way, Prince's Gardens, London SW7 1LU. © **020/ 7594-9507**. Fax 020/7594-9504. www.ad.ic.ac.uk/conferences. 608 units. £40.50 ($65) single; £61 ($98) twin. Rates include full English breakfast. MC, V. Open Easter and summer vacations. Tube: South Kensington. No children under 10. **Amenities:** Restaurant; bar; sports center with pool; game room; tour desk; salon; coin-op washers and dryers. *In room:* no phone.

Swiss House Hotel ☞   If you've just gotta have your space, man, then Swiss House could be the answer to your prayers. If they're available, Peter Vincenti lets out his huge quads to two people as a double room for £99 ($158). But you don't have to splurge because the standard doubles are a good size, too, and this is a lovely place. Guests walk past a curtain of greenery—plants hang from every window ledge, railing, and balcony—and under an old-fashioned canopy to the front door. Inside, chintz, dried flowers, and original fireplaces create a homey, country-style atmosphere. Traffic noise can be a problem on Old Brompton Road, so try to get a room at

---

The Difference Between Singles, Twins & Doubles

In British English, a **single** is a room with one bed for one person. A **twin** has two beds, each for one person. A **double** has one bed big enough for two.

Where to Stay from Knightsbridge to Earl's Court

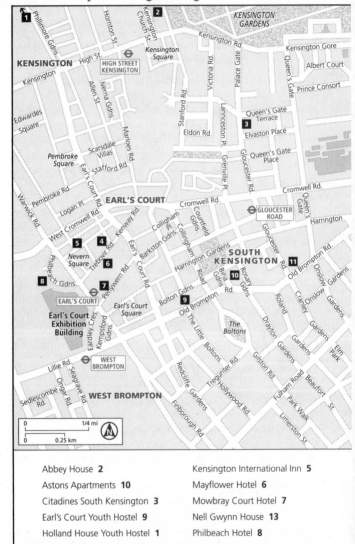

Abbey House **2**

Astons Apartments **10**

Citadines South Kensington **3**

Earl's Court Youth Hostel **9**

Holland House Youth Hostel **1**

Kensington International Inn **5**

Mayflower Hotel **6**

Mowbray Court Hotel **7**

Nell Gwynn House **13**

Philbeach Hotel **8**

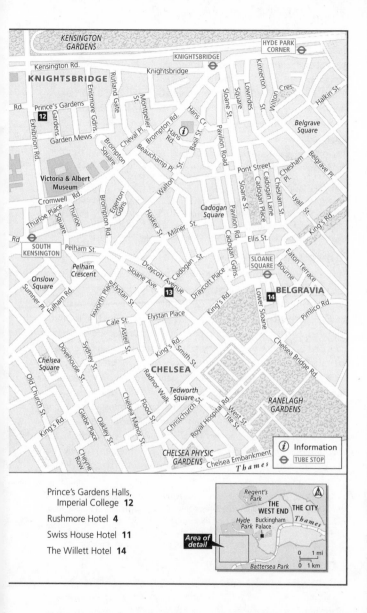

KENSINGTON GARDENS

HYDE PARK CORNER

KNIGHTSBRIDGE

Kensington Rd.

KNIGHTSBRIDGE

Knightsbridge

Kinnerton St.

Lowndes St.

Willow Cres.

Halkin St.

Prince's Gardens

12

Rutland Gate

Montpelier St.

Ensmore Gdns.

Rd.

Exhibition Rd.

Prince's Gardens

Garden Mews

Cheval Pl.

Brompton Square

Brompton Rd.

Hans Rd.

Sloane Square

Pavilion Road

Belgrave Square

Beauchamp Pl.

Hans Cr.

Basil St.

Chesham Pl.

Belgrave Pl.

Victoria & Albert Museum

Cromwell Rd.

Thurloe Place

Thurloe Square

Thurloe

Egerton Gdns

Walton

Pont Street

Sloane St.

Cadogan Lane

Cadogan Place

Chesham St.

Lyall St.

King's Rd.

Brompton Rd.

Hasker St.

Milner St.

Cadogan Square

Pavilion Rd.

Cadogan St.

Cadogan Gdns.

Ellis St.

SOUTH KENSINGTON

Pelham St.

Pelham Crescent

Draycott Avenue

Cadogan St.

Draycott Place

SLOANE SQUARE

Eaton Terrace

Bourne

Onslow Square

Summer Pl.

Fulham Rd.

Ixworth Place

Elystan St.

Sloane Ave.

13

King's Rd.

Lower Sloane

BELGRAVIA

14

Pimlico Rd.

Cale St.

Astell St.

Elystan Place

Chelsea Bridge Rd.

Chelsea Square

Dovehouse St.

Sydney St.

King's Rd.

Smith St.

CHELSEA

Old Church St.

King's Rd.

Glebe Place

Oakley St.

Chelsea Manor St.

Flood St.

Radnor Walk

Tedworth Square

Christchurch St.

Royal Hospital Rd.

Tite St.

West St.

RANELAGH GARDENS

Cheyne Row

CHELSEA PHYSIC GARDENS

Chelsea Embankment

T h a m e s

(i) Information

TUBE STOP

Prince's Gardens Halls,
Imperial College **12**

Rushmore Hotel **4**

Swiss House Hotel **11**

The Willett Hotel **14**

Regent's Park

THE WEST END

THE CITY

Hyde Park

Buckingham Palace

Thames

Area of detail

Battersea Park

0   1 mi
0   1 km

the back looking over the peaceful communal garden (you'll have to be content with looking though; it's not open to guests). The proprietor is an extremely welcoming and helpful host, providing room service of soups and "monster" sandwiches from midday until 9pm. You can also pay a £6 ($10) supplement for a full English breakfast. Someone will carry your bags up and buy your favorite newspaper. Swiss House is popular with families, but around 80% of its guests are middle-aged U.S. tourists.

171 Old Brompton Rd., London SW5 0AN. ℂ 020/7373-2769. Fax 020/7373-4983. www.swiss-hh.demon.co.uk. 16 units, 15 with bathroom (most with shower only). £51 ($82) single without bathroom; £71 ($114) single with bathroom; £89–£104 ($142–$166) double/twin with bathroom; £120 ($192) triple with bathroom; £134 ($214) quad with bathroom. Rates include continental breakfast. Discount of 5% for 1-wk. stay and cash payment (U.S.$ accepted). AE, DC, MC, V. Tube: Gloucester Rd. **Amenities:** Secretarial services; limited room service; babysitting arranged; laundry service; nonsmoking rooms. *In room:* TV, hair dryer.

SUPER-CHEAP SLEEPS

Holland House Youth Hostel 𝕬   This hostel is located right in the middle of a leafy public park that used to be the grounds for Holland House (1607), a redbrick and white-stone Jacobean mansion that was partially destroyed by bombs in World War II. The youth hostel splits its accommodation between what's left of the house and a second building from the 1950s. In the summer, open-air opera is staged in the ruins of Holland House (see the box "Performers in the Park," p. 162). Residents can sit in the courtyard and enjoy the music for free. The hostel has all the normal useful stuff like a kitchen, TV room, quiet room, and Internet access. The cafeteria has a liquor license and serves cheap meals from 5 to 8pm. The only drawback is that a lot of school groups stay here. Some dorms sleep 6 to 8, but most sleep 12 to 20 people, and there are no family bunkrooms. But you're only a 10-minute walk from a tube station and a quick ride into the middle of town.

Holland Walk, Holland Park, London W8 7QU. ℂ 020/7937-0748. Fax 020/7376-0667. www.yha.org.uk. 201 units, none with bathroom. £21 ($34) per adult; £18.75 ($30) per person under 18. Rates include full English breakfast. AE, MC, V. Tube: Holland Park, High St. Kensington. **Amenities:** Restaurant; coin-op washers and dryers; communal kitchen; Internet access; garden. *In room:* no phone.

DO-IT-YOURSELF DEALS

Astons Apartments 𝕬𝕬   Behind the redbrick facades of three Victorian townhouses you'll find the very model of a modern apartment hotel. Maids swoop through every day. You can see your face in the lovely, polished, wood handrail on the stairs. The reception desk, where you can send a fax or drop off your dry cleaning or have someone order a theater or tour ticket, is manned until 9pm. Prices verge on being a splurge for budget travelers, but you get good value for your money and the website often has hot deals. If money is tight, forget the singles and the great family room in the basement with its proper open-plan kitchen and sofa bed for the kids. You can do better elsewhere. But the rest of the studios should impress even the most exacting guests. A dozen were recently refurbed, with more in the works. The Executive doubles and quads are larger and have some extra amenities, including larger bathrooms. Bathrooms throughout are tiled and have showers. All the studios have fully equipped kitchenettes, hidden behind foldaway doors, and there's a big supermarket nearby.

31 Rosary Gardens, London SW7 4NH. ℰ 800/525-2810 or 020/7590-6000. Fax 020/7590-6060. www.astons-apartments.com. 54 units. Standard studios: £65 ($104) single; £90 ($144) double, £125 ($200) triple; Executive studios: £125 ($200) double; £165 ($264) quad. Discount available for Frommer's readers; inquire when booking. Children stay free in parents' room. AE, DISC, MC, V. Tube: Gloucester Rd. **Amenities:** Business center; nonsmoking rooms. *In room:* TV, dataport, kitchenette, coffeemaker, hair dryer.

WORTH A SPLURGE

The Willett Hotel 𝓻𝓻   Part of a quiet redbrick terrace, The Willett is noteworthy for its mansard roof, bay windows, and a host of the other Victorian architectural details. This is a dream location for shopaholics, just off Sloane Square and a 5-minute walk to Chelsea's King's Road. The Willett has been refurbished throughout in a heavily traditional style to match the building. All the rooms are different, standards are very high. Deluxe rooms have canopies over the beds, voluptuous swagged curtains, and matching armchairs, and nice but not terribly large bathrooms. You'll probably want to avoid the tiny standard twins where you sleep head to head along one wall, but the small double is a fantastic value for this swanky area. The porter will stagger upstairs with your bags. Reception can order your favorite newspaper. And, best of all, guests can relax in the secluded communal garden. It's all just so civilized.

32 Sloane Gardens, London SW1 8DJ. ℰ 800/270-9206 in the U.S., or 020/7824-8415. Fax 020/7730-4830. www.eeh.co.uk. 19 units, all with bathroom (most with shower only). £90 ($144) small double/twin; £100 ($160) standard double/twin; £145 ($232) deluxe double/twin; £155 ($248) triple. Rates do not include 17.5% VAT. Include full English breakfast. AE, DC, MC, V. Tube: Sloane Sq. **Amenities:** Limited room service; laundry service; dry cleaning. *In room:* TV, fridge, coffeemaker, hair dryer.

Earl's Court

Mayflower Hotel 🏆 With its black pillars and showy window boxes, this hotel is determined to look a cut above its cut-price competitors in Earl's Court. Fortunately, the inside lives up to the promise. The owners have just refurbished every bedroom and bathroom, giving the rooms (all decorated differently) a subdued, minimal elegance with wood floors, sumptuous fabrics, and gorgeous marble showers. Generally, the rooms aren't a bad size for London. There's a great second-floor family room that leads onto the front porch, and there's even an elevator. The staff here have always been solicitous, lending out irons, hair dryers, and adapter plugs, and making life easy for their guests. Now the owners are aiming for even smoother service, "like the Holiday Inn." It's a good deal all round, especially at this budget price.

The Mayflower also has 35 attractive self-catering accommodations, the **Court Apartments,** on busy Warwick Way. Studios start at £69 ($110) per night, or £420 ($672) per week.

26–28 Trebovir Rd., London SW5 9NJ. ✆ **020/7370-0991.** Fax 020/7370-0994. www.mayflowerhotel.co.uk. 48 units, all with bathroom (some with tub only). £59–£75 ($94–$120) single; £69–£99 ($110–$163) double/twin; £89–£109 ($142–$174) triple, £99–£130 ($158–$208) family room. Rates include continental breakfast. Discount available for 3-day and weekday stays. AE, MC, V. Tube: Earl's Court. **Amenities:** Secretarial services; limited room service; dry cleaning; nonsmoking rooms. *In room:* TV, coffeemaker.

Mowbray Court Hotel 🏆🏆 (Kids) Brothers Tony and Peter Dooley run this spotlessly clean hotel, which their parents opened 41 years ago. Mowbray Court is a very friendly, very good value, old-fashioned budget hotel. It's comfortable without being glamorous and even has a bar and a lounge with Internet service. The rooms tend to be basic, most with prefab bathroom units with shower, basin, and toilet. Otherwise, four bedrooms share every public bathroom. There's a family room with seven beds in the basement of the main building and a triple with a little kitchen in the annex. Rooms at the back face the overground Tube line, but double-glazing keeps out the noise. The party-wall paneling in the breakfast room is a bit grim. The hotel will arrange shuttle-bus service to and from Heathrow for £15 ($24) and £22 ($35) to Gatwick. There's even a Vidal Sassoon–trained visiting hairdresser. Present your Frommer's guide and they'll give you a 5% discount.

28–32 Penywern Rd., London SW5 9SU. ✆ **020/7373-8285.** Fax 020/7370-5693. www.m-c-hotel.mcmail.com. 82 units, 70 with bathroom (most with shower only).

£45 ($72) single without bathroom, £52 ($83) single with bathroom; £56 ($90) double without bathroom, £67 ($107) double with bathroom; £69 ($110) triple without bathroom, £80 ($128) triple with bathroom; £84 ($134) quad without bathroom, £95 ($152) quad with bathroom; £100 ($160) family room without bathroom, £115–£125 ($184–$200) family room with bathroom; £145 ($232) 7-bed room with bathroom. Rates include continental breakfast. AE, DC, MC, V. Tube: Earl's Court. **Amenities:** Bar; babysitting arranged; laundry/dry cleaning; 15 non-smoking rooms, airport shuttle. *In room:* TV, hair dryer, safe, pants press.

Philbeach Hotel 🎇   The Philbeach is a one-stop entertainment bonanza for gay travelers and somehow manages to do it at budget rates. It's a really friendly place and attractive, too. The whole building was recarpeted and most of the rooms got new beds in 2000. Some of the rooms are small so go for one of the little mezzanine doubles. They share a terrace overlooking the lovely garden. One is en suite, and the other shares a bathroom. It's about four bedrooms to every public facility. The Philbeach gets rowdier the higher you go up the house. This isn't the place to come if you want a quiet hidey-hole. The Princess Restaurant, with its conservatory setting, serves Thai cuisine and residents get a 20% discount. The hotel has a cozy basement bar, and the Monday party nights are a blast. There's a terrace, a dance floor, and a dressing service with wigs, clothes, shoes, and make-up for cross-dressers.

30–31 Philbeach Gardens, London SW5 9EB. 𝄢 **020/7373-1244.** Fax 020/7244-0149. www.philbeachhotel.freeserve.co.uk. 40 units, 15 w/bathroom (most w/shower only). £35–£50 ($52–$80) single w/o bathroom, £60 ($96) single w/bathroom; £65 ($104) double w/o bathroom, £90 ($144) double w/bathroom; £75 ($120) triple w/o bathroom, £100 ($160) triple w/bathroom. Rates include continental breakfast. Discount available for 1-wk. stays. No 1-night stays on Sat. AE, DC, MC, V. Tube: Earl's Court. **Amenities:** Restaurant; bar; garden, nonsmoking rooms. *In room:* TV, coffeemaker, hair dryer, iron, safe.

Rushmore Hotel 🎇🎇   This gracious townhouse hotel makes art directors at interiors magazines go weak in the knees. Italianate classical scenes decorate the hallway and ceilings. The breakfast room is in a limestone-paved conservatory with wrought-iron furniture and potted orchids. Every bedroom is a different exuberant stage set. One has gothic looping curtains and a canopy over the bed. In another, you'll find a chandelier and Louis XIV pale-blue walls, with panels sketched out in gold. There's a marvelous family room under the eaves, and a porter will carry up your bags. The Rushmore will take bookings for specific rooms (there are five for nonsmokers) and you can preview some of them on the website (which features seasonal specials). All the rooms had new carpet a couple of years ago, and the bathrooms were given a tiled makeover in 2003. The welcoming staff will let you send a fax and pick up e-mail. There are irons at reception and safety deposit boxes. If the Rushmore were anyplace other than in Earl's Court, it would certainly bust the budget.

11 Trebovir Rd., London SW5 9LS. ℂ 020/7370-3839. Fax 020/7370-0274. www. rushmore-hotel.co.uk. 22 units, all w/bathroom (most w/shower only). £59 ($94) single; £79 ($126) double/twin; £89 ($142) triple; £99 ($158) family room. Rates include continental breakfast. Discount available for 1-wk. stays. 10% discount for seniors. Under-12s stay free in parents' room. AE, DC, MC, V. Tube: Earl's Court. **Amenities:** Laundry services; dry cleaning; nonsmoking rooms. In room: TV, coffeemaker, hair dryer.

SUPER-CHEAP SLEEPS

Earl's Court Youth Hostel   If you're going to stay somewhere cheap in Earl's Court, you're far better off going to the youth hostel than one of the dozens of super-budget hotels. At least you know what you're getting, and the location is great. This garden square is just north of Old Brompton Road. On the other side of the street, the millionaires' mansions in the Boltons mark the beginning of posh South Kensington. Earl's Court is backpacker central, and they flock to this very lively international hostel. The big, half-stuccoed Victorian building has a good mix of pretty basic dorms, from a few twins up to some with nine beds or more. There are kitchen facilities so you can always supplement the shockingly meager, packed continental breakfast (in fine weather you can take your plate out to the hostel's courtyard garden). When it comes to an evening chowdown, Earl's Court is packed with cheap but often unappetizing restaurants. There are lots of late-night shops, too. If the pennies aren't too tight, head for the more upmarket Gloucester Road, which is almost as close.

38 Bolton Gardens, London SW5 0AQ. ℂ 020/7373-7083. Fax 020/7835-2034. www.yha.org.uk. 159 units, none w/bathroom. £19 ($30) per adult; £16.75 ($27) per person under 18. Rates include bed linen and continental breakfast. MC, V. Tube: Earl's Court. **Amenities:** Game room; travel desk; coin-op washers and dryers; communal kitchen; Internet access; garden. In room: No phone.

WORTH A SPLURGE

Kensington International Inn ✿ (Finds)   This polished and professionally run establishment on an elegant 1860s street just reopened after a half-million-pound overhaul. It's high in style and low in price. The rooms are small to medium in size but the contemporary decor is surprisingly chic, utilizing pale wheaty colors and sleek wooden headboards and furnishings. Bathrooms are also small, with glass-walled showers. There's a hip little bar, a conservatory lounge, and a high standard of service. You may find a lower price on their website than the rack rates listed below.

4 Templeton Place, London SW5 9LZ. ⓒ **020/7370-4333**. Fax 020/7244-7873. www. kensingtoninternationalinn.com. 60 units, all w/bathroom (shower only). £100 ($160) single; £120 ($192) twin/double; £140 ($224) triple. Rates include continental breakfast. AE, DC, MC, V. Tube: Earl's Court. **Amenities:** Bar; nonsmoking rooms. *In room:* TV, coffeemaker, hair dryer, safe, pants press.

4 Notting Hill

Imperial College charges the same rates at the spartan **Pembridge Gardens Halls** (ⓒ **020/7594-9407;** www.ad.ic.ac.uk) as at its main Prince's Gardens campus. That's because the gracious houses on this quiet side street sell for multi-millions and the location, between Portobello Market and Kensington Gardens, is fantastic. Singles cost £40.50 ($65) or £49.50 ($79) with a bathroom; twins are £61 ($98) or £69 ($110) with a bathroom. Guests can use all the campus facilities, three Tube stops away from Notting Hill Gate at South Kensington.

Comfort Inn Notting Hill ⓕ *(Value)*   This is rather a sneaky good deal. Comfort Inn is a franchise but the owners of this hotel actively urge you to book directly with them and not through central reservations. And so do we, because it gets you a rate that's at least 10% lower than the official ones, and often lower still (we've listed their lower "direct booking" rates below). The hotel will make deals based on occupancy levels, so the quoted offer can change every week. Located on a quiet, pretty street off Notting Hill Gate, the Comfort Inn stretches across five terrace houses. The rooms are on the three upper floors (there is an elevator) and are a fair size for London. Rear windows look across fire escapes and rooftops, while second-floor rooms on the front have access to an east-facing balcony. Rooms have been redecorated with a nice business feel and equipped with firm new beds. The bathrooms are also newly renovated. There are a few newly redone and fairly charming rooms on a little internal courtyard. The Comfort Inn is a practical choice in a superb location. Breakfast is a self-service buffet, or you can pay £5.95 ($10) for full English.

6–14 Pembridge Gardens, London W2 4DU. ⓒ **020/7229-6666**. Fax 020/7229-3333. www.lth-hotels.com. 64 units, all w/bathroom. £49–£72 ($78–$115) single; £58–£94 ($93–$150) double/twin; £75–£115 ($120–$184) triple; £92–£129 ($147–$206) quad. Rates include continental breakfast. Lower rates apply mid-July to Aug, Dec–Feb. Discount available for 1-wk. stays. AE, DC, MC, V. Tube: Notting Hill Gate. **Amenities:** Bar; babysitting arranged; laundry service; dry cleaning; Internet access; nonsmoking rooms. *In room:* TV, dataport, coffeemaker, hair dryer, radio, safe.

Where to Stay from Marylebone to Notting Hill

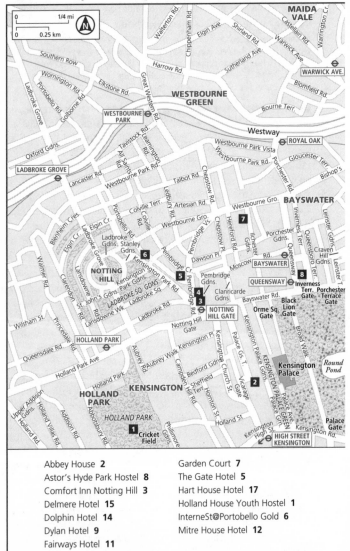

Abbey House **2**
Astor's Hyde Park Hostel **8**
Comfort Inn Notting Hill **3**
Delmere Hotel **15**
Dolphin Hotel **14**
Dylan Hotel **9**
Fairways Hotel **11**

Garden Court **7**
The Gate Hotel **5**
Hart House Hotel **17**
Holland House Youth Hostel **1**
InterneSt@Portobello Gold **6**
Mitre House Hotel **12**

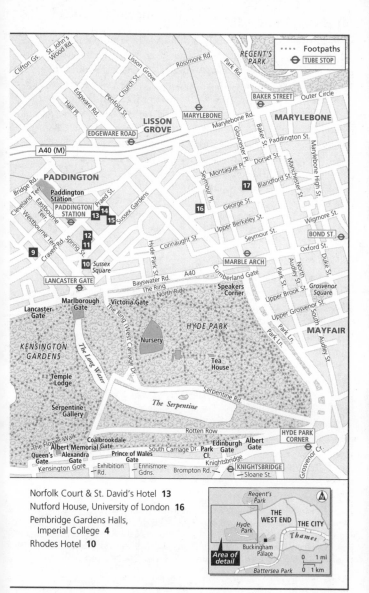

Norfolk Court & St. David's Hotel **13**
Nutford House, University of London **16**
Pembridge Gardens Halls,
    Imperial College **4**
Rhodes Hotel **10**

The Gate Hotel ⏣   Portobello Road is a hot tourist spot because of its market and antiques shops. Which makes The Gate a fun place to stay, if you don't mind crowds of people marching past. The hotel has been in existence since 1932, and the present owners have run it for over 20 years. Look for a tiny, brick, curved-front, late-Georgian house with hanging baskets and a parrot (named Sergeant Bilko) living in a caged-in area in front. Guests eat breakfast in their rooms, which have all been refurbished. The look is attractive, with paneled furniture and blue carpet and linen, and ceiling fans. The bigger rooms each have a small sofa bed for an extra person. Hair dryers are available at reception.

6 Portobello Rd., London W11 3DG. ⏱ **020/7221-0707.** Fax 020/7221-9128. www.gatehotel.com. 6 units, 5 w/private bathroom (most w/shower only). £45–65 ($72–$104) single; £65–£100 ($104–$160) double. Rates include continental breakfast. MC, V. Tube: Notting Hill Gate. *In room:* TV, fridge, radio.

InterneSt@Portobello Gold ⏣ *Finds*   Whatever you do, do not try to make it to InterneSt until at least 6pm if you're arriving on Saturday. The road closes during the day for Portobello Market, and there's zero chance of forcing luggage through the crowds and past the antique stalls set up in front of the building. The conservatory restaurant, with its romantic dining platform, is a local institution and a great deal: two courses could cost you as little as £14.50 ($23). The bar menu is almost as long, and dishes rarely top £6.50 ($10). Guests have unlimited Web access in the second-floor cybercafe or can pay £5 ($8) for a wireless set-up in their room. The rooms are almost unbelievably tiny but freshly decorated. All the rooms have a shower but only three have a toilet; the rest share the facility in the hallway. If you have long legs, ask for the 7-foot-long Captain's bed. For a very special treat, rent the two-story apartment with private roof terrace, then make like a movie star and tour London in Portobello Gold's 1952 Buick convertible (£60/$96 for up to five people).

97 Portobello Rd., London W11 2QB. ⏱ **020/7460-4910.** Fax 020/7460-4911. www.portobellogold.com. 6 units, 3 w/bathroom, 1 apt. £60 ($96) single w/o bathroom; £70 ($112) double w/o bathroom; £75 ($120) single w/bathroom; £85 ($136) double w/bathroom; £180 ($288) apt. Rates include continental breakfast. Lower price Sun–Thurs. Discount for 1-wk. stays. MC, V. Tube: Notting Hill Gate. **Amenities:** Restaurant; bar, free Internet access. *In room:* TV, wireless Internet access.

5 Paddington & Bayswater

Dolphin Hotel ⏣   Mr. and Mrs. Moros have run the Dolphin for over 20 years. It's a nice place, though the lobby smelled of stale cigarette smoke when I visited, and it vies with Norfolk Court (see below) as the best deal in Norfolk Square. The hotel occupies what were once Victorian houses, so the bedrooms vary widely in size. But all are comfortably decorated, with a table and chairs, tiled bathrooms, a fridge, and some with safes, trouser presses, and lovely moldings. The continental breakfast buffet is actually quite an extravaganza, with cheese, cakes, yogurt and honey, eggs cooked any way, and more. If that isn't enough, it will only cost you £2.50 ($4) for full English (we were told that the English breakfast would be free to Frommer's readers, so flash this guidebook). Lower rates below are for bathroomless rooms.

If there's no room at this particular inn, ask about their place next door: **Shakespeare Hotel,** 22–28 Norfolk Sq. (© **020/7402-4646;** fax 020/7723-7233; www.shakespearehotel.co.uk).

34 Norfolk Sq., London W2 1RP. © **020/7402-4943.** Fax 020/7723-8184. www. dolphinhotel.co.uk. 34 units, 22 w/bathroom (most w/shower). £42–£55 ($67–$88) single; £55–£70 ($88–$112) double/twin; £69–£80 ($110–$128) triple; £80–£94 ($116–$150) quad. Rates include continental breakfast. AE, DC, MC, V. Tube: Paddington. *In room:* TV, fridge, coffeemaker, hair dryer.

Dylan Hotel ☞   The recent redecoration of the Dylan resulted in an exuberant decor that mixes dark red, fake-damask wallpaper with red and gold flock and paint. The style fits the date of the house but may not be to everyone's taste. The bedrooms are bright and more restrained. All the en suite rooms have a fridge (relatively rare in this price range and very handy for keeping picnic provisions fresh). No bathroom worries here—they really do sparkle. Try to avoid the top of the house because the stairs go on forever. All in all, the Dylan is a great value. One of the cheaper B&Bs in Paddington, it's off the main drag facing a quiet public square and still only 5 minutes from the Tube station.

14 Devonshire Terrace, London W2 3DW. © **020/7723-3280.** Fax 020/7402-2443. www.dylan-hotel.com. 18 units, 9 with bathroom (some w/shower only). £35 ($56) single w/o bathroom; £52 ($83) double w/o bathroom; £72 ($115) double w/bathroom; £80–£85 ($128–$136) family room. Rates include full English breakfast. Discount for 3-night stays. AE, MC, V. Tube: Paddington, Lancaster Gate. *In room:* TV, coffeemaker, hair dryer, fan.

Fairways Hotel ☞   This is a large, late-Georgian house designed in the 1820s in the style of John Nash. The inside exudes a truly charming English ambience. Stephen James Adams, who took over the management from his parents (they ran the hotel for 25 years), made several improvements in 2002, laying new carpeting and redoing all the communal toilets and showers. The strong personal touch throughout Fairways makes it a home away from home. All the rooms are different, the ones in back much quieter. There's a lovely first-floor double at the back, which has the biggest closet in London, brass fittings in the bathroom, and two boudoir chairs flanking a little lace-covered table. The basic twin is a good deal. The decor is a bit more mix 'n' match, but it's a nice-size room and only shares the bathroom with a single. Guests with a car can park for free in the front. The Mitre Hotel next door is the only other place to offer that.

186 Sussex Gardens, London W2 1TU. ℂ 020/7723-4871. Fax 020/7723-4871. www.fairways-hotel.co.uk. 17 units, 10 w/bathroom (some w/shower only). £52 ($83) single w/o bathroom, £70 ($112) single w/bathroom; £72 ($115) twin w/o bathroom, £80 ($128) double/twin w/bathroom; £110 ($176) triple w/bathroom; £125 ($200) family room w/bathroom. Rates include full English breakfast. Free parking. MC, V. Tube: Paddington. **Amenities:** Nonsmoking rooms. *In room:* TV, coffeemaker, hair dryer, safe, no phone.

Garden Court ⚘   There are cheaper B&Bs in Bayswater but what you won't find elsewhere is such out-and-out appeal, such high standards, or such a genuinely warm welcome. Edward Connolly's grandfather opened Garden Court in 1954 in a pair of pretty Victorian town houses. Inside, it's not luxe—except for the swanky new entrance hall, it's more like a much-loved home. The main lounge has some fine old furniture, ancestral portraits, fat novels to borrow, and free hot drinks. The best value are the rooms without private bathrooms (they all have washbasins), because only two rooms share each public facility. Otherwise, the prices are a little high for Queensway. The rooms are all different: One has pretty yellow wallpaper and white painted furniture, another broad blue stripes. Second-floor, front bedrooms lead out onto balconies. The hotel has a small private terrace at the back and access to the public garden square opposite. Breakfast is called "continental" but you can get eggs and bacon if you want. The lower prices below are for rooms without private bathrooms.

30–31 Kensington Gardens Sq., London W2 4BG. ℂ **020/7229-2553**. Fax 020/ 7727-2749. www.gardencourthotel.co.uk. 32 units, 16 w/bathroom (some w/shower only). £39–£58 ($62–$93) single; £58–£88 ($93–$141) double/twin; £72–£99 ($115–$158) triple; £82–£120 ($131–$192) family room. Rates include continental breakfast. MC, V. Tube: Bayswater, Queensway. **Amenities:** Garden. *In room:* TV, hair dryer.

Mitre House Hotel ⚘⚘ *Kids*   This fine hotel stretches across four Georgian town houses and is kept in tiptop shape by the Chris brothers, who recently took over management from their parents. It's a great family hotel because of the assortment of accommodations.

There are rooms with a double bed and 2 singles, 2-bedroom family suites with a private bathroom, and superior family suites that face quiet, leafy Talbot Square and have a toilet and tub-shower off a little private corridor. Junior suites, with lots of extra amenities and a Jacuzzi in the bathroom, make a good splurge choice. All the rooms are above average size for London; those at the back are quieter, though the view north across back alleys to Paddington isn't very inspiring. Mitre House may not be the cheapest deal around, but it's a good value. Hair dryers and tea/coffeemakers are available at the reception desk. There's a big and very pleasant lounge and bar, and even an elevator.

178–184 Sussex Gardens, London W2 1TU. © 020/7723-8040. Fax 020/7402-0990. www.mitrehousehotel.com. 69 rooms, all w/bathroom (some w/shower only). £60£70 ($96–$112) single; £80 ($128) double/twin; £90 ($144) triple; £100 ($160) family room; £110 ($176) junior suite. Rates include full English breakfast. Free parking. AE, DC, MC, V. Tube: Paddington. **Amenities:** Bar; babysitting arranged; laundry service; dry cleaning. *In room:* TV, radio.

Norfolk Court & St. David's Hotel *(R)* In early 2002, George and Foulla Neokleos finished the mammoth job of refurbishing all four of their buildings. The new look is unusual but appealing, with vanilla-colored walls and moldings and original fireplaces highlighted with yellow. Norfolk Court & St. David's is a treasure trove of architectural details. One room has a domed ceiling, and there's a lovely, stained-glass window on the stairs of no. 20. These Victorian houses have balconies across the front from which guests on the second floor can admire the pretty communal gardens. In the basement, there's a truly enormous and a very good value family room that can fit five people and has a proper built-in shower. The others are drop-in units that vary in size depending on what each bedroom can cope with. Irons and hair dryers are available at reception. When they say "full English breakfast" here, it really does mean full, with mushrooms, tomatoes, and baked beans on top of all the rest. All in all, this is a very good good-value choice. Lower prices listed below are for rooms without bathrooms.

14–20 Norfolk Sq., London W2 1RS. © 020/7723-4963. Fax 020/7402-9061. www.stdavidshotels.com. 70 units, 60 w/bathroom (most w/shower only). £39–£49 ($62–$78) single; £59–£69 ($94–$110) double; £70–£80 ($112–$128) triple; £80–£90 ($128–$144) quad. All rates include full English breakfast. AE, DC, MC, V. Tube: Paddington. *In room:* TV, coffeemaker.

Rhodes Hotel *(R)(R) (Kids)* Chris Crias, the owner of the Rhodes since 1978, recently spruced up the entire hotel with an £80,000 ($116,000) decorating extravaganza. The velvet-curtained lounge and the downstairs dining room now boast handpainted Greek-inspired murals, and painted angels gaze down from the ceiling on the way to the second floor. Other recent improvements include air-conditioning in the main part of the hotel (though not in the annex, which is why the rooms are cheaper there) and dataports for Internet access (free except for phone charges) in all the rooms. The bedroom decor is quite simple and comfortable. Number 220 has its own little private roof terrace, complete with table and chairs. The bunks in the family room are the nicest I've seen, dark wood and 3 feet wide. The continental breakfast includes ham and cheese; you can order an English breakfast for £3 ($4.80).

195 Sussex Gardens, London W2 2RJ. ✆ **020/7262-0537.** Fax 020/7723-4054. www.rhodeshotel.com. 18 units, all w/bathroom (most w/shower only). £50–£60 ($80–$96) single; £75–£85 ($120–$136) double/twin; £85–£90 ($136–$144) triple; £100–£110 ($160–$176) quad. Discount available for weekday and 3-day stays. Rates include continental breakfast. MC, V. Tube: Paddington. *In room:* TV, hair dryer, coffeemaker, fridge, dataports.

SUPER-CHEAP SLEEPS

Astor's Hyde Park Hostel ✴ These three Georgian terrace houses have survived through years as a bargain sleep with their gracious internal spaces and beautiful moldings unmolested. Astor's even decreed that the crazy murals, a hallmark of its hostels, be painted on removable boards here at Hyde Park. The company has turned this into its London flagship. The dorms have anything from 4 to 10 bunks, hence the wide price range, and there are great discounts to be had in winter. But the changes have been much bigger than a lick of paint and new carpet. As well as replacing the bathrooms, Astor's has taken advantage of the existing commercial kitchen to open the ITA (International Travellers Association) club, bar, and canteen-style cafe. Different DJs guest each night—guests get to DJ themselves on Wednesdays. Meals rarely cost more than £3 ($4.80). And beer starts at £1 ($1.60) during happy hour. If you check out the other amenities, you'll see these guys have thought of everything necessary to create a community for travelers. The 18–35 age restriction, unique in the London hostels reviewed, reinforces that spirit. Astor's has two other hostels in Queensway: **Leinster Inn,** 7–12 Leinster Sq., London, W2 4PR (✆ **020/7229-9641;** fax 020/7221-5255), famed for its weekend club nights, and the smaller, more laid-back **Quest,** 45 Queensborough Terrace, London, W2 8SY (✆ **020/7229-7782;** fax 020/7727-8106). There is a fourth hostel in **Victoria** and the long-established **Museum Inn** in Bloomsbury.

2–6 Inverness Terrace, London W2 3HY. 📞 **020/7229-5101**. Fax 020/7229-3170. www.astorhostels.com. 200 units, none w/bathroom. £12.50–£17.50 ($20–$28) per person in a dorm; £45 ($72) twin. Rates include bed linen and continental breakfast. Discount available for 1-wk. stays off-season. MC, V. Tube: Queensway, Bayswater. 18–35 age restriction. **Amenities:** Bar; cafe; club; game room; coin-op washers and dryers; Internet access; communal kitchen; safe. *In room:* No phone.

WORTH A SPLURGE

Delmere Hotel 🏃🏃 Keep an eye on the Delmere's website because there' usually a promotion that makes the cost comparable to the local B&Bs. The Delmere calls itself a "boutique town house hotel," hence the gold nameplates and charming window boxes along the top of the late-Georgian porch, and the real-flame fire in the lounge. It caters to a mix of business and pleasure travelers. The rooms, all recently refurbished and with new bathrooms, are very comfortable, but the decor is a bit too safe for real elegance except for the more expensive Crown Room up under the eaves, which has a Jacuzzi in the bathroom, a canopied bed, frilled tablecloth, and ruched blind that gives it the air of a rich widow's cabin on a cruise liner. Check out the bedrooms in the annex, which feel like you're in your own place. The windows look onto a small courtyard, though, so you may be able to hear the music from the hotel's jazz bar. Avoid the lower floor, which is a real hole in the ground. The La Perla restaurant does three-course meals for around £20 ($32).

130 Sussex Gardens, London W2 1UB. 📞 **020/7706-3344**. Fax 020/7262-1863. www.delmerehotels.com. 36 units, all w/bathroom (most w/shower only). £86 ($138) single; £107 ($171) double/twin. Rates include continental breakfast (full English £6/$10). AE, DC, DISC, MC, V. Tube: Paddington. **Amenities:** Restaurant; bar; limited room service; dry cleaning. *In room:* TV, dataport, coffeemaker, hair dryer, safe, radio.

6 Marylebone

Nutford House, University of London 🏃 *(Finds)* If you don't mind classic student sleeping arrangements, then this is an absolutely fantastic deal. It's hugely popular with 20-something and retired travelers. You get to stay in a quiet side street, just north of Marble Arch, for half the price of anywhere else in the neighborhood. Nutford House is a marvelous redbrick building put up during World War I as a hostel for "distressed gentlewomen." All the rooms are singles, basic but in good, clean condition. There are kitchenettes for making snacks on all four floors—there is an elevator—and five people share each public shower or tub. The twin rooms, which also have kitchenettes, are in three terrace houses across the road. Dining in the canteen is a great deal, too;

dinner is practically given away at £5 ($8) for two courses. An army could march for days on the breakfast menu, which changes daily. And both meals include vegetarian options. Nutford House is nonsmoking throughout and it has a blissfully peaceful walled garden at the back. Don't forget to pack a bath towel.

Brown St., London W1H 6AH. ✆ 020/7685-5000. Fax 020/7258-1781. www.lon. ac.uk/accom. 180 units, none w/bathroom. £23 ($37) single; £27.50 ($44) single w/evening meal. Rates include bed linen, hand towel, and full English breakfast. 10% discount for 1-month stays. Minimum stay 2 nights. Open Easter and summer vacations. No credit cards. Tube: Marble Arch. **Amenities:** Restaurant; coin-op washers and dryers; nonsmoking rooms; communal kitchens; garden. *In room:* No phone.

WORTH A SPLURGE

Hart House Hotel 👁👁   Andrew Bowden, who took over the management of Hart House from his parents, has one of the most welcoming and professionally run B&Bs in London. This Georgian town house, built in 1782, was used by members of the French nobility during the French Revolution. It has retained its dignified entrance hall (with a huge fragrant bouquet of white lilies when we visited) and polished paneling that gives way to pretty floral wallpaper. The rooms (all nonsmoking) are attractive and comfortable with small but immaculate bathrooms. Double-glazing screens out the traffic roar on Gloucester Place, the busy road from Oxford Street to Baker Street. The top floor double is a peaceful high-up hideaway, but there's no elevator to reach it. Room 6, a huge twin at the back with a marvelous leaded-glass bay window and its bathroom up a little flight of stairs, is another sought-after room. Reception has cots to lend out. And best of all, prices have actually come down since our last edition!

51 Gloucester Place, London W1H 3PE. ✆ 020/7935-2288. Fax 020/7935-8516. www.harthouse.co.uk. 15 units, all w/bathroom (some w/shower only). £65 ($104) single; £95 ($152) double/twin; £120 ($192) triple; £150 ($240) quad. Rates include full English breakfast. Discounts for 6 nights or more. AE, MC, V. Tube: Marble Arch, Baker St. **Amenities:** Babysitting arranged; laundry service; dry cleaning; nonsmoking rooms. *In room:* TV, coffeemaker, hair dryer.

7 Soho & Oxford Circus

SUPER-CHEAP SLEEPS

Oxford Street Youth Hostel   This excellent cheap sleep is above some offices, in a location most people would kill for—the northern border of Soho. The legendary Carnaby Street, where London first took off as cult fashion capital in the swinging 1960s, is just around the corner, and hip new fashion shops are finally pushing back the trashy tourist traps. All the rooms are the same size—small. So, if you've got the cash, ask to share with one other person because the four-bedders feel like a cabin on a sleeper train. The bunks are nice sturdy wooden ones, with crisp cotton sheets. There are soft drinks and snack machines, as well as Internet access, in the lounge. The hostel is too small to have a restaurant and provides a very declinable £3.30 ($5) continental breakfast pack. The communal kitchen is a great excuse for a 5-minute walk to Berwick Street market. The hostel also changes money.

14–18 Noel St., London W1. ℂ **020/7734-1618.** Fax 020/7734-1657. www.yha. org.uk. 75 units, none w/bathroom. £22 ($35) adult, £17.75 ($28) under-18s. Rates include bed linen. MC, V. Tube: Oxford Circus. No children under 6. **Amenities:** Lounge, coin-op washers and dryers; communal kitchen; Internet access. *In room:* No phone.

WORTH A SPLURGE

Regent Palace Hotel 🎯 *Value*   This London behemoth, located smack dab in the center of the West End just off Piccadilly Circus, was built in 1915, long before travelers expected private bathrooms in their rooms. In recent years it's been gradually upgrading by installing pre-fab shower/toilet/basin units in some of the rooms, sprucing up room decor, and making the endless hallways more welcoming. The rooms without "en suite facilities" are actually preferable because they have a bit more space (they're also cheaper). The public bathrooms are kept locked to make sure they're spotless; if you need to use a shower, the housekeeper will ride the elevator up at any time with the key and fresh towels. That's quite a deal at a weekday price that knocks socks off many B&Bs. The decor is comfortable if plain, and some of the beds aren't as firm as Americans like them; the spruced-up lobby looks like an air terminal, right down to the weekend check-in queues. Breakfast is extra, but we recommend that you skip it and find some charming cafe in nearby Soho instead. That's really the selling point of the Regent Palace— its fabulous location right in the heart of everything. This hotel has a history of offering cheap rates through a host of accommodation sites, so plug the name into a search engine and see what you come up with. The higher prices listed below are for weekends.

Glasshouse St., Piccadilly Circus, London W1A 4BZ. ℂ **020/7734-0716.** Fax 020/ 7734-6435. 887 units, 383 w/bathroom (shower only). £64–£75 ($102–$120) single w/o bathroom; £69–£89 ($110–$142) double/twin w/o bathroom, £119–£129 ($190–$206) double/twin w/bathroom; £95–£105 ($152–$168) triple w/o bathroom; £119–£138 ($190–$221) quad w/o bathroom. 32 units adapted for travelers w/disabilities. Lower rates apply Sun–Thurs. Discount available for long stays. AE,

Where to Stay in the West End

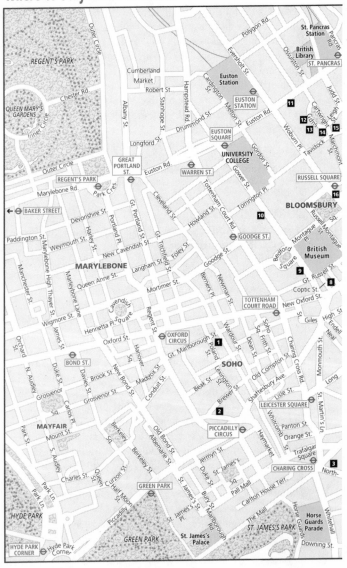

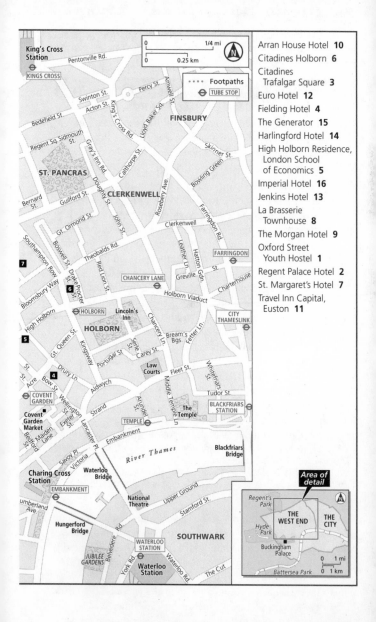

King's Cross Station

Pentonville Rd.

KINGS CROSS

Swinton St.

Acton St.

Percy St.

Amwell St.

Bedefield St.

Regent Sq. Sidmouth St.

Gray's Inn Rd.

King's Cross Rd.

Calthorpe St.

Lloyd Baker St.

FINSBURY

Skinner St.

Bowling Green

ST. PANCRAS

Doughty St.

Guilford St.

Gt. Ormond St.

John St.

CLERKENWELL

Roseberry Ave.

Farringdon Rd.

Bernard St.

Southampton Row

Boswell St.

Drake St. Procter St.

Theobalds Rd.

Red Lion St.

Clerkenwell

Leather Ln.

Hatton Gdn.

FARRINGDON

Charterhouse

Bloomsbury Way

High Holborn

6

HOLBORN

Greville St.

St.

Holborn Viaduct

CHANCERY LANE

CITY THAMESLINK

5

Lincoln's Inn

HOLBORN

Gt. Queen St.

Kingsway

Chancery Ln.

Serle St.

Portugal St.

Carey St.

Bream's Bgs.

Fetter Ln.

Whitefriars St.

4

Drury Ln.

Bow St.

COVENT GARDEN

Wellington St.

Aldwych

Law Courts

Fleet St.

Middle Temple Ln.

Tudor St.

BLACKFRIARS STATION

Acre

St.

Covent Garden Market

Bedford St.

Maiden Lane

Exeter St.

Strand

Lancaster Pl.

Arundel St.

TEMPLE

The Temple

Embankment

River Thames

Blackfriars Bridge

Charing Cross Station

EMBANKMENT

Savoy Pl.

Victoria

Waterloo Bridge

National Theatre

Upper Ground.

Blackfriars Bridge

umberland Ave.

Hungerford Bridge

Belvedere Rd.

Stamford St.

SOUTHWARK

JUBILEE GARDENS

WATERLOO STATION

York Rd.

Waterloo Station

Waterloo Rd.

The Cut

0   1/4 mi
0   0.25 km

•••• Footpaths
⊖ TUBE STOP

Arran House Hotel **10**
Citadines Holborn **6**
Citadines Trafalgar Square **3**
Euro Hotel **12**
Fielding Hotel **4**
The Generator **15**
Harlingford Hotel **14**
High Holborn Residence, London School of Economics **5**
Imperial Hotel **16**
Jenkins Hotel **13**
La Brasserie Townhouse **8**
The Morgan Hotel **9**
Oxford Street Youth Hostel **1**
Regent Palace Hotel **2**
St. Margaret's Hotel **7**
Travel Inn Capital, Euston **11**

Area of detail

Regent's Park

THE WEST END

THE CITY

Hyde Park

Buckingham Palace

Battersea Park

0   1 mi
0   1 km

DC, MC, V. Tube: Piccadilly Circus. **Amenities:** Pub; coffee bar; concierge; limited room service; laundry service; dry cleaning; nonsmoking rooms. *In room:* TV, coffeemaker, radio.

8 Bloomsbury

Travel Inn Capital (② **020/7554-3400;** fax 020/7554-3419; www. travelinn.co.uk), reviewed under "Just South of the River," later in this chapter, has another great value hotel at 1 Dukes Rd., WC1H 9PJ. It has similar rates, decor, and amenities as its hotel in South Bank (for this one, take the Tube to Euston).

Arran House Hotel ⋆⋆ (Kids)   It's hard to get excited by something as ordinary as a kitchen, but most B&Bs don't let guests use theirs, and apart from Wigmore Court in Marylebone, none of the others that do are as welcoming or as nice as this one. Heat up your own supper—great for budget travelers and parents with kids—and dine in style in the pleasant breakfast room. Proprietor John Richards has started a round of refurbishments to spruce up the place. The bedrooms are simple, light, and homey. If you go for one with a shower but no toilet you'll get one of the best deals on Gower Street. The public bathrooms and showers are perfectly clean, though a bit worn. Avoid the tiny basic twins where the beds are head to head along one wall. The front rooms are double-glazed, which cuts out the traffic hum. The coin-operated Internet terminal in the comfy lounge lets you pick up your e-mails and there are self-service laundry facilities. Arran House is very family-friendly; cribs are free. And you won't find a more beautiful garden in London. The lower prices below are for rooms without en suite bathrooms or showers.

77 Gower St., London WC1E 6HJ. ② **020/7636-2186** or 020/7637-1140. Fax 020/ 7436-5328. 28 units, 13 w/bathroom (shower only). £45–£55 ($72–$88) single; £62–£85 ($99–$136) double; £80–£103 ($128–$165) triple; £86–£107 ($138–$171) quad; £95–£120 ($152–$192) quint. Rates include full English breakfast. MC, V. Tube: Goodge St., Russell Sq. **Amenities:** Lounge; use of kitchen; babysitting arranged; laundry facilities; garden; Internet access. *In room:* TV, hair dryer.

La Brasserie Townhouse ⋆ (Finds)   If you're up for something out of the ordinary, this is one of those secret London places that make for a truly memorable stay. Only a tiny handful of hotels so centrally located can match the twin-room price—most are at least £10 ($16) a night more expensive. The singles are even more of a steal, a few pounds more than what you'd pay to sleep at a youth hostel. That's because the rooms really are one-person big. The other *quid pro quo* for the low price is that there is only one public bathroom for what could be six guests. But so what? There's a real charm in this place, which is above the small La Brasserie Townhouse restaurant and run by the same team. The rooms are pleasantly minimalist, the furniture white and the decor vanilla. Room 201 is definitely the best choice. You'll pay more for a room with breakfast, but it's a full English breakfast and you can have it served anytime between 9:30am and noon. You do have to wait until 4pm to check in, though. Presumably, that's when there's a lull in the brasserie, where Chef Raoul Duclos from Lyon recently took over operations. The cuisine is classic French with a nouvelle twist and prices for a fixed-price meal are low enough to make dining here as affordable as staying here. Did I mention that the location, a 2-minute walk from the British Museum, is outstanding?

24 Coptic St., London WC1A 1NT. ⓒ 020/7636-2731. labrasserietownhouse@ hotmail.com. 4 units, none w/bathroom. £28 ($45) single w/o breakfast, £32 ($51) single w/breakfast; £50 ($80) double w/o breakfast, £60 ($96) double w/breakfast. AE, DC, MC, V. Tube: Holborn, Tottenham Ct. Rd. **Amenities:** Restaurant; bar; limited room service; nonsmoking rooms. *In room:* TV, hair dryer, iron, no phone.

Euro Hotel ⓖ (Kids) The kids' drawings that festoon the walls behind reception are a pretty heavy clue as to where the hotel's strength lies—as a favorite of families on holiday. Generally, prices are high-ish for Cartwright Gardens, a Georgian crescent in north Bloomsbury that is more expensive than Gower Street but has more of a neighborhood feel to it. However, the Euro does do a good value rate for children under 16 who share a room with their parents. You pay the normal single or double price, depending on the number of adults, plus £10 ($16) per child. Toddlers under 2½ stay free, and you can borrow a high chair and crib at the reception desk. The Euro was recently repainted throughout and it is a clean, pleasant, friendly, and attractive place with comfortable rooms. The shared bathrooms have just been totally renovated. The hotel offers guests videos, use of the office safe and fax machine, and e-mail pick-up, all for free. And if the kids still need wearing out after a day on the tourist trail, you can play tennis in the gardens opposite. The Euro can lend you rackets and balls. The only potential drawback: no elevator. The higher prices below are for rooms with bathrooms.

53 Cartwright Gardens, London WC1H 9EL. ⓒ 020/7387-4321. Fax 020/7383-5044. www.eurohotel.co.uk. 35 units, 10 w/bathroom (some w/shower only). £49–£70 ($78–$112) single; £69–£89 ($110–$142) double/twin; £85–£105 ($136–$168) triple; £95–£115 ($152–$184) family room. Rates include full English breakfast. Special rates for children under 16. Discount of 10% for 1-wk. stays off-season. AE, MC, V. Tube: Euston, Russell Sq. **Amenities:** Lounge; tennis court; garden. *In room:* TV, coffeemaker, radio.

Harlingford Hotel ✸✸   Andrew Davies is the third generation of his family to run this B&B, a dignified, dove-gray, Georgian-era building on the corner of Marchmont Street and Cartwright Gardens. A perfectionist by nature, he recently oversaw the smart, designer-aided overhaul of the hotel interiors, which use neutral colors and bright splashes of color. The bathrooms are small but adequate. With their gracious arched windows and high ceilings, the lounge and breakfast rooms on either side of the white, airy entrance hall are a real asset. The breakfast room is modern and cheery. As a guest, you can get a key and enjoy the communal gardens opposite the hotel. The only downside: no elevator.

61–63 Cartwright Gardens, London WC1H 9EL. ✆ 020/7387-1551. Fax 020/7387-4616. www.harlingfordhotel.com. 44 units, all w/bathroom (shower only). £72 ($115) single; £90 ($144) double/twin; £100 ($160) triple; £108 ($173) quad. Rates include full English breakfast. AE, DC, MC, V. Tube: Euston, Russell Sq. **Amenities:** Lounge. *In room:* TV, coffeemaker.

Jenkins Hotel ✸   Jenkins has been a hotel since the 1920s and appeared in the PBS mystery series *Poirot*. Today the style is trad-lite, very English but relaxed about it. Sam Bellingham and his partner Felicity Langley-Hunt recently refurbished the entire hotel, putting en suite bathrooms in all but one of the rooms. A double with private bathroom is still a few pounds cheaper here than elsewhere in Cartwright Gardens. Rivals score points for having lounges but Jenkins offers better in-room amenities. There's one nice double room (no. 10) on the fourth floor (no elevator), but the top choice is the second-floor room 5, where two rooms on the front, with floor-to-ceiling windows, have been knocked into one. The room to avoid is the pretty but cavelike basement double. Sam's two friendly Labradors, Tiggy and George, hang out in the kitchen which, with its huge pine table, doubles as reception. There are rackets and balls to borrow if you want to play tennis in communal gardens opposite. Jenkins is completely nonsmoking.

45 Cartwright Gardens, London WC1H 9EH. ✆ 020/7387-2067. Fax 020/7383-3139. www.jenkinshotel.demon.co.uk. 13 units, 12 w/bathroom (most w/shower only). £52–£72 ($83–$115) single; £85 ($136) double/twin; £105 ($168) triple. Rates include full English breakfast. MC, V. Tube: Euston, Russell Sq. **Amenities:** Nonsmoking rooms; garden. *In room:* TV, fridge, coffeemaker, hair dryer, safe.

The Morgan Hotel ✸✸   It's a real treat to find a B&B with air-conditioning and double-glazing, particularly in an elegant 18th-century terrace house. It makes staying at the Morgan Hotel a pleasure. It's more expensive than other local B&Bs (still cheaper than Cartwright Gardens), but then, period-style decoration does tend to bump the price up. There are pretty floral bedspreads and decorative borders on the walls, and every room is different. If there are two of you, go for the first-floor room that opens onto the garden at the back, which no one else gets to use. The basic single room is absolutely tiny, and there are much better single rooms elsewhere. Otherwise, it's almost worth staying here just to see the oak-paneled breakfast room with its wooden booths. A few doors away, the Morgan has four wonderful one-bedroom apartments, which go for £125 ($200) a night including breakfast, or £175 ($280) if you want to have a foldaway bed and sleep three.

24 Bloomsbury St., London WC1B 3QJ. ℭ 020/7636-3735. Fax 020/7636-3045. 15 units, all w/bathroom (most w/shower only). £65–£80 ($104–$128) single; £95 ($152) double/twin; £125 ($200) triple. Rates include full English breakfast. MC, V. Tube: Goodge St., Tottenham Court Rd. In room: A/C, TV, hair dryer.

St. Margaret's Hotel ℛℛ The welcome here inspires devoted loyalty. One guest stayed for 28 years, then asked to have her ashes buried in the back garden! Mrs. Marazzi is the second generation of her family to run this nonsmoking B&B, which rambles over four houses. The rooms are simple, and no two are alike. Budget travelers should go for the cheap double, which has the toilet just outside. The Marazzis recently created some beautiful extra public bathrooms, so it's easy to survive the sharing experience. If you can afford it, room 53 is a marvelous first-floor triple, which normally costs £125 ($200) but which two people can take for £100 ($160). It has a king-size bed, a single bed, and a gray-tiled, private bathroom with a corner tub. And off it is a small private conservatory, looking onto the quiet communal garden that all the guests can use. St. Margaret's has two lounges, one with a TV and the other for guests who prefer peace and quiet. Newspapers are delivered. You'll pay an extra £1 ($1.60) if you stay only 1 night.

26 Bedford Place, London WC1B 5JL. ℭ 020/7636-4277. Fax 020/7323-3066. www.stmargaretshotel.co.uk. 64 units, 10 w/bathroom (most w/shower only). £50.50 ($81) single w/o bathroom; £64.50 ($103) double w/o bathroom, £78–£95 ($125–$152) double w/bathroom. Rates include full English breakfast. MC, V. Tube: Russell Sq., Holborn. **Amenities:** Lounge; babysitting arranged; nonsmoking rooms; garden. In room: TV.

SUPER-CHEAP SLEEPS
The Generator ℛ Hidden away in Tavistock Place, this new-style hostel opened in 1995 in what used to be a police section house. Inside, it's like a cross between the set of *Alien* and a hip Soho coffee bar. Aluminum pipes and blue neon lights snake across the ceiling in reception. The different floors are called Level 01, 02, and so on. And

all the signage, including room numbers, is spray-stenciled, packing-crate-style. The spartan bedrooms, all nonsmoking and with bunks, are equipped with funky metal basins, and it's about eight people to every shower. The 800-bed Generator is more expensive than its private sector rivals, except in the biggest dorms. Breakfast is self-service in the Fuel Stop canteen. There is no self-catering, which can be a bind when you're traveling on this kind of budget. The bar is very Soho, but prices are lower than even a local pub's, and it stays open until 2am. In fact, the only real drawback to The Generator is that it caters for a lot of groups, so be prepared for hordes of kids on tour.

Compton Place, off 37 Tavistock Place, London WC1H 9SD. ⓒ 020/7388-7666. Fax 020/7388-7644. www.the-generator.co.uk. 217 units, none w/bathroom. £35–£37 ($56–$59) single; £40–£46 ($64–$74) twin; £54–£60 ($86–$96) triple; £10–£12 ($16–$19) per person in a dorm. Rates include bed linen, towels, and continental breakfast. Discount available for 5-night stays and for groups. MC, V. Tube: Russell Sq. **Amenities:** Bar; game room; nonsmoking rooms; Internet access. *In room:* No phone.

WORTH A SPLURGE

Imperial Hotel ⓖ *Value*   A few pounds more expensive than Bloomsbury's toniest B&Bs, the Imperial is both a splurge and a good deal. The decor isn't particularly plush. What you get, though, is an affordable, full-service hotel just a stone's throw from Covent Garden and Soho, right on the eastern side of Russell Square. There are nine floors of bedrooms, and the third is nonsmoking. The hotel does a lot of tour-group business, but the rooms have stood up well to the traffic. They're all a decent size, have unusual triangular-shaped bay windows, and excellent storage space. In most of the doubles and twins, the en suite toilet and tub/shower are handily separate. The Imperial has a vineyard to make its Bordeaux house wine and a farm just outside London, which delivers produce every day to be served up in the Elizabethan Restaurant. Otherwise, the Day & Night Bar, an oasis of up-to-the-minute style with Internet sites, is open for light food and drinks until 2am. If you'd rather forego the amenities and pay a few pounds less, check out the website because the company owns five other Bloomsbury hotels, all a few pounds cheaper than the Imperial.

Russell Sq., London WC1B 5BB. ⓒ **020/7278-7871.** Fax 020/7837-4653. www. imperialhotels.co.uk. 448 units. £73 ($117) single; £98 ($157) double/twin. Rates include full English breakfast. AE, DC, DISC, MC, V. Tube: Russell Sq. **Amenities:** Restaurant; cafe/bar; access to nearby health club; concierge; limited room service; babysitting; laundry service; dry cleaning; nonsmoking rooms. *In room:* TV, trouser press, coffeemaker, radio.

9 Covent Garden, the Strand & Holborn

High Holborn Residence, London School of Economics ✸ 𝘒𝘪𝘥𝘴
This is a tip-top student residence in a tip-top location, with double-glazed windows to cut down on the traffic noise of High Holborn. It's right in the middle of Theatreland and a 5-minute walk to Covent Garden, which is why it can charge B&B hotel rates. That, and the fact that the beds have the fattest, most civilized mattresses I've ever seen in a student hall. It's very popular with moms and pops, who pay £5 ($7.25) a night for a foldaway bed plus the same again for an extra breakfast, making this one of the cheapest family rooms in town. Blocks of six rooms lock together and share a toilet, shower, and kitchen (bring your own utensils). Every second floor has two extra shared tubs, and everything is in very good shape. Downstairs, there's a huge breakfast room-cum-lounge with vending machines for snacks. For a modest fee you can use the open-air pool at the Oasis Sports Centre next door. The hall is open from early July to the end of September.

178 High Holborn, London WC1. ℂ **020/7955-7575.** Fax 020/7955-7676. www. lsevacations.com. 428 units, 24 w/bathroom (shower only). £36 ($58) single w/o bathroom; £58 ($93) twin w/o bathroom, £68 ($109) twin w/bathroom, £78 ($125) triple. 4 units adapted for travelers w/disabilities. Rates include continental breakfast. Open summer vacation. MC, V. Tube: Holborn. **Amenities:** Game room; coin-op washers and dryers; communal kitchen; Internet access. *In room:* No phone.

DO-IT-YOURSELF DEALS

Citadines Trafalgar Square ✸   The French company Citadines pioneered the "aparthotel" concept in London. It opened its Trafalgar Square flagship in a 1930s building in 1998, then totally refurbished the premises in 2001. Unfortunately, the prices have shot up quite a bit since our last edition, pushing this property into the splurge category, but four people sharing a one-bedroom still make the rate competitive for the area. Fill a bigger duplex and you'll get a bargain. The inside is all marble-tiled and corporate looking, with an impeccable 24-hour welcome. The studios sleep two on a deluxe sofa bed and have fully equipped kitchenettes. The apartments have the same arrangement, with the tub-shower and toilet separate to cut down on awkward traffic jams. Every unit controls its own heating and air-conditioning, and the phones have handy voice-mail. Reception can lend you a crib, bottle warmer, and changing mat. It will also organize extra maid services, otherwise it's one towel change a week. Citadines has a breakfast room where you can have

The Bargain Business

Business hotel chains need to fill their beds when lucrative corporate customers go home so they offer special rates (often called Leisure Breaks, or Super Savers). These put city-center 3- and even 4-star sleeps on a par with a pricey B&B and may even make posher hotels an affordable splurge. What you'll actually pay will fluctuate according to seasonal demand, so always ask for the best deal. Savvy bargain hounds know it's always worth surfing hotel chain websites for e-deals. The rates below are for two people sharing a room and bed-and-breakfast. These were some of the specials available as of press time.

• **Best Western** (⟨ 08457/747474; www.bestwestern.co.uk): Getaway Breaks any day; from £68 ($109). The best value Best Western hotel is Raglan Hall in Highgate. Only 15 minutes by Tube from the West End, it's in a quiet residential area and has a delightful garden and terrace.

• **Hilton** (⟨ 08705/909090; www.hilton.com): Leisure Breaks; from £119 ($190) for 2 nights. Several of the hotels do great 1-night Sunday Specials all year round: and there's a 2-night Winter Break for £169 ($270), with dinner, at the fab 4-star Hilton Hyde Park, which has Nintendo consoles in every room if the notorious British weather turns against you.

an expensive continental breakfast for £8 ($13) if you don't want to cook yourself. For a cheaper central sleep, try the clone: **Citadines Holborn,** 94–99 High Holborn, London, WC1V 6LF (⟨ 020/7395-8800; fax 020/7395-8789; Tube: Holborn). Studios cost from £97 ($155) a night if you stay 1 week; special offers sometimes bring the week-long price down as low as £81 ($130) per night.

18–21 Northumberland Ave., London WC2N 5BJ. ⟨ 0800/376-3898, or 020/7766-3700. Fax 020/7766-3766. www.citadines.com. 187 units. £120–£145 ($192–$232) studio; £172–£206 ($275–$333) 1-bedroom apt.; £232–£245 ($371–$392) 2-bedroom apt. Lower rates apply to 1-wk. stays. 16 studios and a 1-bedroom apt. suitable for travelers w/disabilities. AE, DC, MC, V. Tube: Charing Cross, Embankment. **Amenities:** Coin-op washers and dryers; dry cleaning; non-smoking rooms. *In room:* A/C, TV, kitchenette, fridge, iron, safe.

- **Holiday Inn** (© 0800/897121; www.basshotels.com/holiday-inn): Offers various Smart Breaks and advance purchase specials from £69 ($110) in the Holiday Inn Express Southwark; prices go up to £97.50 ($156) for the swanky and centrally located Crowne Plaza.

- **Jarvis Hotels** (© 01494/436256; www.jarvis.co.uk): Leisure breaks any day; from £66 ($106) for a 1-night stay at the centrally located Ramada Jarvis Hyde Park.

- **Radisson Hotels** (© 0800/374411; www.radisson.com): Super Savers from £89 ($142). This hotel group aims for classic English style. Go for the good value Radisson Edwardian, which is right in the thick of things on Great Russell Street. And ask about theater packages—oddly, they are sometimes cheaper than a basic bed-booking.

- **Thistle Hotels** (© 0800/181716; www.thistlehotels.com): Leisure Breaks any day; minimum 2 nights; from £116 ($185). For the best deal but scant aesthetic stimulation, go for the modern London Ryan Hotel in King's Cross. For a few pounds more, though, you can buy a more traditional sleep at the brilliantly located Bloomsbury Park (between Russell Square and Holborn).

WORTH A SPLURGE

The Fielding Hotel ⍟   Just an aria away from the Royal Opera House in Covent Garden, this famous hotel is a clean, tidy, and regularly renovated 1970s time warp. The very narrow hallways and stairs are brown and orange, and metallic glam-rock pictures and chocolate-box alpine scenes cover the walls. Other than that, the bedrooms are attractive with comfortable new beds and faded coverlets and curtains. The Fielding has finally upgraded its famously antiquated electrics and plumbing, so there are nice new bathrooms throughout. Breakfast is not included. The hotel doesn't score marks for extra bits-and-bobs, but for London picturesque and convenience to the West End it can't be beat. It sits in a pretty, pedestrian street just minutes from the action at Covent Garden. And it really is one of a kind.

4 Broad Court, Bow St., London WC2B 5QZ. ☎ 020/7836-8305. Fax 020/7497-0064. www.the-fielding-hotel.co.uk. 24 units, all w/bathroom (shower only). £76 ($122) single; £100 ($160) double/twin, £115 ($184) superior double/twin; £130 ($208) double suite w/sitting room. Rates do not include breakfast. No 1-night bookings on Sat. AE, DC, MC, V. Tube: Covent Garden. No children under 13. *In room:* TV, coffeemaker.

10 Victoria & Westminster

Collin House 𝒜   You could easily walk straight past the discreet slate nameplate announcing Collin House. That would be a shame because it's one of the best B&Bs on Ebury Street. For a start, it's well worth foregoing a private bathroom, even though all the showers are new, because there are never more than two bedrooms sharing each public facility. You'll also get a room at the back, which is blissfully quiet. All the rooms with private bathrooms look out onto Ebury Street, and there is no soundproofing. Most of the rooms have been redecorated over the past couple of years and there is new carpeting on the stairs. Last year the first-floor bedroom at the front was converted into an attractive lounge. None of the other Ebury Street B&Bs listed here have got one, as the buildings are quite small. The small basement breakfast room has bench seating and a skylight. The look is half-canteen, half-chapel. Collin House is non-smoking throughout.

104 Ebury St., London SW1W 9QD. ☎/fax 020/7730-8031. www.collinhouse.co.uk. 12 units, 8 w/bathroom (shower only). £55 ($88) single w/bathroom; £68 ($109) double/twin w/o bathroom, £82 ($131) double/twin w/bathroom; £95 ($152) triple w/o bathroom. Rates include full English breakfast. MC, V. Tube: Victoria. **Amenities:** Lounge; nonsmoking rooms. *In room:* TV, no phone.

James & Cartref House 𝒜   Ebury Street calls itself Belgravia, but this is no hushed tycoon's enclave. There are dozens of places to stay on either side of the junction with Elizabeth Street. James House and Cartref House are separate B&Bs on opposite sides of the road, both run by the very welcoming Derek and Sharon James. The main difference between the two B&Bs is in the number of private bathrooms. All 10 rooms in James House have one, but they're very small, so you might be better off without, especially since only three rooms share each immaculately kept bathroom at Cartref house. All the bedrooms are nicely decorated—nothing fancy, but comfortable. Fans have been installed in all the rooms, a boon during summer heat waves. There's a delightful conservatory dining

Where to Stay & Dine in Victoria & Westminster

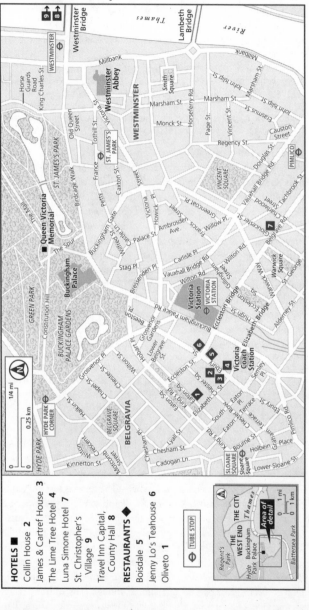

HOTELS ■
Collin House 2
James & Cartref House 3
The Lime Tree Hotel 4
Luna Simone Hotel 7
St. Christopher's
Village 9
Travel Inn Capital,
County Hall 8
RESTAURANTS ◆
Boisdale 5
Jenny Lo's Teahouse 6
Oliveto 1

room. Two things to note: breakfast stops at 8:30am, and kids have to be over 12 to stay in the top bunk in the James House family room. Both houses are totally nonsmoking. Lower rates below are for rooms that share bathrooms.

108–129 Ebury St., London SW1W 9DU. ℭ 020/7730-7338 or 020/7730-6176. Fax 020/7730-7338. www.jamesandcartref.co.uk. 19 units, 13 w/bathroom (shower only). £52–£62 ($83–$99) single; £70–£85 ($112–$136) double/twin; £95–£110 ($152–$176) triple; £135 ($216) family room w/bathroom. Rates include full English breakfast. AE, MC, V. Tube: Victoria. **Amenities:** Nonsmoking rooms. *In room:* TV, coffeemaker, hair dryer, fan, no phone.

Luna Simone Hotel *ℛℛ* *(Finds)*   This family-run hotel stands out by a mile on this scruffy terrace. The outside of the big stucco-fronted house gleams bright white and has glass panels etched with the hotel name around the entrance porch. The Desiras have worked wonders on the inside, too. They've renovated all the bedrooms and put private bathrooms in all but two singles. The rooms vary widely in size, but with their blue carpeting and cream-colored walls and newly tiled bathrooms, they beat all the dowdy, badly designed hotels and B&Bs for miles around. The beechwood and marble-clad reception area is all new, too, as is the smart-looking breakfast room, now totally nonsmoking. The look throughout is light, simple, and modern, a refreshing change from the interiors of so many Victorian buildings.

47–49 Belgrave Rd., London SW1V 2BB. ℭ 020/7834-5897. Fax 020/7828-2474. www.lunasimonehotel.com. 36 units, 34 w/bathroom (shower only). £40 ($64) single, £60–£80 ($96–$128) double/twin; £80–£100 ($128–$160) triple. Rates include full English breakfast. MC, V. Tube: Victoria, Pimlico. **Amenities:** Internet access; lounge. *In room:* TV, coffeemaker, hair dryer, safe.

WORTH A SPLURGE
The Lime Tree Hotel *ℛ*   David and Marilyn Davies ran Ebury House, across the road, until 1994 when they moved to The Lime Tree Hotel. Mr. Davies is something of a champion when it comes to award-winning window boxes; there are twice as many at the Lime Tree than on any other hotel in the street. The hotel is just as attractive inside, with deep cornices in the hall and statues and flowers in the alcoves up the stairs. The more expensive rooms are quite luxurious, with swagged curtains, canopied beds, and pretty furniture. There is one on the first floor that leads out to a table and chairs on its own little terrace. The lower price applies to doubles and twins on the upper floors, which are more restrained but still very attractive. Don't expect a lift as part of your splurge, though. The authorities are very stringent about what they'll let people do to historic Victorian

houses. The bathrooms are spotlessly clean with glass-doored show-ers. The dining room is on the first floor, and in the summer, many guests take their breakfast out into the rose garden.

135–137 Ebury St., London SW1W 9RA. ℂ 020/7730-8191. Fax 020/7730-7856. www.limetreehotel.co.uk. 26 units, all w/bathroom (most w/shower only). £75 ($120) single; £105–£115 ($168–$184) double/twin; £145 ($232) triple; £165 ($264) quad. Rates include full English breakfast. AE, DC, MC, V. Tube: Victoria. No children under 5. **Amenities:** Garden. *In room:* TV, coffeemaker, hair dryer, safe.

11 Just South of the River

Travel Inn Capital, County Hall 🅁🅁 *(Kids)*   No budget hotel ever had a better location. County Hall is a mammoth 1920s monument to civic pride, across the Thames from the Houses of Parliament. It used to be home to the Greater London Council until Margaret Thatcher abolished it in 1986. Now millionaires at the Marriott, which occupies the plum parts of County Hall, enjoy *the* London view. Guests at the Travel Inn, sadly, do not. Some rooms look downriver, but you can't see much because the 135-foot-high British Airways London Eye observation wheel is located right next door. Most rooms face into a big central courtyard or out at luxury apart-ments behind. Inside there are six floors (five nonsmoking) of bland identical corridors, but that's what budget chains do. The rooms are of a decent size, the decor good quality, and the price is an absolute steal. All rooms are standard doubles and the rate is the same even if the room is made into a twin, triple, or quad. In the family rooms, maximum capacity is two kids under 16 on the sofa bed, one tod-dler under 2 in a crib, and two grown-ups. There are no adult-only triples or quads. Breakfast is not included. Continental costs £4.95 ($8), full English is £6.95 ($11), and under-10s can eat what they want for £3 ($4.80). The restaurant also serves a children's dinner menu. There's a McDonald's and a Yo! Sushi down below in County Hall, as well as the London Aquarium, the Dali Universe exhibition, and the new Saatchi Gallery of contemporary art.

There are several other Travel Inn Capitals, of which the best located is **Euston. Putney Bridge** is near the river in quite a chi-chi bit of West London. **Tower Bridge** is less sexy than it sounds, too far into no man's land south of the river to be convenient.

Belvedere Rd., London SE1 7PB. ℂ 0870/242-8000. Fax 020/7902-1619. www.travel inn.co.uk. 313 units. £79.95–£82.95 ($117–$133) single, double/twin, and family room; lower rates are for weekends. Units adapted for travelers w/disabilities. Rates do not include breakfast. AE, DC, MC, V. Tube: Waterloo, Westminster. **Amenities:** Restaurant; bar; nonsmoking rooms; Internet access. *In room:* TV, coffeemaker, hair dryer, radio.

SUPER-CHEAP SLEEPS

St. Christopher's Village ★★   Only Astor's is cheaper, but even its swanky Hyde Park hostel can't boast a hot tub as part of the deal. In 1999, St. Christopher's gutted some marvelous old buildings on busy Borough High Street and turned them into what it calls a "hostel with attitude." The American diner-style bar called Belushi's puts on endless low-rent alcohol-fueled entertainment, from guest DJs to quiz nights. The hostel lounge has a dance floor too. Or you can chill out on the rooftop deck where the hot tub and sauna are located. Instead of the usual self-catering arrangements, St. Christopher's subsidizes the food (£1.50/$2.20 for cooked breakfast) and drink. The company has two other hostels on Borough High Street. The first is above the historic St. Christopher's Inn (no. 121) where the floors are wonky, the rooms are clean, and the showers are all new. (Don't stay here for the weekend if you're an early-bedder, because the pub goes ballistic and the floors are paper-thin.) The second is above the Orient Espresso coffee bar just up the road (no. 59). This is much quieter and suits post–Generation X-ers and families with children. Southwark is still a bit grotty but it's on the rise, with the Tate Modern, Shakespeare's Globe, and the mouthwatering Borough Market only a few minutes away.

St. Christopher's also has hostels in **Camden, Greenwich,** and **Shepherds Bush.** You can book them all through the telephone number and website below.

165 Borough High St., London SE1 1NP. ✆ 020/7407-1856. Fax 020/7403-7715. www.st-christophers.co.uk. 164 units, none w/bathroom. £15–£23 ($24–$37) per person in a 2-to-14-bed dorm. Full facilities for travelers w/disabilities. Rates include linen and continental breakfast. Discount available off-season and for 1-wk. stays. MC, V. Tube: London Bridge, Borough. **Amenities:** Two bars; hot tub; sauna; coin-op washers and dryers; Internet access. *In room:* No phone.

12 Near the Airport

Hotel Ibis Heathrow (✆ 020/8759-4888; fax 020/8564-7894; www.ibishotels.com) is at 112–114 Bath Road, at the end of a long row of more expensive suburban-looking hotel chains. Recently refurbished, the amenities and decor at this Ibis replicate the Ibis Euston (see "Bloomsbury," earlier in this chapter), without the railway theme. An en suite double/twin is £69.95 ($112) during the week, but a bargain £49.95 ($80) at weekends. Breakfast is £4.50 ($7) extra, but not particularly appetizing. To get here from the airport, take the Hotel Hoppa bus: H3 from Terminals 1 to 3 or H13 from Terminal 4.

Harmondsworth Hall ★★ *Finds*   Harmondsworth is the perfect place to get over jet lag or catch a last glimpse of picture-book England before you go. This pretty little village has two pubs, an old-fashioned post office, and an 800-year-old church mentioned in the Domesday Book. It takes only 15 minutes to get to one of the world's busiest airports, yet the village isn't even under the flight path. Harmondsworth Hall is a rambling, 17th-century, redbrick house, with wrought-iron gates leading into a lovely country garden where there's even a Tudor cannon. The inside is beautiful, with a checkerboard floor in the hall, coffered ceiling in the wood-paneled breakfast room, an elegant drawing room, and Turkish carpets everywhere. It may sound like a museum, but it feels more like a cherished home. The rooms have lovely old furniture, and each one is decorated differently. Number 6 is a huge double with a polished wood floor. Rooms in what was originally a separate cottage are relatively modern and have less character. Elaine Burke will organize your transport to and from Heathrow if you give her enough warning. She has a lot of loyal regulars, and it's easy to see why.

Summerhouse Lane, West Drayton, Middlesex, UB7 0BG. ☎ **020/8759-1824.** Fax 020/8897-6385. www.harmondsworthhall.com. 10 units, 7 w/bathroom (shower only). £45 ($72) single w/o bathroom, £55–£65 ($88–$104) double/twin w/bathroom; £75 ($120) family room w/bathroom. Rates include full English breakfast. Discount available for longer stays. V. Bus: U3 from Heathrow Terminals 1–3 or West Drayton train station. **Amenities:** Lounge; garden. *In room:* TV, coffeemaker, hair dryer.

4

Great Deals on Dining

The Brits get really bored by the constant slurs cast on their cooking. It can even cause them to forget their manners. And rightly so. That old cliché is about as accurate as the one that says the city is permanently enveloped in a pea-soup fog. The last 2 decades have seen an explosion of new eateries, new tastes, and new celebrities in the kitchen. Today, London is one of the great food capitals of the world. The only problem is, eating out at the best restaurants costs a small fortune.

But don't despair, because it's still possible to eat out, eat creatively, and eat well, without breaking the bank.

Restaurant hours vary, but lunch is usually noon to 2:30pm and dinner 6 to 10:30pm. Some eateries shut down on Sundays or, if not, for one weekday meal. You'll never go hungry, though, because the city is stuffed with all-day cafes and diners. Except for these super-cheapies, most restaurants accept reservations and it is always wise to call ahead, especially from Thursday night through the weekend.

1 How to Eat Without Losing £s

Brace yourself: a meal for two with wine in a good Central London restaurant is now reckoned to cost around £80 ($128)! But don't choke on the news, because there are many great places for travelers on a budget (most of us) to dine. Here's a short checklist of ways to keep meal costs down in this super-expensive city:

- **Go for fixed-price menus.** You'll notice from the reviews in this chapter that many restaurants offer great-value set meals at lunch, dinner, or for pre- and post-theater.
- **Check the Charges.** Left to their own devices, Brits tip 10%, and so should you. However, some restaurants automatically add an "optional" 12% to 15% service charge. Knock it off if you're at all dissatisfied.
- **Don't double tip**. If the menu states that a service charge has been added to your bill, don't add an additional 10% to the gratuity portion of your credit-card receipt.

- **Bring Your Own Booze.** There are still a few unlicensed eateries left in London. You can take your own drink, saving pounds on inflated restaurant prices. Some charge a small fee per bottle, known as "corkage."

2 Knightsbridge

Pan-Asian Canteen @ Paxton's Head *(Finds* GASTROPUB/ PAN-ASIAN   There's been a pub on this spot since 1632 but the present one dates from the turn of the last century. Every inch of it, inside and out, is paneled in polished mahogany. So the new Pan-Asian Canteen upstairs comes as a bit of a surprise. The cool, modern, Bangkok-green dining room has three big teak tables, which can seat 12 people each, eating communal style. Depending on the day and time, you could have one to yourself or be elbow-to-elbow with businessmen, backpackers, and babes on a shopping break. The fixed-price dinners are a great value, and the regular prices make this a perfect light meal break. The menu is very strong on seafood, from the fishcake starter to clams, red snapper, and deliciously juicy king prawns revved up with chili. But there's lots to tempt vegetarians and carnivores, too. The pork ribs sprinkled with sesame seeds make a very tasty starter and there's always a chicken curry. The pub has several real ales on tap.

153 Knightsbridge, SW1. ☎ 020/7589-6627. Reservations not accepted. Main courses £5.50–£7.25 ($9–$12). Fixed-price dinners £16–£20 ($26–$32). AE, MC, V. Mon–Sat noon–10:30pm; Sun 12:30–9pm. Tube: Knightsbridge.

Pizza on the Park *(K* PIZZA & PASTA   This is one of the most popular jazz venues in London and pulls in all the big names. Unfortunately, you have to pay extra for the basement gigs—from £16 ($26) depending on who's playing—and you must book ahead. But come here Sunday lunchtime and there's live background music (not usually jazz) upstairs as well. This is a very classy pizza joint, with high ceilings, dramatic pillars, and tables set with fresh flowers. The pizzas have lots of tomato on the base and interesting toppings. The *Quattro Formaggi* with four cheeses is great, but anyone prone to cheese-induced nightmares ought to avoid it because it's super-rich. The pastas aren't always so successful. Pizza on the Park also does breakfast until 11:30am. The nicest view is from the inside looking out at the park. Pavement tables are a bit too close to heavy traffic.

11 Knightsbridge SW1. ☎ 020/7235-5273. Reservations required for music room. Breakfast £4.95 ($8); main courses £6.95–£13 ($11–$21). AE, DC, MC, V. Daily 8:30am–midnight. Tube: Hyde Park Corner.

Where to Dine from Knightsbridge to Earl's Court

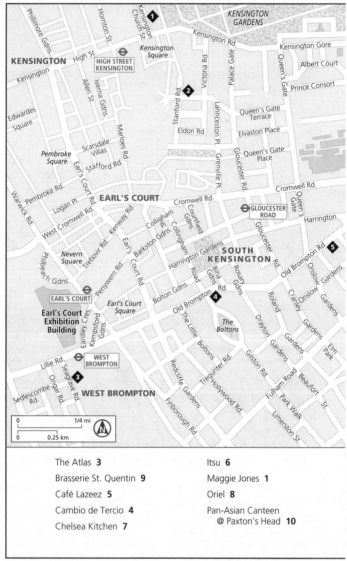

KENSINGTON GARDENS

Phillimore Gdns.
Hornton St.
Kensington Church St.
Kensington Rd.
KENSINGTON
High St.
HIGH STREET KENSINGTON
Kensington Square
Kensington
Allen St.
Iverna Gdns.
Edwardes Square
Marloes Rd.
Scarsdale Villas
Pembroke Square
Stafford Rd.
Earl's Court Rd.
Pembroke Rd.
Logan Pl.
Warwick Rd.
West Cromwell Rd.
EARL'S COURT
Cromwell Rd.
Nevern Square
Trebovir Rd.
Penywern Rd.
Kenway Rd.
Earl's Court Rd.
Barkston Gdns.
Collingham Pl.
Collingham Gdns.
Courtfield Gdns.
Harrington Gardens
Bolton Gdns.
Bina Gdns.
SOUTH KENSINGTON
Rosary Gdns.
Philbeach Gdns.
EARL'S COURT
Eardley Cres.
Kempsford Gdns.
Earl's Court Square
Earl's Court Exhibition Building
Old Brompton Rd.
The Little Boltons
The Boltons
Drayton Gardens
Roland Gardens
Cranley Gardens
Onslow Gardens
Elm Park
Lillie Rd.
WEST BROMPTON
Seagrave Rd.
Ongar Rd.
Sedlescombe Rd.
WEST BROMPTON
Redcliffe Gardens
Tregunter Rd.
Gilston Rd.
Fulham Road
Beaufort St.
Park Walk
Finborough Rd.
Hollywood Rd.
Limerston St.

Stanford Rd.
Victoria Rd.
Palace Gate
Kensington Gore
Queen's Gate
Albert Court
Prince Consort
Eldon Rd.
Launceston Pl.
Grenville Pl.
Queen's Gate Terrace
Elvaston Place
Queen's Gate Place
Gloucester Rd.
Cromwell Rd.
GLOUCESTER ROAD
Queen's Gate
Harrington
Gloucester Rd.
Old Brompton Rd.
Onslow Gardens

0   1/4 mi
0   0.25 km

The Atlas **3**

Brasserie St. Quentin **9**

Café Lazeez **5**

Cambio de Tercio **4**

Chelsea Kitchen **7**

Itsu **6**

Maggie Jones **1**

Oriel **8**

Pan-Asian Canteen
@ Paxton's Head **10**

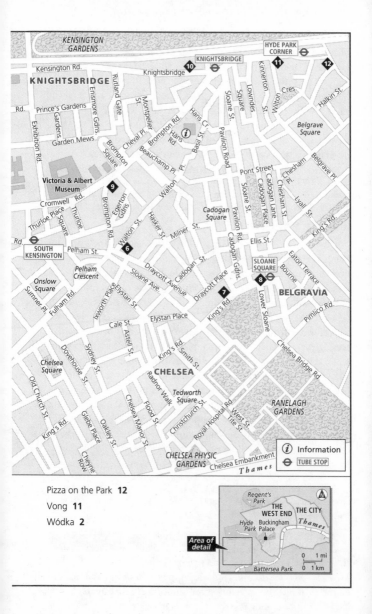

Pizza on the Park **12**

Vong **11**

Wódka **2**

Brasserie St. Quentin ⟨⟨ FRENCH BRASSERIE   This attractive brasserie with chandeliers, etched mirrors, and well-starched table-cloths is right on the border between Knightsbridge and South Kensington and caters to a pretty affluent clientele (there's a reassuringly high number of French patrons, too). But the brasserie has excellent value fixed-price meals, two or three courses, both at lunch and pre-theater. These offer a blend of classic and updated French fare, from navarre of lamb with root vegetables to seared white seabass. Vegetarian options include spinach ravioli and warm leek salad.

243 Brompton Rd., SW3. ⟨⟩ **020/7589-8005.** Reservations recommended. Main courses £8.95–£22 ($14–$35). Fixed-price lunch/pre-theater menus £14.50–£16.50 ($23–$26), £12.50 ($20) vegetarian. AE, DC, MC, V. Daily noon–3pm; Mon–Sat 6–11:30pm; Sun 6:30–10:30pm. Tube: Knightsbridge, South Kensington.

WORTH A SPLURGE

Vong ⟨⟨⟨ THAI–FRENCH   This is the London outpost of famous chef Jean-Georges Vongerichten, though you probably won't find him in the kitchen. Make sure to dress up for the occasion because you'll have to make an entrance from the reception area down into the chic basement dining room where single-stem orchids decorate the tables. The Thai–French cuisine includes a delicious lobster daikon roll with rosemary ginger dip. This is one of the five appetizers that make up the black plate pre- and post-theater menu. You'll also get a crab spring roll with tamarind dipping sauce, prawn satay with fresh oyster sauce, tuna and vegetables wrapped in rice paper, and quail rubbed with Thai spices and served with a cress salad. Seafood lovers can ditch the quail and take salmon slices in a scallion pancake with green peppercorns instead. Vegetarians can swap selections, too. If you can, add on the divine warm Valrhona chocolate cake with lemongrass ice cream.

Berkeley Hotel, Wilton Place, SW1. ⟨⟩ **020/7235-1010.** Reservations essential. Main courses £16–£32 ($23.20–$46.40); fixed-price lunch £18.50–£20 ($30–$32); black plate menu pre-/post-theater £22.50 ($36). AE, DC, DISC, MC, V. Mon–Fri noon–2:30pm; Sat–Sun 11:30am–2pm; Mon–Sat 6–11:30pm; Sun 6–10pm. Tube: Hyde Park Corner, Knightsbridge.

3 Kensington & Chelsea

Itsu ⟨⟨⟨ PAN-ASIAN/SUSHI   This is the brainchild of Julian Metcalfe, who created Pret a Manger, the chain of hip and healthy sandwich shops that revolutionized the British lunch market. Itsu has the super-fashionable conveyor belt, with circling food on white, red, black, and gold plates to show the different prices. The menu subverts tradition with pan-Asian and Western influences. On the cheapest white plates you'll find salmon sushi and a sweet omelet roll with chives. Salmon plays a big part on the menu, from the smoked variety with avocado and flying-fish eggs, to some marinated with chives, or turned into sashimi. The gold plates include tasty grilled chicken with green soba noodles. Itsu is evangelically healthy, except for the oddball crème brûlée on the black-plate list, and is nonsmoking. There's sometimes a £1 ($1.60) per plate special between 4 and 6pm and 10:30 and 11:30pm. A new Soho branch opened at 103 Wardour St., W1 (✆ **020/7479-4794**; Tube: Leicester Square, Piccadilly Circus).

118 Draycott Ave., SW3. ✆ **020/7590-2401**. Colored plate selections £1.95–£5.95 ($3–$10). AE, MC, V. Mon–Thurs noon–11pm; Fri noon–midnight; Sat 12:30pm–midnight; Sun 1–11pm. Tube: South Kensington.

Maggie Jones's ✰ TRADITIONAL BRITISH   This 40-year veteran bistro has a charming staff and a quirkily cozy atmosphere that pulls in a diverse clientele. Maggie Jones's is like a junkshop crammed with farmhouse kitchen ephemera—copper warming pans, toddlers' rocking horses, and sheaves of dried corn hang down from the ceiling. The food is hearty farmhouse-style, too—big portions, not much finesse—from slices of eggy quiche to wild boar sausages and mash, as well as duck, venison, guinea fowl, and rabbit. And the menu tosses avocado about with 1970s abandon. The three-course Sunday lunch is a classic, offering such national culinary treasures as roast beef with Yorkshire pudding and apple crumble. There's only a cover charge in the evening, but the bill includes a 12.5% service charge, so watch for the total left blank on your credit card slip.

6 Old Court Place, off Kensington Church St., W8. ✆ **020/7937-6462**. Reservations essential at dinner and for Sunday lunch. Main courses £7–£22.95 ($11–$37). Fixed-price Sunday lunch £15.50 ($25). Cover charge at dinner £1 ($1.60). AE, DC, MC, V. Daily 12:30–2:30pm; Mon–Sat 6:30–11pm; Sun 6:30–10:30pm. Tube: Kensington High St.

Oriel FRENCH BRASSERIE *(Kids*   Oriel is in a fantastic location, right on the corner of Sloane Square, and everyone knows it. It's always hopping, so if you're planning to eat rather than grab a coffee or a quick drink (wine by the glass is very reasonably priced), try to arrive a little ahead of normal mealtimes. The upstairs is classic brasserie, with big mirrors, square-topped tables, and high ceilings. There are a few pavement tables for people-watching. Downstairs, marshmallow-soft sofas make you never want to leave. The food is a good value, from *moules marinières* (mussels) to salads or sausage and mash. Oriel has vegetarian dishes and will provide reduced-price portions for the kids.

50–51 Sloane Sq., SW1. ✆ 020/7730-2804. Main courses £8.45–£13.95 ($14–$22). AE, DC, MC, V. Mon–Sat 8:30am–10:45pm; Sun 9am–10pm. Tube: Sloane Sq.

SUPER-CHEAP EATS

Chelsea Kitchen BRITISH DINER   This is a sister to the Stock-pot chain, which also has a diner on King's Road. The Chelsea Kitchen is a lot more convenient, and the food is a little better. The cuisine is not remotely haute by any stretch of the imagination, but it's a fantastically good deal. The menu never changes. It runs from omelets and burgers to salads and more substantial hot dishes, such as goulash, spaghetti bolognese, and braised lamb chops. Chelsea Kitchen is no-frills on the decor side, too, with polished wooden tables and bum-numbing booths. The service sometimes sorely lacks a smile. But the prices are so "Old World" that it gets scream-ingly busy, particularly in the evening.

98 King's Rd., SW3. ✆ 020/7589-1330. Main courses £3–£6.10 ($4.80–$10); fixed-priced meal £6–£6.70 ($10–$11). No credit cards. Mon–Sat 7:30am–11:45pm. Tube: Sloane Sq.

GREAT DEALS ON FIXED-PRICE MEALS

Café Lazeez ⟨⟩ INDIAN   A two-time winner of Carlton TV's Best Indian Restaurant award, this is another place that has ditched flocked wallpaper and canned ethnic music for a cool modern approach, evolving new dishes but losing nothing of its authenticity in the kitchen. There's a bar/brasserie on the ground floor with the dining room upstairs. In summer, diners hang out on a terrace framed with flower boxes. There's so much good stuff to choose from and at such a range of prices, that you'd have to go back several times to work out which is the best deal. The £39 ($62) fixed-price menu for two starts with delicious barbecued kebabs and chicken tikka with naan bread. The main course includes spicy sautéed chicken, lamb, aubergines, cumin potatoes, dhal, rice, more naan, and coffee. Alternatively, the £15.50 ($25) House Feast—a host of different meats cooked in the tandoor oven—could easily feed two people. Just ask for extra cutlery. There are two other branches: at 88 St. John St., EC1 (✆ 020/7253-2224; Tube: Barbican, Farringdon), and at the Soho Theatre, 21 Dean St., W1 (✆ 020/7434-9393; Tube: Tottenham Court Rd.).

93–95 Old Brompton Rd., SW7. ✆ 020/7581-9993. Reservations recommended. Main courses £7.25–£16.95 ($12–$27); fixed-price meals £10–£12.75 ($16–$20). AE, DC, MC, V. Mon–Sat 11am–1am; Sun 11am–10:30pm. Tube: South Kensington.

Wódka POLISH   This friendly Kensington restaurant takes a new look at classic Polish dishes, served amid the simple modern decor. The two- and three-course fixed-price lunches are a great value. You might start with a meal-in-itself, such as *zur* (sausage and sour rye soup), or light fluffy blinis with aubergine mousse. The main courses are likely to include at least one Western European dish, like the delicious fishcakes. If you've got a bit of spare cash, come in the evening instead. It's a much better time to enjoy Wódka's real specialty: the mile-long menu of vodkas, served by the shot or carafe. There's every flavor under the sun, from bison grass to rose petal, or a honey one that's served hot. Wódka is a firm favorite with locals and not-so-locals who want to kick up their heels.

12 St. Alban's Grove, W8. ⓒ 020/7937-6513. Reservations recommended. Main courses £10.90–£13.50 ($17–$22); fixed-price lunch £11.50–£14.50 ($18–$23). AE, DC, MC, V. Daily 7am–11:15pm. Tube: High St. Kensington, Gloucester Rd.

WORTH A SPLURGE

Cambio de Tercio 𝓡𝓡 SPANISH   Several changes of chef have done nothing to dent the standards or popularity of the stylish Cambio de Tercio. The dramatic interior is decorated in a rich yellow with damask-spread tables and chairs swathed in burgundy cloth. The walls are hung with pictures of bullfights and a matador's cloak and swords. The charming Spanish staff guides you through a menu of regional delights. Ham is the house specialty—from the expensive plate of ham Jabugo, made from acorn-fed black pig, to the suckling pig Segovia style. But you could also get dishes like poached eggs with grilled asparagus, Basque wine mousseline, and sautéed foie gras. You should dress up a bit for this place and starve yourself beforehand.

163 Old Brompton Rd., SW5. ⓒ 020/7244-8970. Reservations required for dinner. Main courses £10.50–£15 ($17–$24). AE, MC, V. Daily noon–2:30pm; Mon–Sat 7–11:30pm; Sun 7–11pm. Tube: Gloucester Rd., South Kensington.

4 Earl's Court

The Atlas 𝓡𝓡 GASTROPUB/MEDITERRANEAN   The doors open for drinkers at noon here, and that's when you should come if you want to get a table (especially one outside). The Atlas is incredibly popular, and rightly so: the food is delicious, the ambience laid-back, and it has a real neighborhood feel. The Manners brothers run the place, with George as the chef and grand creator of grilled Tuscan sausages with Puy lentils, or pan-fried calves liver. While he is big on balsamic vinegar, pancetta, and parmesan, the rich flavors characteristic of Spanish and North African cooking spice up both starters and main courses made from the freshest of whatever's in season. And do leave space for dessert, because George's are some of the best in town. Choose from the menu chalked up on the board and order at the bar. The Atlas has several ales on tap and around 10 wines available by the glass.

16 Seagrave Rd., SW6. © 020/7385-9129. Main courses £7–£12 ($11–$19). MC, V. Food served daily 12:30–3pm; Mon–Sat 7–10:30pm; Sun 7–10pm. Tube: West Brompton.

5 Notting Hill

Mandola ⚘ SUDANESE   This little local restaurant started out as the half-hearted annex to the take-out joint next door. Now it has grown into an attractive and mildly eccentric restaurant with very good food but unbelievably slow service. The best deal is the £11 ($18) starter, which gives two diners free run at everything the salad bar has to offer—though to call it just a "salad bar" doesn't do it justice. Options include white cabbage in peanut sauce, aubergine *salata aswad,* and Sudanese falafel. Each would cost over £2 ($3.20) on its own, and you get pita bread to accompany them. Main courses are just as simple, from super-tender lamb and chicken in pungent sauces to the vegetarian stews. Mandola is unlicensed, so you can bring your own wine for a £1 corkage fee per bottle.

139–143 Westbourne Grove, W11. © 020/7229-4734. Reservations recommended for dinner. Main courses £5.25–£11 ($8–$18). AE, MC, V. Mon–Sun noon–midnight. Tube: Notting Hill Gate.

Portobello Gold *(Finds* INTERNATIONAL   In December 2000 Bill Clinton popped into this little local pub-restaurant, and popped

---

(Finds Much More Than Just a Bookshop

The first muffins come out of the oven at 10am, filling **Books for Cooks** with heavenly smells. This mecca for gastronomes, which stocks nearly 12,000 titles, has a little test kitchen at the rear and a handful of tables where browsers can settle down for a cup of coffee and a freshly-baked cake. Light lunches are a steal at £5 ($8)—hot soup and bread in the winter, a salad or homemade savory tart in the summer. It's just off the Portobello Road at 4 Blenheim Crescent, W11 (© 020/7221-1992; Tube: Ladbroke Grove, Notting Hill Gate). Open daily 10am–6pm; closed last 3 weeks in August.

---

out of it again without paying, while Hillary did her Christmas shopping in Portobello Market. Clinton and his secret service guys stuck to the all-day bar menu—jumbo sandwiches, salads, nibbles and dips, pâtés, and sweet temptations, all for under £6.50 ($10). This restaurant also has one of the most romantic dining spots in town: the "hippy balcony," as long-time owner Mike Bell describes it, is under the conservatory greenery, with a low Indian table and squashy cushions. Starters are fishy or vegetarian, except for the bacon in the tasty smoked eel and anchovy salad. The hearty main courses, like calves' liver with basil and parmesan polenta, make up for it, though. Portobello Gold also has an Internet cafe and a handful of B&B bedrooms (see p. 56). It's happy hour in the bar every day from 5:30 to 7pm. This is a nutty, chaotic place, but great fun, especially on Saturdays.

95–97 Portobello Rd., W11. ℂ 020/7460-4900. Reservations recommended for dinner and Sunday lunch. Main courses £7.95–14.75 ($13–$24). DC, MC, V. Restaurant Mon–Sat noon–5pm, 7:30–11:15pm; Sun 1–5pm, 7:30–9:30pm. Tube: Notting Hill Gate.

6 Paddington & Bayswater

Royal China 𝒜𝒜 CHINESE   The plaudits keep rolling in for Royal China's dim sum, which is reckoned by many to be the best in London. The decor is marvelously over-ornate, with Hong Kong casino-style, black-and-gold paneling. But you don't have to be a high roller to dine here: A dim sum extravaganza is unlikely to set you back much more than £10 ($16). The most popular dish, and deservedly so, is the roast pork puff. The touch is always light as air, whether on the standard menu dumplings or daily specials, such as a delicate mange tout (snowpeas) combination. No wonder Sundays here are as big a scrum as the Harrods sale. Come during the week when it's a lot more peaceful, and the staff are more likely to have their happy faces on.

13 Queensway, W2. ℂ 020/7221-2535. Reservations recommended. Main courses £6–£40 ($10–$64); fixed-price dinner £28–£36 ($45–$58). AE, DC, MC, V. Mon–Thurs noon–11pm; Fri–Sat noon–11:30pm; Sun 11am–10pm; dim sum to 5pm daily. Tube: Bayswater, Queensway.

7 Marylebone

The Chapel 𝒜 GASTROPUB/MODERN EUROPEAN   The Chapel is one place that deserves to be called a gastropub. The food is ambitious, beautifully executed, and primarily modern European. The blackboard lists a handful of daily starters, from brie en croute

Where to Dine from Marylebone to Notting Hill

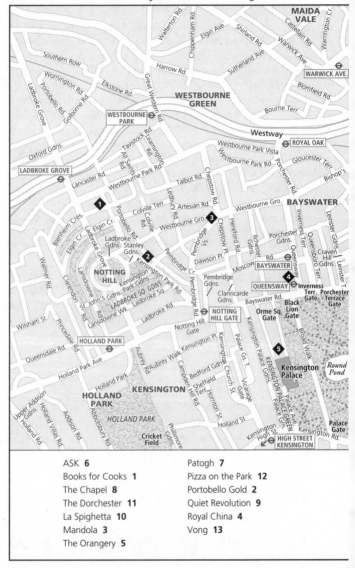

ASK **6**	Patogh **7**
Books for Cooks **1**	Pizza on the Park **12**
The Chapel **8**	Portobello Gold **2**
The Dorchester **11**	Quiet Revolution **9**
La Spighetta **10**	Royal China **4**
Mandola **3**	Vong **13**
The Orangery **5**	

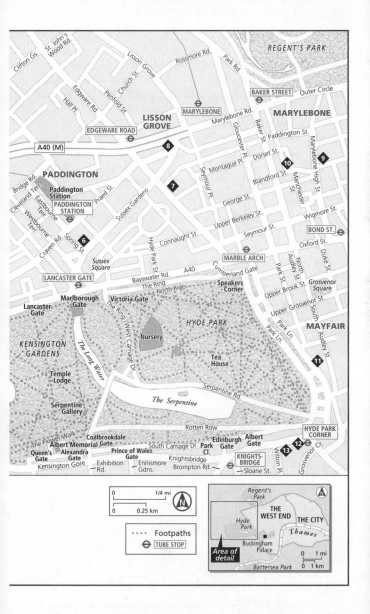

Clifton Gs.
St. John's Wood Rd.
Lisson Grove
Rossmore Rd.
Park Rd.
REGENT'S PARK

Edgware Rd.
Penfold St.
Church St.
BAKER STREET — Outer Circle
Hall Pl.

MARYLEBONE
LISSON GROVE
EDGEWARE ROAD
Marylebone Rd.
MARYLEBONE
Paddington St.
Baker St.

A40 (M)
8
Gloucester Pl.
Dorset St.
Marylebone High St.
9

PADDINGTON
Bridge Rd.
Montague Pl.
10
Blandford St.
Manchester St.

Paddington Station
7
Seymour Pl.
George St.

PADDINGTON STATION
Praed St.
Sussex Gardens
Upper Berkeley St.
Wigmore St.

Cleveland Terr.
Eastbourne Terr.
Westbourne Terr.
Craven Rd.
Spring St.
6
Connaught St.
Seymour St.
BOND ST.

Hyde Park St.
MARBLE ARCH
Oxford St.
North Audley St.
Duke St.

Sussex Square
LANCASTER GATE
Bayswater Rd.
The Ring
A40
Cumberland Gate
Marble Arch
Park St.
Grosvenor Square

North Ride
Speakers Corner
Upper Brook St.

Marlborough Gate
Victoria Gate
HYDE PARK
Upper Grosvenor St.

Lancaster Gate
The Ring (West Carriage Dr.)
Park Ln.
MAYFAIR

KENSINGTON GARDENS
The Long Water
Nursery
Audley St.

Temple Lodge
Tea House
11

Serpentine Gallery
Serpentine Rd.

The Flower Walk
The Serpentine

Rotten Row
HYDE PARK CORNER

Coalbrookdale
Albert Memorial Gate
Prince of Wales Gate
South Carriage Dr.
Park Cl.
Edinburgh Gate
Albert Gate
Wilton Pl.
Grosvenor Cr.

Queen's Gate
Alexandra Gate
Ennismore Gdns.
Knightsbridge
KNIGHTS-BRIDGE
13 **12**

Kensington Gore
Exhibition Rd.
Brompton Rd.
Sloane St.

| 0 | | 1/4 mi |
| 0 | 0.25 km | |

···· Footpaths
⊖ TUBE STOP

Regent's Park
THE WEST END
THE CITY
Hyde Park
Thames

Area of detail
Buckingham Palace
Battersea Park
0 — 1 mi
0 — 1 km

to parma ham and Tuscan bean salad in a phyllo basket. Main courses that sound traditional (many don't) have a very modern twist, like the pork with caramelized apples and fluffy fishcakes. Don't graze too enthusiastically at the complimentary basket of delicious breads because the desserts are extremely wicked and deserve close attention. The interior is bright and spacious, but the bareboard floor makes it rather noisy. In the summer, head out to the garden where you can escape the cigarette smoke and sip a glass of wine (25 are available by the glass) or a pint of London Pride.

48 Chapel St., NW1. ✆ 020/7402-9220. Main courses £8.50–£13 ($14–$21). AE, DC, MC, V. Daily noon–2:30pm and 7–10pm. Tube: Edgware Rd.

La Spighetta ✿✿ PIZZA & PASTA   This little basement eatery is the better-value sister of Spiga in Covent Garden. It was "created," as the higher echelons of the restaurant world say, by Giorgio Locatelli, who is chef and part owner of Knightsbridge's illustrious and molto pricey Zafferano. The menu is as authentic and uncomplicated as the decor, using an Italian wood-fired oven for the pizzas. The ingredients are simple: mozzarella, artichoke, spicy salami, pecorino cheese, and so on, all melting together on superbly crispy bases. There are nine main pasta dishes and lots of meat and fish main courses. The menu changes every week but maybe you'll find the marvelous wind-dried tuna starter, one of several dishes that show La Spighetta's posh pedigree. Cheaper children's portions are available on request, though I doubt the kids would thank you for sparing them even one mouthful of the homemade ice cream. This place is justly popular for working lunches and for R&R after the day is done.

43 Blandford St., W1. ✆ 020/7486-7340. Reservations recommended. Main courses £7–£11 ($11–$18). AE, MC, V. Mon–Sat noon–2:30pm, 6:30–11:30pm; Sun 6:30–10:30pm. Tube: Baker St.

SUPER-CHEAP EATS

Patogh IRANIAN   If you like simple Persian cooking, you'll love Patogh. The kebabs are legendary. Left to marinate overnight, the organic lamb or chicken practically melts in the mouth. The skewers come on a huge circle of seeded bread, with yogurt dips and Middle-Eastern salad. If kebabs ain't your thing, there are plenty of other choices, from chicken pieces to a whole host of ready-prepared salads and starters. There's hummus, marinated tomato, and other *meze* (small entrees). You could stack a plate high without coming close to busting the budget. Patogh is unlicensed, too, so you can bring your own bottle of wine or beer, and you won't even be charged any corkage.

8 Crawford Place, W1. ✆ **020/7262-4015**. Reservations recommended. Main courses £5.50–£10 ($9–$16). No credit cards. Daily 1:30–11:30pm. Tube: Edgware Rd.

Quiet Revolution BRITISH DINER/SOUP   Originally a soup manufacturer, Quiet Revolution has won awards for its certified organic concoctions like the Polska Tomato soup—suitable for vegans, 35 calories per 100g, 5g of carbohydrate, 1.3g of fat. It branched out into a daytime cafe-diner in 2000 to serve its super-healthy food direct to the public. No meat is served, but there are always good fish and veggie options such as ratatouille.

28 Weymouth St., off Marylebone High St., W1. ✆ **020/7487-5683**. Main courses £5.95–£8.95, soups £3–£5.50 ($4.80–$9). MC, V. Mon–Fri 9am–7pm; Sat 9am–6pm. Tube: Baker St..

8 Soho & Chinatown

Andrew Edmunds ☆ *Finds* MODERN BRITISH   This charming Soho restaurant started life as a wine bar and is attached to the print gallery next door. Popular for business lunches by day, at night it becomes the haunt of romantic young couples eating dinner by candlelight. They have to whisper their sweet nothings because the tables are pretty close together. The handwritten menu changes frequently but always offers modern European cuisine in healthy portions. Menu offerings might include grilled sardines with balsamic vinegar, white bean and lemon soup, or black pudding and caramelized apples with watercress salad and chive crème fraîche. The desserts are delicious classics, from tiramisu to almond tart. Finish up with a portion of Stilton.

46 Lexington St., W1. ✆ **020/7437-5708**. Reservations recommended. Main courses £8.25–£13.50 ($13–$22). AE, MC, V. Mon–Sat 12:30–3pm and 6–10:45pm; Sun 1–3pm and 6–10:30pm. Tube: Oxford Circus, Piccadilly Circus.

Golden Dragon ☆☆ CANTONESE   The crowds of local Chinese diners who come here back up the claim that the Golden Dragon serves up some of the best dim sum in town. There can be nothing but praise for the honey-glazed spare ribs, steamed eel with black-bean sauce, and sliced marinated duck with garlic dipping sauce. The service is variable because the staff is usually so busy. If you decide on dim sum, make sure to try the steamed scallop dumplings and prawn cheung fen. A real blowout shouldn't cost you more than £15 ($24), but you'll have to get here before 5pm. And reserve in advance, especially on Sundays when the place is packed.

28–29 Gerrard St., W1. ✆ **020/7734-2763**. Reservations recommended. Main courses £6–£18 ($10–$29); fixed-price menus £12.50–£22.50 ($20–$36). AE, DC,

MC, V. Mon–Thurs noon–11:30pm; Fri–Sat noon–midnight; Sun 11am–11pm. Tube: Leicester Sq.

Incognico 🅖🅖 MODERN FRENCH   The £12.50 ($20) set menu comprises three courses, with a choice of two dishes at each stage, which is great value in itself, but even better when you realize it offers superlative French cooking in the style of Michelin-star-winning Nico Ladenis, who's still the owner but now retired from his various kitchens. Ladenis' signature dish, pan-fried foie gras with brioche and caramelized orange, is on the a la carte menu here as a starter for £11 ($18). Otherwise, Incognico prices compare favorably with other mid-range London restaurants. With its bar, heavy paneling, and starched white tablecloths, it looks like an international bourgeois brasserie. The fish is delicious, and there are great vegetarian choices, such as Parmesan risotto with mushrooms. Unlike many of London's eateries, where the food is only part of the entertainment, eating here feels like a very special gastronomic experience.

117 Shaftesbury Ave., WC2 🅒 020/7836-8866. Reservations essential. Main courses £12.50–£18.50 ($20–$30). Fixed-price lunch and pre-theater meal £12.50 ($20). AE, DC, MC, V. Daily noon–3pm; Mon–Sat 5:30–midnight. Tube: Leicester Sq., Tottenham Ct. Rd.

Mr Kong 🅖 CANTONESE   This rather shabby restaurant is so popular that it's busy long past midnight every night of the week. The cheaper fixed-price menu includes soup, a choice of three main courses—beef with black bean sauce, for instance—and rice. The more expensive one covers four courses and is a lot better value. Over 150 dishes are listed on three different menus. The daily specials are generally a bit cheaper and less exotic. Or you can choose from the regular selection: Sliced pork, salted egg, and vegetable soup is a house specialty. The service is friendly and the menu translated into English.

21 Lisle St., WC2. 🅒 020/7437-7341. Reservations required for weekend dinners. Main courses £10–£18 ($16–$29); fixed-price dinner £9.30–£22 ($15–$35). AE, DC, MC, V. Daily noon–2:30am. Tube: Leicester Sq., Piccadilly Circus.

YO! Sushi 🅚🅘🅓🅢 SUSHI   In the 6 years since it opened, the relentless self-congratulation of this fast expanding chain has become something of a turn off. But you can still enjoy this original Soho sushi bar with its blitz of brand messages because it remains a novel experience. YO! Sushi rivals NASA for hi-tech gadgets. Talking drink trolleys circle the restaurant like R2D2, and diners pick out what they want. Sushi-making robots turn out 1,200 pieces an hour, which circle around on a 60-meter conveyor belt. The different colored plates

Where to Dine in Soho & Chinatown

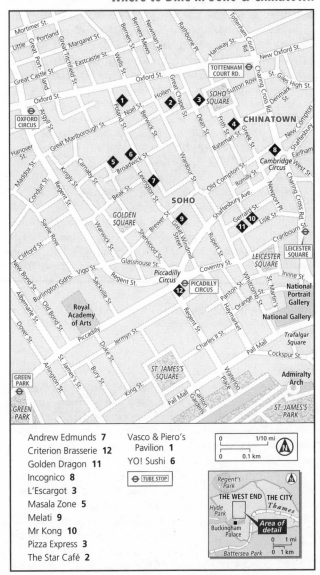

Andrew Edmunds **7**

Criterion Brasserie **12**

Golden Dragon **11**

Incognico **8**

L'Escargot **3**

Masala Zone **5**

Melati **9**

Mr Kong **10**

Pizza Express **3**

The Star Café **2**

Vasco & Piero's
Pavilion **1**

YO! Sushi **6**

⊖ TUBE STOP

indicate the price. Diners tuck into tuna, sashimi, and so on, until full
enough to ask for a plate count. Do keep a running tally, or this could
turn out to be a budget-buster. At the branches other than this one,
kids eat for free from Monday to Friday and they'll love it. There are
scaled down and toned-down dishes for them, from chicken nuggets
to cigar-shaped fish fingers.

Other good lunchtime deals are the £5 ($8) bento box and a beer
at **YO! Below,** the Japanese beer and sake hall downstairs at Poland
Street (© **020/7439-3660**), and below the new YO! Sushi at 95
Farringdon Rd., EC1 (© **020/7841-0785** restaurant, 020/7841-
0790 YO! Below; Tube: Farringdon). This latter is now the biggest
YO! and it has a kids' eating zone. So does the one at the Harvey
Nichols store in Knightsbridge, SW1 (© **020/7235-6114**). Others
useful to know about are at Selfridges on Oxford Street, W1 (© **020/
7318-3944**); the Whiteleys shopping center in Queensway (© **020/
7727-9293**); at Bloomsbury's Myhotel, 11–13 Bayley St., WC1
(© **020/7667-6000;** Tube: Goodge St., Tottenham Ct. Rd.); and at
County Hall on the South Bank by the London Eye (© **020/
7928-8871;** Tube: Waterloo, Westminster), which is the only one
that accepts reservations.

52 Poland St., W1. © **020/7287-0443.** Sushi selections from £1.50–£3.50 ($2.20–
$6) per plate; children's dishes £1.50–£2 ($2.20–$3.20). AE, DC, MC, V. Daily noon–
midnight. Tube: Oxford Circus. No smoking.

SUPER-CHEAP EATS

The Star Café ⊱ BRITISH DINER   This ex-pub has been run by
the same family for 68 years and is proud to boast of being the oldest cafe in Soho. The walls of the main floor are hung with old
enamel shop signs and radio sets. The no-frills menu includes staples
like jacket potatoes, toasted sandwiches, and pasta, with daily lunch-
eon specials such as roast chicken with crispy bacon stuffing, steak
and onion pie, or salmon filet with broccoli. Most people come for
the all-day, full English breakfast, including vegetarians, who get a
very superior spread with peppers and diced roast potatoes. Unfortunately, The Star Café closes after lunch and at the weekends.

22 Great Chapel St., W1. © **020/7437-8778.** Reservations recommended. Main
courses £4.95–£6.50 ($8–$10). No credit cards. Mon–Fri 7am–3:30pm. Tube: Tottenham Court Rd.

GREAT DEALS ON FIXED-PRICE MEALS

Masala Zone ⊱⊱ *Kids* INDIAN   Like Mela in Shaftesbury
Avenue, Masala Zone reacts against the determined upward mobil-
ity of London's Indian restaurants (never mind that its owners run

Veeraswamy, one of the poshest of the lot). Masala Zone was one of the first restaurants that attempted to introduce Britain to the way India really eats at home—off *thalis* and at the roadside chaat stall. A thali is a fixed-price meal on a tray, including a curry, bowls of vegetables, dal, yogurt curry, rice, poppadums, chapattis, chutneys, and raita. The street food is often Anglo-influenced comfort food, like *gosht dabalroti,* a lamb curry with white bread mixed in and topped by crispy fried noodles. Masala Zone is in the bottom of a concrete block near Carnaby Street. Two Indian tribal artists came all the way from Maharashtra to decorate the inside. Long teak tables invite shared eating. There's also a takeaway counter. Another plus: it's smoke free.

9 Marshall St., W1. © 020/7287-9966. Reservations not accepted. Main courses £4.75–£7 ($6.90–$10.15). Fixed-price meals £6–£9 ($9–$13); children's meal, available at weekends, £3.75 ($6). MC, V. Mon–Fri 11am–11pm; Sat 5:30–11:30pm; Sun 6–10:30pm. Tube: Oxford Circus.

Vasco & Piero's Pavilion ITALIAN This cozy, comfortable restaurant attracts a business and sophisticated older crowd who consider it their secret favorite hideaway—folks like "Call me Ken" Livingstone, London's mayor. Unfortunately, so many of them have written glowingly about it in newspaper columns that you must book ahead. The Matteucci family has run the restaurant for 33 years, and the welcome is one of the warmest around. Vasco still does much of the cooking. The unpretentious cuisine is light on butter and cream, with flavors clear as a bell, whether marinated anchovies or asparagus perfectly cooked al dente. Many of its ingredients come from local producers in Umbria, except for the pasta, which they make themselves. The fixed-price menus change daily, and you can choose either two or three courses from a fantastic selection of seven or eight of each. Ask what's best that day, and order it. Calves' liver, allegedly the best in London, is a house specialty.

15 Poland St., W1. © 020/7437-8774. Reservations recommended. Main courses £10.50–£15.50 ($16–$23) at lunch; fixed-price dinners £14.50–£23.50 ($23–$38). AE, MC, V. Mon–Fri noon–3pm and 6–11pm; Sat 7–11pm. Tube: Oxford Circus.

PRE-THEATER BARGAINS

L'Escargot TRADITIONAL FRENCH Dining in a Michelin 1-star restaurant for £14.95 ($24) is a fantastic value. This is serious food, in seriously elegant surroundings, and you ought to dress up and make a real occasion of it. The walls are hung with works by Marc Chagall, Joan Miró, and David Hockney. The first-floor restaurant's fixed-price menu changes every week. Diners get to choose from three starters, main courses, and desserts, all classic French dishes perfectly executed. For example, you could have tartare of red mullet, followed by ravioli langoustine; or swap one of those for chocolate tart with praline ice cream. Choices are limited for vegetarians. Prices are higher in the upstairs Picasso Room, but the service is uniformly impeccable.

48 Greek St., W1. ℂ 020/7437-2679. Reservations recommended. Main courses £12.95 ($21); fixed-price lunch and pre-theater menu £14.95–£17.95 ($24–$29). AE, DC, MC, V. Mon–Fri 12:15–2:15pm; Mon–Sat 6–11:30pm. Pre-theater dinner served from 6 to 7pm. Tube: Leicester Sq., Tottenham Court Rd.

WORTH A SPLURGE

Criterion Brasserie ✿ MODERN FRENCH   This used to be the only place where diners could sample the cooking of Michelin 3-star bad boy Marco Pierre White without remortgaging their homes. Now his superlative restaurant Mirabelle, in Curzon Street (reviewed below), offers a fixed-price lunch for a similar price. But it is still well worth coming to the Criterion. The inside is like a Byzantine palace with its fantastic gold vaulted ceiling. The staff is often pressed for time, but the cuisine is superb. Don't try the three-course early dinner, unless you eat at the speed of lightning. Save the Criterion for a lunchtime blowout. Big favorites are ballotine of salmon with herbs and *fromage blanc,* and risottos are always real star performers.

224 Piccadilly, W1. ℂ 020/7930-0488. Reservations essential. Main courses £12–£15 ($19–$22); fixed-price lunch £14.95–£17.95 ($22–$29); fixed-price dinner £14.95 ($22), order before 6:30pm. AE, DC, MC, V. Mon–Sat noon–2:30pm, 5:30–11:30pm. Tube: Piccadilly Circus.

9 Mayfair

Browns TRADITIONAL BRITISH   Browns takes the brasserie idea and makes it terribly English. The food is pretty predictable, but it's robust, generally well put together, and a good value for the money. That's a rare treat in Mayfair, where restaurants tend to cater to the super-affluent and child-free. Browns is divided into two sections, filled with wood paneling and mirrors. The restaurant is at the back beyond the bar, which is a popular after-work meeting point. The food ranges from pastas, salads, and sandwiches to main courses such as steak, mushroom, and Guinness pie. There are lighter, more modern dishes, too, like chargrilled chicken breast with tarragon butter. For dessert, the fudge brownie is a firm favorite. There are six other branches: the most central is located at 82 St. Martins Lane, WC2 (ℂ 020/7497-5050).

47 Maddox St., W1. © **020/7491-4565**. Hot sandwiches and main courses £6.95–£13.95 ($11–$22). AE, DC, MC, V. Mon–Sat noon–10pm. Tube: Oxford Circus.

GREAT DEALS ON FIXED-PRICE MEALS

Veeraswamy 🦚 INDIAN   This will probably be the most extraordinary Indian restaurant you'll ever encounter. Established in 1926 by a general and an Indian princess, Veeraswamy claims to be the oldest Indian restaurant in London. Over the years, it's been the haunt of princes and potentates, from the Prince of Wales to King Hussein and Indira Gandhi. Nowadays it's very hip, painted in vibrant colors, with frosted-glass panels dividing up the sections, and ultra-modern furniture. For starters, the stir-fried oysters with coconut and Kerala spices are sublime. For an exotic and only mildly hot choice, try the shanks of lamb curried in bone stock and spices. Unless you're in the mood to splurge, this isn't the place to sample lots of different dishes. Go for a great-value fixed-price menu and enjoy the best of new Indian cuisine. **Masala Zone,** its new sister restaurant in Soho, is much cheaper and much praised: see p. 96.

99–101 Regent St., W1. © **020/7734-1401**. Reservations recommended. Main courses £10–£14.50 ($16–$23); lunch and pre-/post-theater menu £12.50–£14.75 ($20–$24); Sun menu £15 ($24). AE, DC, MC, V. Mon–Sat noon–2:30pm and 5:30–11:30pm; Sun 12:30–3pm and 5:30–10:30pm. Tube: Piccadilly Circus.

WORTH A SPLURGE

Mirabelle 🦚🦚 MODERN EUROPEAN   As long as you don't indulge your urge to wash down your meal with a £30,000 ($48,000) bottle of 1847 Chateau d'Yquem, this is the best value mouthful of Marco Pierre White's cooking you will ever eat. The lower priced, two-course, fixed-price lunch may be a splurge but it costs less than most of his main courses. And the food is sensational, made with tricky ingredients timed perfectly. The entrance to Mirabelle is pretty nondescript but behind it lies a lounge decorated with tongue-in-cheek murals, then the long bar, and finally the brasserie-style restaurant. Diners are a little cramped, but don't seem to care. On sunny days, you can sit out on the terrace. The menu changes seasonally but includes MPW classics. The two courses could be terrine of duck with foie gras and potatoes in a beetroot dressing, and then ballotine of salmon or caramelized wing of skate with winkles and jus a la Parisienne. A few extra pounds will get you a dessert or a selection of creamy French cheeses. This offer is only on at lunchtime.

56 Curzon St., W1. © **020/7499-4636**. Reservations essential. Main courses £14.50–£28.50 ($23–$46); fixed-price lunch £16.50–£19.95 ($26–$32). AE, DC, MC, V. Daily noon–2:30pm, 6–11:30pm. Tube: Green Park.

Where to Dine in the West End

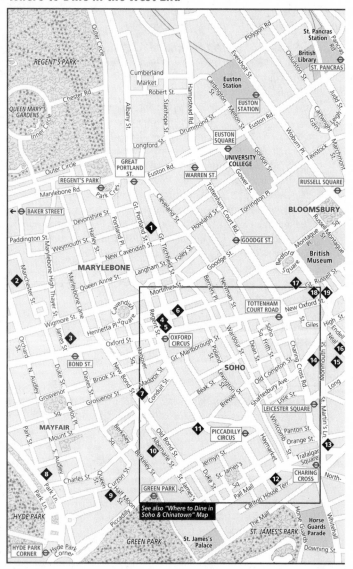

See also "Where to Dine in Soho & Chinatown" Map

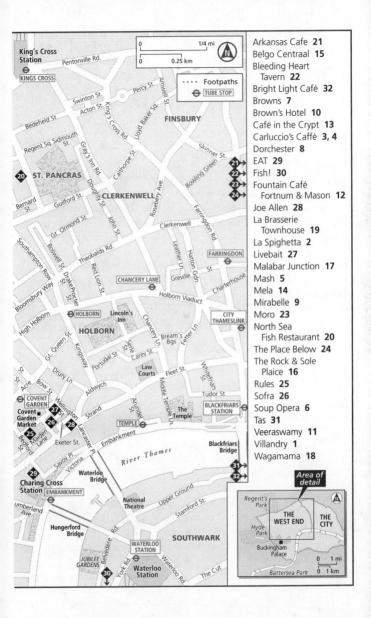

Arkansas Cafe **21**
Belgo Centraal **15**
Bleeding Heart
  Tavern **22**
Bright Light Café **32**
Browns **7**
Brown's Hotel **10**
Café in the Crypt **13**
Carluccio's Caffè **3, 4**
Dorchester **8**
EAT **29**
Fish! **30**
Fountain Café
  Fortnum & Mason **12**
Joe Allen **28**
La Brasserie
  Townhouse **19**
La Spighetta **2**
Livebait **27**
Malabar Junction **17**
Mash **5**
Mela **14**
Mirabelle **9**
Moro **23**
North Sea
  Fish Restaurant **20**
The Place Below **24**
The Rock & Sole
  Plaice **16**
Rules **25**
Sofra **26**
Soup Opera **6**
Tas **31**
Veeraswamy **11**
Villandry **1**
Wagamama **18**

10 Bloomsbury & Fitzrovia

The Bar at Villandry ✦ INTERNATIONAL   This new offshoot of the famous gourmet hotspot is a godsend for budget travelers. You can swing by any time of day, without a reservation. The menu changes every week and picks the best of everything in season. In the early evening, the bar raids the Villandry foodstore for produce to make its snacks. The typically English ploughman's lunch with farmhouse Stilton and onion marmalade is pricier than the average pub version, but the cheese is creamy and moist. Tiger prawns with chili and lemon dipping sauce could use a little more oomph. All in all, the Bar at Villandry is an exuberant place where you can feel wicked and wholesome at the same time. But be careful with the Red Hot Villandry cocktail, an explosive mix of tomato juice and tequila.

The refectory-style restaurant serves Modern British cuisine at lunch every day and dinner from Monday to Saturday. It is totally nonsmoking, unlike the smoky bar. The restaurant is open Monday through Saturday noon to 10:30pm and Sunday noon to 4pm. The Villandry foodstore closes an hour earlier than the bar (same time on Sunday).

170 Great Portland St., W1. ✆ 020/7631-3131. Main courses in bar £3.95–£11.50 ($6–$19), main courses in restaurant £11–£21 ($18–$34). AE, DISC, MC, V. Mon–Sat 8am–11pm; Sun 11am–4pm. Tube: Great Portland St.

North Sea Fish Restaurant ✦ FISH & CHIPS   Locals love North Sea's version of what is, of course, the national dish. Here the look is country-cozy, even down to the stuffed fish on the walls. Diners at the rear of the chippie sit on velvet-covered chairs at wooden tables. You'll find a good mix of cabbies on a tea break, local academics, and tourists here. Dining in, you could do two starters—smoked mackerel and scampi, perhaps—or one and a portion of deliciously crispy fat chips, for under £7 ($11). The best deal, though, is the enormous seafood platter, which comes with bite-size, battered pieces of lots of different sorts of fish and seafood. You can go for straight cod, of course, or skate, haddock, plaice, all brought in fresh from Billingsgate every morning. And after all that, I'll salute any diner who's got room for one of the traditional desserts. North Sea also does take-away.

7–8 Leigh St., WC1. ✆ 020/7387-5892. Reservations recommended for dinner. Main courses £8.30–£16.95 ($13–$27). AE, DC, MC, V. Mon–Sat noon–2:30pm, 5:30–10:30pm. Tube: Russell Sq., King's Cross.

Wagamama ✦ JAPANESE NOODLES   I eat at one or more of the Wagamamas every time I'm in London, and crave the yaki soba when I'm away. At this branch and the one in Soho, stairs lead down to a dining room set up with ranks of long shared tables like a traditional Japanese noodle bar. Staff punch food orders into handheld electronic keypads that send a radio signal to the kitchen. The thread noodles come in soups, pan-fried, or else served with various toppings. The menu actually tells you to slurp because the extra oxygen adds to the taste. For a hearty dish, try the chili beef ramen—char-grilled sirloin, chilies, red onion, parsley, and spring onions served in a chili-soup base. It's up to you to add as much or as little parsley, pickled pepper, bean sprouts, and lime as you want. Each dish is cooked and served immediately, so if you're dining with a group, be prepared for individual meals to arrive at different times. And don't expect to linger too long in the bus-station bustle. Wagamama is also in the basement of Harvey Nichols (see p. 150); at 10a Lexington St., W1 (© 020/7292-0990); 101a Wigmore St., W1 (© 020/7409-0111); 26a Kensington High St., W8 (© 020/7376-1717); and 11 Jamestown Rd., Camden Town, NW1 (© 020/7428-0800). All are nonsmoking.

4a Streatham St. (off Coptic St.), WC1. © **020/7323-9223.** Main courses £5.20–£8.50 ($8–$14). AE, DC, MC, V. Mon–Sat noon–11pm; Sun 12:30–10pm. Tube: Tottenham Court Rd.

SUPER-CHEAP EATS

Carluccio's Caffè *Kids* ITALIAN   Antonio Carluccio was one of the first celebrity chefs in Britain. That the locals no longer think of Italian cuisine simply as pizza and soggy lasagna is largely due to him. The cafe uses many imported ingredients and still manages to be a mega-cheap eat. Make a quick lunch stop for soup and antipasti starting at £3.60 ($6), or come for an evening reviver. Even if you choose the most expensive items for each course—a huge plate of antipasti, followed by moist grilled swordfish, then a culinary tour of regional Italian cheeses—and have the most expensive aperitif, glass of wine with the meal, and coffee, you'd still spend under £30 ($48). Choose the cheapest, and it'd be £16.50 ($26), including drinks. There are cheaper dishes for kids, the deli can provide top picnic pickings, and Carluccio's will even sell you a Vespa! A new branch opened last year in St. Christopher's Place, W1 (© 020/7935-5297; Tube: Bond St.), and there are seven others scattered all over London.

8 Market Place, W1. © **020/7636-2228.** Main courses £4.50–£7.50 ($7–$12). AE, MC, V. Mon–Fri 8am–11pm; Sat 11am–11pm; Sun 11am–10pm. Tube: Oxford Circus.

GREAT DEALS ON FIXED-PRICE MEALS

Malabar Junction ⟨ SOUTH INDIAN   After a bar meal here I can almost guarantee that you'll want to come back. Okay, so the choice is limited—chicken, lamb, or vegetarian—but a bumper plate of curry for just £3.50 ($6)? This attractive restaurant serves South Indian cuisine, specifically from Kerala. Behind an unprepossessing entrance, the domed dining room is furnished with potted palms, and exudes a languid tropical air. The four-page menu starts with a long list of mix-and-match house specialties: *masala dosa,* a traditional Kerala pancake, filled with potato *masala* and served with *sambar* and chutney; and *rasa vada,* a lentil doughnut in a hot spicy tomato and tamarind broth. Fish is another specialty, cooked in combinations of coconut, turmeric, ginger, chili, garlic, cumin and curry leaves. Every dish is a taste sensation: Try the green bananas flavored with spices and onions. After 7pm, the minimum check is £10 ($16).

107 Great Russell St., WC1. ℂ **020/7580-5230.** Reservations essential. Fixed-price bar meal (served noon–5pm) £3.50 ($6); main courses £7.50–£9.50 ($12–$15). AE, MC, V. Daily noon–3pm, 6–11:30pm (until 11pm Sun). Tube: Tottenham Court Rd.

WORTH A SPLURGE

Mash ⟨ MODERN EUROPEAN   You splurge here for the buzz rather than for ambrosial food. The Love Machine at the entrance flashes romantic epigrams as people open the doors. That gimmick and the video screens in the women's toilets giving glimpses into the men's (not vice versa) are why people either love or hate Mash. Oliver Peyton opened this sleek and gargantuan resto-deli in 1998. It was one of London's first microbreweries, with huge tanks visible at the back of the first-floor cafe. Couches invite customers to linger. The cuisine is modern Mediterranean-Italian, of sorts: Paper-thin pizzas, with bizarre toppings such as crispy duck, cucumber, Asian greens, and hoisin sauce, appear from a wood-fired grill. Main courses are either baked (like whole sea bass with gherkin and caper mayonnaise) or roasted (like the pork cutlet with wilted radicchio, new potatoes, French beans, and anchovy butter). This is a great place to come for a full-works brunch on the weekend: Your choice of Mash menu, American, or vegetarian costs £10 ($16).

19–21 Great Portland St., W1. ℂ **020/7637-5555.** Main courses £9.50–£15.50 ($15–$25); brunch £10 ($16). AE, DC, MC, V. Restaurant: Mon–Fri noon–3:30pm; Sat–Sun noon–4pm; Mon–Sat 6–11pm. Bar: Mon–Sat 11am–2am; Sun noon–4pm. Tube: Oxford Circus.

11 Covent Garden & the Strand

The Rock & Sole Plaice 🍴 FISH & CHIPS   Endell Street is a peaceful oasis only 1 block away from Covent Garden's unrelenting crowds. But it's best to avoid The Rock & Sole Plaice in the early evenings, when it's crowded with theater-goers. It opened in 1871 and claims to be London's oldest surviving fish-and-chip shop. The decor is very Covent Garden, with theatrical posters and pavement tables. The Dover sole certainly has to be the cheapest in town at £11 ($18), and the other fish are half that price. Choose from halibut, mackerel, tuna, haddock, plaice, or cod. If you've never tried skate, then do so here–it's a moist, flaky fish with a wonderful flavor. The chips are thick and wedge-shaped, and you can add on mushy peas and pickled onions. For non-fish-eaters, there's steak-and-kidney and several other pies, plus sausage in batter.

47 Endell St., WC2. ✆ 020/7836-3785. Reservations recommended (dinner). Fish-and-chips: Eat in £7.50 ($12); take-out £5 ($8). Main courses: £7.50–£12 ($12–$19). DC, MC, V. Mon–Sat 11:30am–10:30pm (11:45pm for take-out); Sun noon–10pm. Tube: Covent Garden.

SUPER-CHEAP EATS

Café in the Crypt BRITISH DINER   Right on Trafalgar Square, this is a great place to grab a bite to eat between a visit to the National Gallery and marching off down The Mall to Buckingham Palace. Or pop in with the kids after a session at the church's brass rubbing center. Simple healthy food costs a lot less here than at more commercial places. It's a self-service cafeteria, where diners choose from a big salad bar and a choice of two traditional main courses—one might be shepherd's pie. The other light-lunch options include filled rolls and delicious cups of soup. The menu changes daily, but one fixture is that most traditional of British desserts, bread-and-butter pudding (bread soaked in eggs and milk with currants or sultanas and then oven-baked). The door to the crypt is on the right-hand side of the church.

St. Martin-in-the-Fields, Duncannon St., WC2. ✆ 020/7839-4342. Rolls and sandwiches £2.50–£3.10 ($4–$5); main courses £5.95–£6.50 ($9–$10). No credit cards. Mon–Wed 10am–8pm; Thurs–Sat 10am–11pm. Tube: Charing Cross.

GREAT DEALS ON FIXED-PRICE MEALS

Belgo Centraal BELGIAN   Blatant concept restaurants often have a very short life-span, but the Belgian national dish of *moules, frites,* and *bière* (mussels, fries, and beer), served at long refectory tables by staff dressed as monks, has become a London dining staple. A kilo pot of mussels, prepared any one of three ways, will set you back between £10.95 and £11.95 ($18–$20). The only quibble is that sometimes there's too much broth. There are non-seafood dishes, and you'll find them on the fixed-price lunch menu: either wild boar sausages served with Belgian mash and a beer, or two lighter dishes with mineral water. For sheer gluttony, nothing beats the Beat the Clock menu. It runs from 5 to 7pm on weekdays. Whatever time you order, that's what the meal will cost—£5.45 if you order at 5:45, for instance. There are three huge dishes to choose from and wash down with a free drink. This is a fun place, if you can hack the noise and pace, and it's got a Belgian beer hall, too.

Opening times and meal deals vary from branch to branch, so call ahead to check: **Belgo Noord,** 71 Chalk Farm Rd., NW1 (✆ **020/ 7681-8182;** Tube: Chalk Farm); **Belgo Zuid,** 124 Ladbroke Grove, W10 (✆ **020/8982-8400;** Tube: Ladbroke Grove); and the **Bierdrome,** 173 Upper St., NW1 (✆ **020/7226-5835;** Tube: Highbury, Islington, Angel).

50 Earlham St., WC2. ✆ **020/7813-2233.** Reservations recommended. Main courses £7.95–£17.50 ($13–$28); lunch £5 ($8). AE, DC, MC, V. Mon–Thurs noon–11:30pm; Fri–Sat noon–midnight; Sun noon–10:30pm. Tube: Covent Garden.

Mela 🎔🎔 INDIAN   In 2001 this place won the Moët & Chandon award as best Indian restaurant in London. It claims to take its inspiration from Wali Gali, where Delhi's workers go to refuel at midday from a food stall on the street. Lunch here is a fantastic deal: curry or dal of the day, with bread, pickle, and chutney for under £2 ($3.20). That's less than you'd pay for a sandwich in this neck of the woods. Pay a little more and you can build your own version, from lots of different breads and toppings, culminating in the bargain-for-under-a-fiver, which has rice and salad thrown in too. This is a great way for curry novices to have a cheap taster—and to see it being made in the open kitchen. But do come back in the evening for a proper go at the innovative Indian country cuisine. Early birds get three courses. Fixed-price sharers have 10 dishes and accompaniments between them, with the lower prices for the vegetarian versions. The word mela means fair, and Mela the restaurant is energetic in its efforts to create a festive atmosphere.

152–156 Shaftesbury Ave., WC2. ✆ **020/7836-8635.** Main courses £7.95–£18.95 ($13–$30). Light lunches £1.95–£4.95 ($3.10–$8). Fixed-price meal for 2 people £24.95–£34.95 ($40–$56). AE, MC, V. Mon–Sat noon–11:30pm; Sun noon–10:30pm. Tube: Leicester Sq.

PRE- & POST-THEATER BARGAINS

Joe Allen AMERICAN   This dark wood-paneled basement, with its ridiculously discreet entrance, is a Theatreland institution where Londoners dining late rub shoulders with the cream of West End talent. You'll have to splurge to join them or stick to starters and salads where the portions are pretty generous. Joe Allen does have good value pre-theater deals, though, for two or three courses. The menu changes daily, except for the perennial bowl of chili, and the cuisine is a mix of classic down-home dishes and others that look suspiciously like modern British cooking—for instance, roast guinea fowl with new potatoes roasted in balsamic vinegar, served with blueberry and ginger relish. The service is sometimes perfunctory, and the tables are too close together, but the lively atmosphere and live jazz on Sunday nights compensate.

13 Exeter St., WC2. ℂ **020/7836-0651.** Reservations essential at weekends. Main courses £9–£15 ($14–$24); fixed-price lunch and pre-theater menu £14–£16 ($22–$26); weekend brunch menu £17.50–£19.50 ($28–$31). AE, MC, V. Mon–Fri noon–1am; Sat 11:30am–1am; Sun 11:30am–midnight. Tube: Covent Garden.

Livebait ⓡ SEAFOOD   If you like fish so fresh that it still looks surprised, then you'll love this very friendly, white-tiled place. There's a cheap way to enjoy it, too: Settle down in the bar for a bowl of cockles and a mixed-green salad, and it'll only cost you £6.50 ($10). In the restaurant, you have to have a main course. The fixed-price menus are all a steal, and early booking is essential. You get two or three courses, and two dishes to choose from in each. Fish soup with aïoli is a good way to start. Seafood haters should stay away because Livebait makes absolutely no concessions to meat eaters. It has also been spawning new branches: 43 The Cut, SE1 (ℂ **020/7928-7211;** Tube: Waterloo, Southwark); 175 Westbourne Grove, W11 (ℂ **020/7727-4321;** Tube: Bayswater, Queensway); and in Chelsea at 2 Hollywood Rd., SW10 (ℂ **020/7349-5500;** Tube: Earl's Court).

21 Wellington St., WC2. ℂ **020/7836-7161.** Reservations recommended. Main courses £9.25–£15.95 ($15–$26); Livebait platter for 2 £40 ($64); fixed-price lunch and pre-/post-theater menu £12.95–£15.50 ($21–$25). AC, DC, MC, V. Mon–Sat noon–11:30pm. Tube: Covent Garden.

Sofra TURKISH   At this very modern Turkish eating-house the cuisine is completely authentic, although the food is not as spicy as some chili fans would like, nor are the portions as generous at Sofra as they are at more basic ethnic restaurants. But the ingredients are super-fresh and so is the way they're treated. The chef goes light on the oil, chargrilling instead. The fixed-price meals are a fantastic value, comprising 11 mezes and meat dishes—super-tender diced lamb, velvety hummus, the classic Middle Eastern eggplant dish, *Imam Bayildi,* and so on. This place has two little sisters: The best for stopping off mid-shopping in Oxford Street, or for dining outside, is **Sofra Cafe,** 1 St. Christopher's Place, W1 (℃ 020/7224-4080; Tube: Bond St.). For Sunday lunch, head for **Sofra Bistro,** 18 Shepherd St., W1 (℃ **020/7493-3320;** Tube: Green Park, Hyde Park Corner).

36 Tavistock St., WC2. ℃ 020/7240-3773. Mixed meze £5.95 ($10); main courses £6.95–£12.95 ($11–$21); fixed-price lunch £8 ($13); pre- and post-theater menu £10 ($16). AE, DC, MC, V. Daily noon–midnight. Tube: Covent Garden.

WORTH A SPLURGE

Rules ⋪⋪ TRADITIONAL BRITISH   This ultra-British restaurant has been around for 200 years and seems likely to survive another 200. Lily Langtry and Edward VII used to tryst here, and it's about the only place in London where you'll still see a bowler hat these days. But despite the hammy quaintness, Rules is a very modern restaurant operation. It markets the house specialty, "feathered and furred game," as healthy, free range, additive-free, and low in fat. The fixed-price mid-afternoon meal is a splurge, but it's still a great deal because you can select two courses from anything on the menu. Head straight for the biggest budget busters—lobster and asparagus salad with mango dressing, followed by fallow deer with spiced red cabbage, blueberries, and bitter chocolate sauce—and you'll save over £10 ($16). The food is delicious: traditional yet innovative, until you get to the puddings (desserts), which are a mix of nursery and dinner-dance classics. The wine list is pricey, but Rules does have three brown ales, so try one of those instead.

35 Maiden Lane, WC2. ℃ 020/7836-5314. Reservations essential. Main courses £16.95–£22.50 ($17–$36); weekday fixed-price menu (served 3–5pm) £19.95 ($32). AE, DC, MC, V. Mon–Sat noon–11:15pm; Sun noon–10:15pm. Tube: Charing Cross, Covent Garden.

12 Victoria

Jenny Lo's Teahouse ⋪ CHINESE   Jenny Lo's father was Britain's best-known Chinese chef, and this is where he had his cookery school. His restaurant, Ken Lo's Memories of China, is still going strong in nearby Ebury Street but it's very pricey. This teahouse, however, is quite affordable. The decor is simple but stylish, utilizing long shared tables, wooden chairs, and bright splashes of color. There's a short menu, mainly rice, soup noodles, and wok noodles, including ones with a southeast Asian twist (hot coconut). Try the luxurious black-bean seafood noodles. Side dishes include such street-food classics as onion cakes. The staff is extremely friendly and helpful, which helps soothe any irritation you may feel if you have to wait for a table. Jenny Lo has also commissioned her own tonic teas from Chinese herbalist Dr. Xu. Long life and happiness are on the menu here.

14 Eccleston St., SW1. (C) 020/7259-0399. Reservations not accepted. Main courses £5–£7.50 ($8–$12). No credit cards. Mon–Fri 11:30am–3pm; Sat noon–3pm; Mon–Sat 6–10pm. Tube: Victoria.

Oliveto ☞ PIZZA & PASTA   This is a cheaper offshoot spawned by Olivo, the successful Italian restaurant just 'round the corner. Oliveto offers the same quality but simpler, faster food, with the focus on pizza (which is also the cheapest main course). There are 15 different and deliciously crisp pizzas to choose from. One fave is the *quattro stagioni,* a revitalized old favorite made with mozzarella, tomato, sausages, prosciutto, mushroom, and squash; another is made with Gorgonzola, arugula, tomato, and mozzarella. There are always a few pasta dishes—a delicious *linguine al granchio* made with fresh crabmeat, garlic, and chili, for example. The daily specials, tuna or swordfish perhaps, top the price list. Oliveto has a very mixed clientele, from platinum credit-carded families who live in Belgravia to young Pimlico singles out for a relaxed supper. If you're feeling a little more flush, try **Olivo,** 21 Eccleston St., SW1 ((C) **020/7730-2505**). Main courses cost £8.50 to £15 ($14 to $24), and the cuisine is robust, modern Italian.

49 Elizabeth St., SW1. (C) 020/7730-0074. Main courses £9.50–£13 ($13.80–$18.85). AE, MC, V. Mon–Fri noon–3pm; Sat–Sun noon–4pm; daily 7–11:30pm. Tube: Victoria.

GREAT DEALS ON FIXED-PRICE MEALS

Boisdale ☞ SCOTTISH   This is clan territory. Owned by Ranald Macdonald, the very model of a modern chieftain-in-waiting, the Boisdale bar boasts London's biggest range of hard-to-find single malt whiskies and a tartan menu to match. The cheaper fixed-price lunch is a cultural treat you'll want to boast about at home: a hearty fish soup, then haggis made by the world famous McSween in Edinburgh, neeps (mashed swede or turnip), and tatties (mashed potato). This is the dinner that Robert Burns wrote his famous ode in praise of and which guests salute as it's brought to the table at the annual celebration of his birthday on January 25th. If centuries of tradition can't persuade you to try oatmeal and sheep's innards, you can choose from the more expensive fixed-price meal with a wide choice of starters and main courses, which are bound to include venison, salmon, and Scottish beef. You might not want to dine here if you have a strong aversion to smoke: What else would a fat cat want to go with the single malt other than a big fat Cuban cigar?

15 Eccleston St., SW1. ℂ 020/7730-6922. Reservations recommended. Main courses £11.95–£26.50 ($19–$42); fixed-price lunch menu £14.90–£17.45 ($22–$28). AE, DC, MC, V. Bistro Mon–Fri noon–2:30pm; Mon–Sat 7pm–1am. Bar Mon–Sat to 1am. Tube: Victoria.

13 The City & Clerkenwell

THE CITY

Arkansas Café ☆☆ AMERICAN   The U.S. Embassy swears by the barbecuing skills of Keir and Sarah Hellberg. If you're important enough to get onto the Independence Day guest list there, you'll probably find them catering the party. And this is *the* place to come on Thanksgiving (the only time it's open in the evening except for parties of 25 people or more). Arkansas Café is at Old Spitalfields Market, and diners sit out in the covered central space and enjoy the sizzle and delicious smells while the Hellbergs cook steaks, lamb, sausages, ribs, and corn-fed chicken to order. Mr. Hellberg personally selects the best cuts of meat from Smithfield market. Go for a jumbo sandwich as a cheaper option or take the meat on its own. The beef brisket and ribs are home-smoked, the desserts fabulous.

Unit 12, Old Spitalfields Market, E1. ℂ 020/7377-6999. Main courses £4.90–£13 ($8–$21). MC, V. Mon–Fri noon–2:30pm; Sun noon–4pm. Tube: Liverpool Street.

The Place Below VEGETARIAN   St. Mary-le-Bow is a beautiful Christopher Wren church built on the site of a much earlier one. Today, the arched Norman vaults are home to one of the most atmospheric and delicious cheap eateries in The City. The menu changes daily but you'll always find a hot dish of the day, two salads (one dairy-free), and a quiche. Because The Place Below gets so busy at lunchtime, it offers £2 ($3.20) off all main course prices between 11:30am and noon. You'll save about the same amount on most dishes if you take out rather than eat in. Soup is a dynamite deal at £3.10 ($5). The Place Below has just had a tart up, introducing a new espresso and sandwich bar, and extending its hours to 3:30pm.

So you could just come for a rich chocolate brownie and a cappuccino. There is seating for 50 outside in Bow Churchyard—good for outcast smokers.

St. Mary-le-Bow, Cheapside, EC2. © 020/7329-0789. Main courses £5.50–£7.50 ($9–$12). MC, V. Mon–Fri 7:30am–3:30pm. Tube: St. Paul's, Bank.

CLERKENWELL

Bleeding Heart Tavern 介介 GASTROPUB/MODERN BRITISH Beautiful 17th-century it-girl Lady Elizabeth Hatton was murdered in Bleeding Heart Yard while strolling with the European ambassador during her annual winter ball. Today, there's a remarkable gastropub on the site. The restored 1746 tavern is the London flagship of regional brewery and wine merchant Southwold Adnams. It is *the* place to quaff real ale (from £2.50/$4 a pint) while enjoying earthy dishes such as deep-fried Somerset brie with gooseberry compote, ale-fed Suffolk pork sausages with mash and cider onion gravy, and sticky apple pie.

There are two other parts to this trencherman's heaven, with successively higher prices. Though you can drink wine in the tavern, the choice represents a mere fraction of the miraculous wine list in the bistro, from £10 ($16) a bottle or £2.50 ($4) a glass. Three courses of a similar style cuisine costs a couple of pounds more than in the tavern. For a real splurge (£15.45/$25 minimum for two courses), head for the ever-so French restaurant downstairs.

Bleeding Heart Yard, off Greville St., EC1. © 020/7404-0333. Reservations essential in restaurant. Main courses, tavern £6.95–£10.95 ($11–$18), bistro £7.50–£12.50 ($12–$20), restaurant £9.95–£16.95 ($16–$27); bar menu £3.50–£6.95 ($6–$11). AE, DC, MC, V. Tavern Mon–Fri 11am–11pm; bistro Mon–Fri noon–3pm and 6–10:30pm; restaurant Mon–Fri noon–2:30pm and 6–10:30pm. Tube: Chancery Lane, Farringdon.

WORTH A SPLURGE

Moro 介介 NORTH AFRICAN/SPANISH Clerkenwell, on the run-down fringes of the City, has become a very hip neighborhood in recent years. If you didn't know that, then an evening at Moro will quickly put you in the picture. It opened 7 years ago, has amassed a pot full of awards, and gets better every day. The decor is modern and minimalist with bare walls and stripped wood and a quieter conservatory corner. The Spanish and North African cuisine is earthy and powerful. You can dine very reasonably on delicious tapas, but splurge, if you can, because the kitchen uses only the best ingredients, organic whenever possible, in its daily-changing menu.

The charming staff will explain any of the menu's exotic mysteries. Highly recommended are the wood-roasted bream with fennel, garlic, and paprika, and the stewed longhorn beef with prunes, chard, and potatoes. Two courses will probably set you back around £20 ($32). Giving up dessert isn't too much of a sacrifice, as the choice is limited.

34–36 Exmouth Market, EC1. © 020/7833-8336. Reservations recommended. Main courses £12.50–£16.50 ($20–$26); tapas £2.50–£4.50 ($4–$7). Mon–Fri 12:30–10:30pm; Sat 6:30–10:30pm. AE, DC, MC, V. Tube: Angel, Farringdon.

14 Just South of the River

GREAT DEALS ON FIXED-PRICE MEALS

Tas *(Finds)* TURKISH   This bright bustling restaurant lists more than 100 dishes, which is ridiculous even for a meze-style meal. So go for one of the set menus. Even the cheapest will bring you three courses, and for well under a tenner. And the food is very good, from the complementary appetizer, cheese and herb dip, to the homemade pita bread, and eggplant in any number of different incarnations. A "tas" is a Turkish cooking pot, and casseroles are a main-course specialty—chicken and almond, for instance, with a side of apricot rice. Tas stocks Turkish wine, as well. The great value and the fact that SE1 has hitherto been a culinary wasteland mean large crowds at lunch and in the evening. So if you hate noise, it probably isn't for you.

33 The Cut, SE1. © 020/7928-1444. Reservations recommended. Main courses £6.25–£14.45 ($10–$23). Fixed-price menu £18.50 ($30), fixed-price mezes £7.25–£9.95 ($12–$16). AE, MC, V. Mon–Sat noon–11:30pm; Sun noon–10.30pm. Tube: Southwark.

SUPER-CHEAP EATS

Bright Light Café *(Finds)* MODERN EUROPEAN   If dreary weather has dogged your London vacation, it might be worth your while to spend a couple of hours under the fake-sunshine lighting, the kind designed to combat Seasonal Affective Disorder, at this permanently sunny cafe. If that doesn't work, the food will. Local deli Konditor & Cook runs this brasserie, which stretches all the way across the front of the Young Vic theater. It dishes up scrumptious quick bites, from soup to sandwiches, and good-value light meals. You might find warm potato cakes with smoked salmon, or a delicious spinach ricotta tortellini. The bright lights switch off a little earlier in the evening if there's no performance, so call ahead to check.

Young Vic, 66 The Cut, SE1. © 020/7620-2700. Main courses £5.25–£9.25 ($8–$15). MC, V. Mon–Fri 8:30am–11pm; Sat 10:30am–11pm (closes 8pm if no performance). Tube: Waterloo, Southwark.

WORTH A SPLURGE

Fish! 🤹🤹 *Kids* SEAFOOD   Tate Modern is turning Southwark into one of the hippest neighborhoods in London. Another draw is the Borough Market, the foodie mecca where you'll find Fish! This futuristic diner is all glass and steel, and very noisy, especially when it's full of families at weekend lunchtimes. The restaurant has high chairs, toys, and a two-course children's menu with things like tuna bolognese. For the grown-ups, evangelical notes on the place mats detail why fish is good for you and how it should be caught. The choose-your-own menu lists 20 fish with ticks against those that are available that day, to be grilled or steamed as you like, with a choice of five accompanying sauces. Big thumbs up for the tender halibut and scallops. Chips cost extra but are perfectly cooked and well worth it. There are several new branches, including one a couple of miles upriver at **County Hall;** call the central reservations number below.

Cathedral St., Borough Market, SE1. ✆ **020/7407-3803.** Reservations recommended. Main courses £8.95–£16.50 ($14–$26); fixed-price children's meal £6.95 ($11). MC, V. Mon–Sat 11:30am–11pm; Sun 11:30–10pm. Tube: London Bridge, Borough.

15 Best of the Budget Chains

The past 2 decades have brought a massive explosion in restaurant chains to Britain. It began with bland *faux*-French cafes. Now no high concept eatery seems to be without a business plan to clone itself in as many places as possible. London's sushi and noodle bars are a prime example, as you'll see from the reviews. Apart from them, the best budget spots are a mix of fast-ish food clichés and snack-stops riding the health fad.

Pizza Express introduced the Italian staple to Britain when even metropolitan Londoners talked about filthy foreign muck. It's still the quality benchmark, and a pizza will cost you £4.95 to £7.75 ($8–$12). There are over 60 branches across London, most of them in very upscale-looking premises. One of the liveliest is in Soho: 10 Dean St., W1 (✆ **020/7437-9595;** Tube: Tottenham Court Rd., Leicester Sq.). Surf the website for a full list (www.pizzaexpress.co.uk). Newcomer **ASK** is putting up a very worthy challenge. It uses fancy ingredients familiar in upmarket cuisine—goat cheese, sun-dried tomatoes, and so on. It's a restaurant, not a joint, with cool modern decor and smooth service. Yet pizza prices are very reasonable at £4.85 to £7.10 ($8–$11). There are about 20 ASKs—look for the blue neon signs.

The one in Paddington, at 41–43 Spring St., W2 (℡ **020/ 7706-0707**) is handy for budget hotels along Sussex Gardens.

Healthy meals-in-a-cup are definitely big in London. Prices at **Soup Opera** include a piece of bread and fruit, and start at £2.95 ($5) for a 12 oz. carton. There are 10 branches; I'd try the one near Oxford Circus at 6 Market Place, W1 (℡ **020/7631-0777;** www. soupopera.co.uk).

A big cup of soup costs £1.95 to £2.95 ($3.10–$4.75) at **EAT,** a healthy cafe chain that has blossomed into 25 central London branches from the original Embankment branch at 39–41 Villiers St., WC2 (℡ **020/7839-2282**). It has won prizes for its hot sandwiches and yummy tortilla wraps (99p–£2.90/$1.60–$4.60), and does sushi, too. Although West End branches stay open until 7pm, this is mostly a daytime snack stop, as is **Pret a Manger,** a top-notch chain of sandwich shops which use good breads and fresh ingredients; sandwiches range in price from £1.95 to £4.50 ($3.10–$7). Besides sandwiches you can grab a cappuccino, sushi box, or a piece of cake. There are nearly 70 branches in London.

16 Afternoon Tea

KENSINGTON

The Orangery ⟨⟨ ⟨*Kids* AFTERNOON TEA   The cakes here are homemade English treats, from Victoria sponge on the cheapest set menu to the Belgian chocolate on the priciest. There are three teatime blowouts to choose from: level one gets you sandwich, shortbread, and the aforementioned cake; add £1 to swap the sandwich for a scone with cream and jam; and the top treat assembles all of the above, plus a glass of bubbly. The atmosphere is lovely in this elegant 18th-century conservatory by Kensington Palace, yet the prices make most tea spots look like a real rip-off.

Kensington Palace, Kensington Gardens, W8. ℡ **020/7376-0239.** Fixed-price teas £6.95–£13.95 ($11–$22). MC, V. Daily 10am–6pm (5pm Oct–Easter); tea served from 3pm. Tube: Kensington High St., Queensway. No smoking.

MAYFAIR

Brown's Hotel ⟨⟨ AFTERNOON TEA   This quintessentially understated, oh-so English hotel (the oldest 5-star in London) is justifiably famous for its country-house afternoon tea. Tailcoated waiters tend to guests reclining in armchairs in the paneled drawing room. It's a lot of money, but you certainly won't need dinner after a session here. Tea starts with a fine array of ham and mustard, smoked salmon, egg, and many other sandwiches. Scones with clotted cream and jam follow that. And then you'll have your pick of scrumptious cream cakes and pastries. Brown's serves its own blended tea, among a long list of others. You don't have to dress up, but it somehow seems part of the occasion to do so.

Albemarle and Dover sts., W1. ℂ 020/7493-6020. Reservations required for 2, 3:45 and 5:30pm sittings on weekdays. £25 ($40). AE, DC, MC, V. Daily 3–6pm. Tube: Green Park.

Dorchester ℛ AFTERNOON TEA   The Promenade may not have quite the limitless luxury of the Ritz's Palm Court, but it comes pretty close. Gold decoration and marble floors and pillars make this a very posh corridor in which to take afternoon tea. The Dorchester is famed for its pastries: The fluffy scones that follow the sandwich first course and the strawberry tart, white chocolate parcel, coffee éclair, and the host of other cakes will send you out into the Mayfair early evening with a real sugar rush. The higher priced tea includes a glass of champagne. Don't wear jeans or tennis shoes; the dress code is "smart casual."

54 Park Lane, W1. ℂ 020/7629-8888. Reservations recommended. Fixed-price tea £23.50–£29.50 ($38–$47). Daily 3–6pm. AE, DC, MC, V. Tube: Hyde Park Corner.

ST. JAMES'S

Fountain Restaurant at Fortnum & Mason AFTERNOON TEA   This store is world-famous, and so are its eateries, which are always mobbed with tourists. Unfortunately, the downstairs Fountain restaurant has discontinued its famous ice-cream tea, which was a favorite of kids everywhere. Now you must have your traditional tea upstairs in the St. James restaurant. You'll get a nice spread that includes freshly baked scones with clotted cream and strawberry jam and a slice of cake.

181 Piccadilly, W1. ℂ 020/7734-8040. Afternoon tea £18.50 ($30). AE, DC, MC, V. Tues–Sat tea 3–5:30pm. Tube: Green Park, Piccadilly.

Exploring London

It was nothing short of amazing. In 2001, after months of wheeler-dealering and changes to the tax regulations, London's major national museums dropped their admission charges. Now you can indulge in sci-fi fantasy at the Science Museum for free. You can inhale the aroma of cheesy socks and close-confined unwashed bodies in the Imperial War Museum's submarine simulator for free. At the Natural History Museum you can experience an earthquake and see a fabulous dinosaur collection for free. Without shelling out a pence you can visit, but not bounce on, the Great Bed of Ware in the V&A's remodeled British Galleries. And for nothing more than the cost of your transportation to Greenwich, you can see the original model for Nelson's Column, and the Admiral's bullet-pierced coat, at the National Maritime Museum.

There hasn't been such a museum and gallery boom since the era of the great Victorian philanthropists. All those now-free attractions have recently sprouted new extensions and wings, or had elaborate refurbs. In less than 3 years, the fabulous new Tate Modern opened on Bankside and the Tate Britain embarked on a centenary spruce-up. The Museum of London has also begun a long and complicated renovation. Even the ill-fated Millennium Bridge connecting the Tate Modern to St. Paul's has had its wobblies re-engineered and is ready to take on your pounding feet.

1 How to Spend Less and See More

London will never be a cheap thrill, but fortunately, in addition to the top-dollar tourist draws there are now scads of free museums, galleries, and historic buildings. And remember, London's major national museums are now free.

2 London's Top Attractions

British Airways London Eye ★★★ *Kids*   "Passengers" on the Eye can see straight into the Buckingham Palace garden, much to the Queen's annoyance. And both the Ministry of Defense and Shell have spent thousands spy-proofing their offices after discovering that someone with the right gadgetry could look in and pinch their secrets. At 443 feet high, this is the world's tallest observation wheel (don't say "Ferris," it's a dirty word to these guys). On the south bank, next to County Hall, the ½-hour, very slow-mo "flight" gives a stunning 25-mile view over the capital. It's better when the sun isn't shining, as the glare makes it difficult to see out. And the pod should have a map of the landmarks running round the inside— instead you have to pay £4.50 ($7) for a guidebook. Book your "boarding ticket" in advance to avoid too much hanging about. The Eye will keep spinning at least through December 2003, and probably longer, but they've jacked the prices up in a kind of "last call."

Jubilee Gardens, SE1. © 0870/500-0600. www.ba-londoneye.com. Admission £11 ($18) adults, £10 ($16) seniors, £5.50 ($9) children 5-15. Open daily 9:30am; last admission varies seasonally (May 8 or 9pm; June 9 or 10pm; July–Aug 10pm; Oct–Dec 8pm). Tube: Waterloo, Westminster. River services: Festival Pier.

British Museum 🕮🕮🕮   To get the maximum visual kerpow from your first sight of the **Great Court,** use the main south entrance into the museum—the one with the too-white portico made of the wrong kind of stone. Except for that embarrassing blunder, the £100 million redevelopment of the British Museum, designed by Lord Norman Foster, has won high praise. The 2-acre Great Court used to serve as a giant store cupboard. Now covered by a stunning steel-and-glass roof, it has become the light-filled hub of the Bloomsbury complex, staying open after the galleries close, with an education center, restaurants where you can have supper Thursday through Saturday, and coffee shops. Call for details of talks, performances, and workshops.

But the real excitement is that for the first time, visitors can enter the copper-domed **British Library Reading Room.** The giant drum in the middle of the Great Court is clad in the same too-white stone, while the interior has been restored to its Victorian blue, cream, and gold glory. Designed by Robert Smirke and completed in 1857, it inspired Thomas Carlyle, Virginia Woolf, Mahatma Gandhi, Lenin, George Bernard Shaw, Karl Marx (who wrote *Das Kapital* here), and a host of other great names. It houses the museum's books on the upper floors, with a public reference library and media center down below (the rare books, maps, manuscripts, and historic documents that were once in the Reading Room and museum vaults are now at the British Library, described later in this chapter).

From a collection purchased from Sir Hans Sloane in 1753, the British Museum has grown into one of the richest storehouses of

Central London Attractions

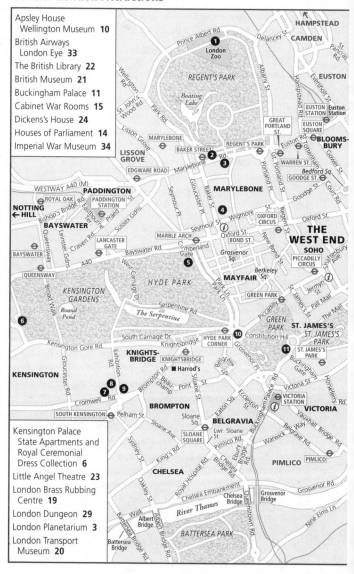

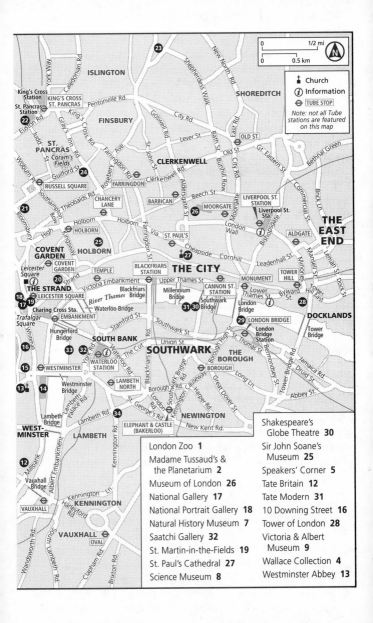

London Zoo **1**

Madame Tussaud's &
the Planetarium **2**

Museum of London **26**

National Gallery **17**

National Portrait Gallery **18**

Natural History Museum **7**

Saatchi Gallery **32**

St. Martin-in-the-Fields **19**

St. Paul's Cathedral **27**

Science Museum **8**

Shakespeare's
Globe Theatre **30**

Sir John Soane's
Museum **25**

Speakers' Corner **5**

Tate Britain **12**

Tate Modern **31**

10 Downing Street **16**

Tower of London **28**

Victoria & Albert
Museum **9**

Wallace Collection **4**

Westminster Abbey **13**

antiquities, prints, drawings, manuscripts, and *objets d'art* in the world, rivaled only by the Smithsonian in Washington, D.C. There are 2½ miles of galleries, so you'll need to weed out what really interests you and make a plan of attack. The £2.50 ($4) *Visit Guide* will help. Otherwise, let the museum take the stress out of deciding: the 90-minute Highlight tour takes place daily at 10:30am, 1pm, and 3pm and costs £8 ($13) for adults, £5 ($8) concessions and under-11s. There are also free single gallery tours, EyeOpeners, which last 50 minutes and take place from 11am to 3pm. You can also rent audio guides for £3.50 ($6).

If you only have time or interest for "the greatest hits," pop in to see the much fought-over **Parthenon Sculptures** formerly known as the Elgin Marbles. The Egyptian antiquities are also a must—they include **mummies,** sarcophagi, and the **Rosetta Stone.** It would also be a shame not to take in a bit of local history, like the leathery remains of garroted **Lindow Man,** or the glittering Anglo-Saxon silver and gold of the **Sutton Hoo treasure.** Then wander into the new **Sainsbury African Galleries,** a modern imaginative exhibition a far cry from the dusty trophy rooms of empire days. Check out the fabulous 1950s fantasy coffins from Ghana: my favorite is one that looks like a white Mercedes, with the number plate RIP2000.

Great Russell St., WC1. ℂ **020/7323-8000,** or 020/7323-8299 info desk. www.the britishmuseum.ac.uk. Main galleries free; £2 ($3.20) donation requested. Special exhibitions £4–£8 ($6–$13) adults, £2–£4 ($3.20–$6) seniors and students, free under-11s. Galleries Sat–Wed 10am–5:30pm; Thurs–Fri 10am–8:30pm. Great Court Sun–Weds 9am–6pm; Thurs–Sat 9am–11pm. Tube: Russell Sq., Holborn, Tottenham Court Rd.

Buckingham Palace ☆ *Overrated*   This is Her Maj's official London residence, and supposedly the one she likes least of all her palatial homes. You know she's there when the royal standard is flying. The Queen and her husband, the Duke of Edinburgh, occupy only 12 of the palace's 600 rooms. The rest are used by the royal household as offices and for royal functions, banquets, and investitures.

King George III and Queen Charlotte bought the house from the Duke of Buckingham in 1762, but it was George IV who converted it into a palace. He commissioned John Nash to pump up the grandeur, which he did by adding wings at the front and extending those at the back, all for £700,000. Neither George nor his brother William IV actually lived here, and by the time Queen Victoria came to the throne, doors wouldn't close, windows wouldn't open, bells wouldn't ring, and the drains were clogged. Victoria sent Nash packing and Edward Blore completed the repairs. But it quickly became too small for an official residence. So, in 1847, the queen had the East Front built, facing The Mall, and moved Marble Arch from the palace forecourt to the top of Park Lane. Sir Aston Webb designed the facade in 1913.

The Queen first opened the 18 formal **State Rooms,** including the **Throne Room,** in 1993 to help raise money to repair Windsor Castle after a fire. Overlooking the 45-acre gardens, where she gives her famous summer parties, they contain priceless pictures, tapestries, and a few pieces of furniture from the royal collections. Queen Victoria's vast ballroom—the ceilings are 45 feet high and there's room to park 35 double-decker buses—is part of the self-guided tour. Although you have to pay an exorbitant price to get in the palace, don't expect a fly-on-the-wall glimpse of royal home life. For a start, you can only visit during August and September when the family is on holiday. And these rooms are not where the Royals put their feet up with a reviving cup of tea—it could be almost any unlived-in stately home or grand private collection. Tickets can be purchased in person, from 9am on the day: Eager tourists start queuing at sunrise, and an hour-long wait is the rule. Booking a fixed-time ticket by phone, or asking the Visitor Office for an application form, is less hassle, but only the regular £12 ($19) adult rate is available in advance.

Much better value is the **Royal Mews** 𝒶𝒶 (entrance in Buckingham Palace Road). These superb working stables house the royal carriages, including the gold state coach used at every coronation since 1831, and the horses that draw them. By tradition, the Queen always has greys.

The newly revamped **Queen's Gallery** 𝒶 displays hundreds of items from the Royal art collection in changing exhibitions.

The Mall, SW1. ✆ **020/7839-1377,** 020/7799-2331 recorded info, 020/7321-2233 credit-card bookings, 020/7839-1377 for visitors with disabilities. www.royal residences.com. State Rooms £12 ($19) adults, £10 ($16) seniors, £6 ($10) under-17s, £30 ($48) family ticket. Aug 1–Sept 28 daily 9:30am–4:15pm (last admittance 3:15pm). Royal Mews £5 ($8) adults, £4 ($6) seniors, £2.50 ($4) under-17s, £12.50 ($20) family ticket. March–July 11am–4pm (last admission 3:15pm); Aug–Sept 10am–5pm (last admission 4:15pm). Queen's Gallery £6.50 ($10), £5 ($8) over 60 and student, £3 ($4.80) under 17. Daily 10am–5:30pm (last admittance 4:30pm). Tube: Victoria, St. James's Park, Green Park.

Hampton Court Palace 𝒶𝒶𝒶 *(Kids* Bring a picnic because a visit to Hampton Court makes a splendid day out. You'll need 2 to 3 hours to look round the palace itself, plus time to wander through the 60 acres of gardens. And then there's the famous **maze,** with its half a mile of twisting paths—most people take 20 minutes or so to extricate themselves from its green clutches.

Hampton Court is about 15 miles southwest of London on the banks of the Thames. Henry VIII's pleasure-loving Lord Chancellor, Cardinal Wolsey, took the house in 1515 as a retreat from the city's poisonous air and water. His grandiose remodeling plan called for 280 rooms, new courtyards and gardens, and 500 staff. When the cardinal fell into disfavor in 1528, the greedy king confiscated his property. Henry spent a whopping £18 million in today's money and turned Hampton Court into a very sophisticated palace with bowling alleys, tennis courts (yes, really), a chapel, pleasure gardens, a hunting park, The Great Hall for dining, and a 36,000-square-foot kitchen.

His daughter, Queen Elizabeth I, planted the gardens with new discoveries, such as tobacco and potatoes brought back by Sir Francis Drake and Sir Walter Raleigh from South America. Under the Stuarts, the palace collections grew with hundreds of new paintings and other lavish objets d'art. Charles II banished the gloom of Cromwell's brief stay here with his lively court and many mistresses. William and Mary found the palace apartments old-fashioned and uncomfortable, so they commissioned Sir Christopher Wren to make improvements and asked such artists as Grinling Gibbons, Jean Tijou, and Antonio Verrio to decorate the rooms. George III ended royal occupation—his grandfather used to box his ears in the State Apartments, so he hated the place.

The highlights for visitors to Hampton Court are the **Tudor Kitchens** and the **King's Apartments,** as well as the **Wolsey Rooms** and **Renaissance Picture Gallery.** One of Henry VIII's wives, the hapless (and ultimately headless) Catherine Howard, has reputedly been sighted several times in the **Long Gallery,** where she ran, terrified, to pound on the king's locked door and plead desperately for her life. Throughout the palace, costumed guides bring the centuries of history to life, as does the full calendar of special events and festivals.

East Molesey, Surrey. ✆ **0870/752-7777** or 0870/753-7777 (tickets by phone). www.hrp.org.uk. Admission £11 ($18) adults, £8.25 ($13) students and seniors, £7.25 ($11) under-16s, £33 ($53) family ticket. Apr–Oct Mon 10:15am–6pm, Tues–Sun 9:30am–6pm (last admission 5:15pm); Nov–Mar Mon 10:15am–4:30pm, Tues–Sun 9:30am–4:30pm (last admission 3:15pm). Park 7am–dusk. Closed Dec 24–26. Train: Waterloo to Hampton Court, 30-min. journey time. River services from Westminster pier (✆ **020/7930-2062;** www.wpsa.co.uk), 3- to 4-hr. journey time; £18 ($29) standard adult return fare; schedules vary seasonally.

Houses of Parliament ⟨★★⟩ This neo-Gothic extravaganza, with its trademark clock tower, is the ultimate symbol of London.

Edward the Confessor built the first palace here, and the site was home to the monarchy and court until Henry VIII's time. In 1834 a fire lit to burn the Exchequer's tally sticks got out of control, sparing only Westminster Hall (1097), which is not open to the public, and the Jewel Tower. Charles Barry designed the Houses of Parliament (1840) you see today. Augustus Welby Pugin created the paneled ceilings, tiled floors, stained glass, clocks, fireplaces, umbrella stands, and even inkwells. There are more than 1,000 rooms, 100 staircases, and 2 miles of corridors. Big Ben, by the way, is not the clock tower itself, as many people think, but the largest bell (14 tons) in the chime.

The parliamentary session runs from mid-October to the end of July, with breaks at Christmas and Easter. Visitors can watch debates from the **Strangers' Galleries** in both houses. Most visitors are struck by how small the **Commons chamber** is. It was rebuilt in precise detail in 1950 after being destroyed during the Blitz of 1941. Only 437 of the 651 MPs can sit at any one time; on the rare occasions when most of them turn up, the rest crowd noisily around the door and the Speaker's chair. The ruling party and opposition sit facing one another, two sword lengths apart, though from the volume of the arguments you'd think it was more like 2 miles. The Mace, on the table in the middle, is the symbol of Parliament's authority. The queue for the **House of Lords** is usually shorter, as debates here are less crucial (some might say inconsequential) and a lot more polite. The Lords' chamber is fantastically opulent, decorated with mosaics and frescoes. The Lord Chancellor presides over proceedings from his seat on the Woolsack, a reminder of the days when wool was the source of Britain's wealth. You'd think such tradition would make the place sacrosanct. Yet, in 2000, New Labour made all the hereditary peers pitch to keep their privileges and ousted 600 of them. And in 2001 it appointed the promised "people's peers," though the prominent professionals chosen seemed scarcely more representative of the general population than the aristocracy.

During the recess (usually mid-July–late Aug or early Sept, and mid-Sept–early Oct; see www.parliament.uk for recess dates), you can take a 75-minute tour of the Houses of Parliament for £7 ($11). It isn't really suitable for young children as rest-stops are limited. You must be there 10 minutes before your timed-entry tour starts. Call ✆ **0870/906-3773** or visit www.firstcalltickets.com for tickets and information.

Bridge St. and Parliament Sq., SW1. ✆ **020/7219-3000** House of Commons or ✆ **020/7219-3107** House of Lords. www.parliament.uk. Free admission to Strangers'

Galleries, subject to recess and sitting times. House of Commons: Mon 1:30–8:30pm,
Tues–Wed 11:30am–7:30pm, Thurs–Fri 9:30am–3pm. House of Lords: Mon–Wed from
2:30pm, Thurs and occasionally Fri from 11am. Queue at St. Stephen's entrance, near
the statue of Oliver Cromwell. Tube: Westminster. River services: Westminster Pier.

Kensington Palace State Apartments and Royal Ceremonial Dress Collection 🍿🍿

The palace has been a pilgrimage site ever
since Princess Diana died in August 1997, when people flocked to
the gates and carpeted the ground with floral tributes. Several of her
best-known designer frocks are now on permanent display here, as
are dozens of dowdy dresses, shoes, and hats worn by the Queen
over the past 50 years.

The asthmatic William and his wife Mary bought this house from
the Earl of Nottingham in 1689 to escape from the putrid air
enveloping Whitehall. Then they commissioned Sir Christopher
Wren to remodel the modest Jacobean mansion. Queen Anne, who
came to the throne in 1702, laid out the gardens in English style, had
the Orangery built after designs by Nicholas Hawksmoor, and died
here in 1714 from apoplexy brought on by overeating. The first two
Georges lived at Kensington Palace. George III abandoned it in favor
of Buckingham House (now Palace). But his fourth son, Edward
Duke of Kent, did have apartments here. Queen Victoria was his
daughter. The Archbishop of Canterbury and the Lord Chamberlain
roused her from sleep here on June 27, 1837, with news of the death
of her uncle, William IV, and her succession to the throne. That
night was the first she had ever slept outside her mother's room.
Three weeks later, aged 18, she moved into Buckingham Palace.

Princess Margaret lived at Kensington Palace until her death in
2002. Today, the Duke and Duchess of Gloucester and Princess
Michael of Kent have apartments there. Only the **State Apartments,**
filled with art treasures from the Royal Collection, and the display of
court fashions and uniforms from 1760 in the **Royal Ceremonial
Dress Collection** are open to the public. See the Cupola Room,
where Queen Victoria was baptized, and marvel at William Kent's
magnificent trompe l'oeils and paintings in the King's Drawing
Room, Presence Chamber, and on the King's Staircase. The audio
guide that comes with your ticket is a good way to self-guide yourself
through the palace. And you can have lunch or tea in The Orangery
(p. 114).

Kensington Gardens. ✆ 020/7937-9561. www.hrp.org.uk. Admission £10 ($16)
adults, £7.50 ($12) seniors and students, £6.50 ($10) under-16s, £28 ($45) family
ticket. Nov–Feb daily 10am–5pm; Mar–Oct daily 10am–6pm. Tube: Queensway,
High St. Kensington.

Madame Tussaud's & the Planetarium *(Overrated* Madame Tussaud had an extraordinary life. Born Marie Grosholtz, she learnt her craft from her mother's doctor employer, who had a talent for wax modeling. Such was her renown that Louis XIV and Marie Antoinette appointed her as their children's art tutor. In an ironic turn of events, in order to prove her loyalty to the revolution and get out of Laforce Prison, Marie had to make the royal couple's death masks after their executions in 1793. You can see several casts from her original molds—a spooky Voltaire, for instance—at this "museum." But most of its space is devoted to modern superstars of dubious fame, from Saddam Hussein to Mel Gibson (the staff once found a pair of ladies underpants in his pockets). Craftsmen take more than 200 measurements from each star sitter. And stars know they're on the wane when Tussaud's boils their figure down and uses the wax to make someone else. The dungeon-level Chamber of Horrors is the stuff tourist traps are made of. It "honors" psychopathic murderers like Charles Manson and Jack the Ripper, offers a rendition of Joan of Arc burning at the stake, and shows the grisly unmentionables done to Gunpowder Plotter Guy Fawkes. Madame Tussaud's is expensive and overrated, but it attracts more than 2.5 million visitors a year. So it has introduced a fast-track system whereby you pre-book time slots. Use it or you may end up queuing for longer than the 2 hours or so it takes to go round.

If you're into stars of the celestial variety, it's worth spending the extra couple of pounds for a combined ticket to Madame Tussaud's and the **London Planetarium** next door. This copper-domed London landmark is the largest planetarium in Europe. Its state-of-the-art Digistar II projection system re-creates an earth-based view of 9,000 stars and planets scattered across the night sky, and takes you on a *Starship Enterprise* journey past exploding nebulae right to the edge of the universe. There are also interactive exhibits to play with.

Marylebone Rd., NW1. (*©* 020/7935-6861 or 0870/400-3000 advance reservations. www.madame-tussauds.com. Madame Tussaud's £14.95 ($24) adults, £11.80 ($19) seniors, £10.50 ($17) under-16s. Combined ticket with planetarium £16.95 ($27) adults, £13.50 ($22) seniors, £12 ($19) under-16s. Madame Tussaud's: opening time varies by season and weekday or weekend (9, 9:30, and 10am), closing at 5:30pm. Planetarium daily 10am–5:30pm. Shows run every 40 min., 12:20–5pm, weekends/holidays from 10:20am. Closed Dec 25. Tube: Baker St.

National Gallery *★★* Britain's national art collection comprises more than 2,300 paintings dating from 1260 to 1900, supplemented by masterpieces on loan from private collectors. The gallery is arranged in four time bands. The **Sainsbury Wing** shows work from 1260 to 1510 by such artists as Giotto, Botticelli, Leonardo da Vinci, Piero della Francesca, and Raphael. The **West Wing** takes on the next 90 years, with El Greco, Holbein, Bruegel, Michelangelo, Titian, and Veronese. The **North Wing** holds the 17th-century masters, Rubens, Poussin, Velázquez, Rembrandt, and Vermeer. Van Dyck's *The Abbé Scaglia* entered the collection in 1999, given by a private owner in lieu of inheritance tax. Works by Stubbs, Gainsborough, Constable, Turner, Canaletto, van Gogh, Corot, Monet, Manet, Renoir, and Cézanne are all in the **East Wing.** From May to September, the National Gallery lets natural daylight illuminate many of the paintings, particularly in the Sainsbury Wing, to magical effect—the colors are truer, and it cuts down on flare and shadow from the frames. You'll need to choose a sunny day for your visit, though, because artificial help steps in if it gets too gloomy. Weekday mornings and late on Wednesday are the quietest times.

There's a free (donation invited) audio guide to every painting on the main floor, and free guided tours start at 11:30am and 2:30pm every day, plus at 6:30pm on Wednesday evenings. Most of the gallery talks are also free. There are two eateries: the Crivelli's Garden Restaurant and Italian Bar (✆ **020/7747-2869**) on the first floor of the Sainsbury Wing, and the Gallery Cafe sandwich cafe in the basement of the main building.

Trafalgar Square, WC2. (✆ **020/7747-2885**. www.nationalgallery.org.uk. Main galleries free; Sainsbury wing, £3–£7 ($6–$11) for some special exhibitions. Daily 10am–6pm (Wed until 9pm). Closed Jan 1, Dec 24–26. Tube: Charing Cross, Leicester Sq.

Natural History Museum ★★ *Kids*   It roars. It opens its jaws and moves its head. And it's the biggest hit the museum has ever had: a **robotic Tyrannosaurus Rex** hovering over a fresh dino-kill. It's worth a trip just to watch the 12-feet-tall toothy beast, driven by motion sensors, react to the appearance of each new human meal (not suitable for young kids). Before you see "T" you'll encounter two cunning-looking animatronic raptors eyeing you from atop a perch. All this takes place in a Victorian hall full of **dinosaur skeletons** and exhibitions about the life of the 'saurs. Head to the **Earth Galleries** for earthquake and volcano simulations that hint at the terror of the real thing. Kids also love the slithery and slimy critters in the **Creepie-Crawlies** exhibit.

Sir Hans Sloane was such a prolific collector that his treasures overflowed the British Museum. Hence the decision to build this palatial building (1881), with its towers, spires, and nave-like hall, fit "for housing the works of the Creator." Yet it, too, can display only a fraction of its specimens—animal, vegetable, and mineral. An exciting project is set to revolutionize all that, opening both the storerooms and the science labs, with their 300 white-coated experts, to public view. The £28 million first phase of the Darwin Centre opened in summer 2002. The museum already has the new Clore Education Centre, where kids can use video microscopes and bug-hunting magnifying glasses, build their own websites, and take part in regular events. Highlight and themed tours start near the entrance to the Life Galleries.

Cromwell Rd., SW7. ℭ 020/7942-5000. www.nhm.ac.uk. Free admission. Mon–Sat 10am–5:50pm; Sun 11am–5:50pm. Clore Education Centre Mon 10:30am–5pm (school holidays); Tues–Fri 2:30–5pm (term-time); Sat 10:30am–5pm; Sun 11:30am–5pm. Closed Dec 23–26. Tours: 45-min introduction to Life and Earth Galleries daily, £3 ($5) adults, £1.50 ($2.40). Tube: South Kensington.

St. Paul's Cathedral ⍟   No one who saw the wedding of Prince Charles and Lady Diana in 1981 will ever forget the image of the royal carriages approaching St. Paul's. In 2002, the Queen had a ceremony of thanksgiving here to celebrate her Golden Jubilee.

This magnificent cathedral is 515 feet long and 360 feet high to the cross on the famous dome, which dominated the skyline until ugly office buildings rose around it after World War II. Christopher Wren laid out the whole base first to thwart interference from his paymasters, who harassed him constantly over the 35 years it took to complete the building (1675–1710). Wren was buried in the crypt; his epitaph reads: *"Lector, si monumentum requiris, circum-spice"* ("Reader, if you seek his monument, look around you"). Many artists worked on the decoration, most notably Grinling Gibbons, who carved the choir screens and stalls. Frescoes depicting the life of St. Paul line the inner dome. You can see them best from the **Whispering Gallery,** famous for its amazing acoustics, which can project a murmur right across the void. A second steep climb leads to the Stone Gallery, and a third to the highest Inner Golden Gallery. In all, it's 530 steps to the top, with the views ever more awe-inspiring.

Ninety-minute "Supertours" of the cathedral and crypt take place at 11, 11:30am, 1:30, and 2pm, and cost £2.50 ($4) for adults, £2 ($3.20) concessions, £1 ($1.60) children, plus admission. Audio guides are available in five languages until 3pm: £3.50 ($6) for adults, £3 ($4.80) seniors and students. "Triforium" tours take in the library, geometric staircase, the West End gallery, and Trophy

Room where Wren's Great Model is on display. Tickets are £11 ($18), including admission. Call Monday to Friday, 9am to 4pm, to book. There are often organ recitals at 5pm on Sunday, at no charge. Fuel up at the Crypt Café first.

St. Paul's Churchyard, EC4. (℃) **020/7246-8348** or 020/7246-8319. www.stpauls. co.uk. Admission £6 ($10) adults, £5 ($8) students and seniors, £3 ($4.80) under-16s. Mon–Sat 8:30am–4pm; Sun for worship only. Tube: St. Paul's, Mansion House.

Science Museum *(Kids)* This is one of the best science museums in the world. The striking new £45 million **Wellcome Wing** houses six new exhibitions presenting the latest developments in science, medicine, and technology. Find out what the kids might look like in 30 years in the *Who am I?* gallery. For a more intimate portrait, check out the gory digital cross-sections in *The Visible Human Project.* This is fantasyland for gadget geeks, who'll love all the interactivity. There's a 450-seat IMAX cinema on the first floor and another huge new gallery, **Making the Modern World,** links the Wellcome Wing to the old museum. Using some of the most iconic treasures of the permanent collection—the Apollo 10 space capsule, an early train known as Stephenson's Rocket, and a fleece from famous Scottish clone, Dolly the Sheep—it charts 250 years of technological discoveries and their effects on our culture.

The new galleries are stunning, but don't let them dazzle you into forgetting the rest of this marvelous museum. It is home to many pioneering machines: Arkwright's spinning machine, for instance, and the Vickers "Vimy" aircraft, which made the first Atlantic crossing in 1919. The basement is dedicated to children, with water, construction, sound and light shows, and games for 3 to 6 year olds in the **garden,** and the **Launch Pad** for 7 to 15 year olds. Of course, the Wellcome Wing is even more ambitious: its first-floor **Pattern Pod** aims to convert kids to science from the age of 3 months!

Exhibition Rd., SW7. (℃) **020/7942-4000** or 0870/870-4771. www.sciencemuseum. org.uk. Free admission. Daily 10am–6pm. Closed Dec 24–26. Tube: South Kensington.

Somerset House The late Queen Mother once remarked how sad it was that the courtyard at Somerset House had become an Inland Revenue car park. It was just the spur needed by the long-running campaign to open up the 1,000-room civil service palace, designed by Sir William Chambers (1724–96), to the public. The government moved its workers out and the Heritage Lottery Fund coughed up the millions needed to restore the buildings, the courtyard with its new fountains, and the river terrace, where there's now a summer cafe (it's cheaper than the new restaurant indoors). A heady mix of high culture and street entertainment, the "new" Somerset House contains three major museums and hosts a program of open-air performances, talks, and workshops (✆ **020/7845-4670,** box office). The restoration is proceeding in phases and you can already visit the **Seamen's Waiting Hall,** where naval officers came to collect their commissions. The 45-minute tours at 11am and 3:15pm on Tuesday, Thursday, and Saturday cost £2.75 ($4.40).

The **Courtauld Gallery** ⚜ (✆ **020/7848-2526;** www.courtauld. ac.uk) has been in Somerset House since 1989. Its chief benefactor, textile mogul Samuel Courtauld, collected impressionist and post-impressionist paintings, which are still the gallery's main strength—Manet's *Bar at the Folies Bergères;* Monet's *Banks of the Seine at Argenteuil; Lady with Parasol* by Degas; *La Loge* by Renoir; Van Gogh's *Self-Portrait with Bandaged Ear;* and several Cézannes, including *The Card Players.* But you'll find work by most great names (lots of Rubens), right up to modern greats Ben Nicholson, Graham Sutherland, and Larry Rivers. At noon on Tuesday, Thursday, and Saturday, 1-hour tours cost £7.50 adults ($12), £7 ($11) concessions.

The **Gilbert Collection** ⚜⚜ (✆ **020/7420-9400;** www.gilbert-collection.org.uk) is also in the South Building, as well as in the vaults beneath the river terrace. The glittering gold, silver, and mosaics were valued at £75 million when Arthur Gilbert donated the 800-piece collection to the nation in 1996. There are objects here from Princess Diana's old home, Althorp. The 1-hour tour on Tuesday, Thursday, and Saturday costs £5.50 ($9) adults, £5 ($8) concessions.

The last and most extraordinary of the treasures of Somerset House are the **Hermitage Rooms** ⚜ (✆ **020/7845-4630;** www. hermitagerooms.com). This offshoot of the State Hermitage Museum in St. Petersburg exhibits pieces from the Russian Imperial collections in changing shows. The Russians are so desperate for money that they're "lending" their national treasures to this and similar museums around the world. Half the tickets are sold in advance (✆ **020/7413-3398;** www.ticketmaster.co.uk), half at the door, for half-hourly timed entry.

Strand, WC2. ✆ 020/7845-4600. www.somerset-house.org.uk. Somerset House free. Courtauld Gallery £5 ($8) adults, £4 ($6) seniors, free under-18s; free Mon 10am–2pm. Gilbert Collection £5 ($8) adults, £4 ($6) seniors, free under-18s. Hermitage Rooms £6 ($10) adults, £4 ($6) concessions, free under-5s. Same-day admission to 2 collections, save £1 ($1.60), all 3, save £2 ($3.20). Courtyard 7:30am–11pm (7pm in winter). Galleries and exhibitions daily 10am–6pm (last admittance 45 min–1 hr earlier). Closed Jan 1, Dec 24–26. Tube: Temple, Covent Garden, Charing Cross.

Tate Britain 🟊🟊   The new Tate Modern at Bankside hogs most of the limelight, but the shifting around of the Tate collections has also seen a huge overhaul at the original gallery, founded in 1897. The refurbished Tate Britain reopened in November 2001 with more exhibition space and a suite of airy new galleries. Having handed International Modernism over to Bankside, Tate Britain now concentrates on British work dating back to 1500. It ditched the chronological displays for a thematic approach. **Art Now** focuses on new media and experimental work by foreign artists living in London and Brits based here and abroad; **Private and Public** includes portraits and scenes of daily life; **Artists and Models** explores nudes and self-portraiture; **Literature and Fantasy** is for visionary artists such as William Blake and Stanley Spencer; and **Home and Abroad** looks at the landscape artist at home and abroad. Juxtaposing very different kinds of work isn't always successful, but the vibrancy of the place can't help but give you a rush. Important artists, like Gainsborough, Constable, Hogarth, and Hockney, get their own rooms, which should pacify the traditionalists.

Guided tours, gallery talks (Mon–Fri 11:30am, 2:30, and 3:30pm, and Sun 3pm), auditorium lectures, and films are mostly free. Tate Britain also has shops, a good cafe and espresso bar, and a well-regarded but pricey restaurant.

Millbank, SW1. ✆ 020/7887-8000, 020/7887-8888 for events. www.tate.org.uk. Permanent collection free; temporary exhibitions £6.50–£8.50 ($10–$14). Daily 10am–5:50pm. Closed Dec 24–26. Tube: Pimlico. River services: Millbank Pier.

Tate Modern 🟊🟊🟊   The Tate Modern, London's new and wildly popular cathedral of modern art, occupies the defunct Bankside Power Station on the South Bank of the Thames opposite St. Paul's Cathedral. Except for a 2-story glass addition on the roof, the vast bunker-like facade looks much as it ever did, right down to the London grime. Then you enter the building, down a ramp into the huge old turbine hall, left empty, and three floors of ultra-plain white galleries. The work is arranged thematically rather than chronologically: **Landscape/Matter/Environment, Still Life/Object/Real Life, History/Memory/Society,** and **Nude/Action/Body.** In some rooms, paintings are next to sculptures next to installations. Others are devoted to a single artist—like the marvelous Joseph Beuys sculptures. The display concept is certainly challenging, but the themes often seem spurious, lacking the quirky spirit of a mixed private collection where one person's taste is the guide.

There's no such thing as a flash visit to Tate Modern. Set aside half a day if you can. Free guided tours start daily at 10:30, 11:30am, 2:30, and 3:30pm, each focusing on one of the four themes. There's also a busy talks program (usually £6/$10; free talks weekdays at 1pm); music; and children's workshops and storytelling sessions. But if you only do one thing at Tate Modern, go up to the glass-roofed level seven to see the spectacular views across the Thames. The cafe there is often mobbed so time your visit for early mealtimes and during the week. It is also open for dinner until 9:30pm on Friday and Saturday but doesn't take reservations.

Bankside, SE1. ℂ 020/7887-8000, 020/7887-8888 for events. www.tate.org.uk. Permanent collection free; temporary exhibitions £5.50–£8.50 ($9–$14). Sun–Thurs 10am–6pm; Fri–Sat 10am–10pm; galleries open at 10:15am. Closed Dec 24–26. Tube: Southwark, Mansion House, St. Paul's (cross over Millennium Bridge). River services: Bankside Pier.

Tower of London 🏰🏰🏰 *Kids*   This is the most perfectly preserved medieval fortress in Britain and you'll need at least 2 or 3 hours for your visit, especially since the restored New Armouries building has opened as a delicious and good-value cafe.

Over the centuries, the Tower has served as a palace and royal refuge; a prison, military base, and supplies depot; home to the Royal Mint and the Royal Observatory; and finally, a national monument. It has only twice come into practical use since the late 19th century: in World War I, 11 spies were executed here; then, in World War II, Rudolph Hess was a prisoner here for 4 days, and another spy was executed. The oldest part is the massive **White Tower,** built in 1078 by the Norman king, William the Conqueror, to protect London and discourage rebellion among his new Saxon subjects. Every king after him added to the main structure, so that when Edward I completed the outer walls in the late 13th century, they enclosed an 18-acre square. Walk round the top of them for a bird's-eye view of how the Tower of London would have looked in its heyday.

The **Crown Jewels,** glittering in the Jewel House in Waterloo Barracks, are the real must-see. No words can do justice to the Imperial State Crown, encrusted with 3,200 precious stones, including a 317-carat diamond. A moving walkway is meant to keep visitors flowing through, but it can still be a long wait. The **Martin Tower** exhibition tells the stories of two of the world's most famous diamonds, the

Koh-i-Noor and Cullinan II, as well as of a botched attempt to steal the State regalia in the late 17th century.

Visitors with a more ghoulish bent should start at **The Chapel Royal of St. Peter ad Vincula,** which contains the graves of all the unfortunates executed at the Tower. The Scaffold Site, where the axeman dispatched seven of the highest-ranking victims, including Henry VIII's wives, Anne Boleyn and Catherine Howard, is just outside. Everyone else met their end on **Tower Green.** Imagine their terror as they arrived by boat at the dread **Traitors' Gate.** The **Bloody Tower** was where Richard of Gloucester locked up his young nephews while he usurped his crusading brother Edward IV. The princes' bodies were later mysteriously found by the White Tower. Today, an exhibit re-creates how Sir Walter Raleigh might have lived during his 13-year imprisonment after the Gunpowder Plot against James I.

The royal menagerie moved out in 1834 to form the new London Zoo—all except the **ravens.** Legend has it Charles II was told that if they ever left the Tower the monarchy would fall. Ever since, a few birds with clipped wings have been kept in a lodging next to Wakefield Tower, looked after by a yeoman warder. The **yeoman warders,** or Beefeaters, have guarded the Tower for centuries. Now usually retired soldiers, they lead tours every half hour from 9:30am to 3:30pm and give vivid talks at 9:30, 10:15, 11:30am, 2:15, 4:30, and 5:15pm (the first one on Sun is at 10:30am). Costumed guides also re-create historic happenings.

As well as the daily **Ceremony of the Keys,** there's a schedule of State events and gun salutes. Call for info. **Beating the Bounds** takes place every third year on Ascension Day, the Thursday 40 days after Easter. The Chief Yeoman Warder leads 31 choirboys around the 31 parish boundary marks in the surrounding streets, beating each one with willow wands, to signal the Tower's independence from the jurisdiction of the city. Now *that's* tradition.

Tower Hill, EC3. Ⓒ **0870/756-6060** or 0870/756-7070 (box office). www.hrp.org.uk. Admission £11.50 ($18) adults, £8.75 ($14) students and seniors, £7.50 ($12) under-16s, £34 ($54) family ticket. Mar–Oct Tues–Sat 9am–6pm, Sun–Mon 10am–6pm; Nov–Feb Tues–Sat 9am–5pm, Sun–Mon 10am–5pm. Last tickets sold 1 hr. before closing. Last entry to buildings 30 min. before closing. Closed Jan 1, Dec 24–26. Tube: Tower Hill. DLR: Tower Gateway. River services: Tower Pier.

Victoria & Albert Museum 𝕮𝕮   Even the staff drop bread crumbs to find their way around this labyrinthine treasure house. Recent plans to extend the 7 miles of galleries devoted to the decorative and fine arts with an ultra-modern, and ultra-controversial, new building by Daniel Libeskind had to be scaled down, but the **British Galleries** reopened in late 2001 after a £31-million over-haul. The revamped galleries reflect a new, non-traditional approach to museum curatorship: instead of showing off dazzling treasures protected in glass cases, there are pieces to handle, video re-creations of how they were used, and commentaries on taste by historical figures and today's top designers. Iconic objects, such as the Great Bed of Ware, which Shakespeare mentions in *Twelfth Night,* tell the story of Britain's 400-year rise (1500–1900) to world power and cultural authority.

Once you've "done" the British Galleries, you'll want to cherry-pick the highlights from the rest of the V&A's collections: the designer dresses in the **Costume Gallery,** textiles, sculpture, furniture, prints, paintings, photographs, silver, glass, ceramics, and jewelry, from Britain and all over the world. Not only is the museum worth a good long visit, but there are so many regular activities you'll want to keep coming back. Free guided tours take place daily every hour, 10:30am to 3:30pm, plus 4:30pm on Wednesday.

Cromwell Rd., SW7. ℂ **020/7942-2000,** 020/7942-2209 events. www.vam.ac.uk. Free admission. Thurs–Tues 10am–5:45pm; Wed and last Fri each mo. 10am–10pm. Closed Dec 24–26. Tube: South Kensington.

Westminster Abbey ⭐⭐⭐   This ancient building is neither a cathedral nor a parish church, but a "royal peculiar," under the juris-diction of the dean and chapter, and subject only to the sovereign. It's also one of the most popular tourist attractions in London and tends to be packed in the high-tourist summer months.

Largely dating from the 13th to 16th centuries, Westminster Abbey has played a prominent part in British history—most recently with the funeral of Princess Diana and, in 2002, of the Queen Mother. All but two coronations since 1066 have taken place here. The oak **Coronation Chair,** made in 1308 for Edward I, can be seen in the **Chapel of Edward the Confessor.** From 1266 when the English seized it until 1998 when it was finally returned to St. Giles Cathedral in Edinburgh, the coronation chair held the ancient Stone of Scone, on which the kings of Scotland were crowned. Visit the **Norman Undercroft** to see the replica coronation regalia.

Five kings and four queens, including half-sisters Queen Elizabeth I and Mary Tudor and Elizabeth's rival for the throne, Mary Queen of Scots, are buried in the beautiful, fan-vaulted **Chapel of Henry VII.**

In 1400, Geoffrey Chaucer became the first literary celebrity to be buried in **Poets' Corner**—in his case, though, it was because he worked for the abbey. Ben Jonson is there, as well as Dryden, Samuel Johnson, Sheridan, Browning, and Tennyson. The practice of putting up literary memorials began in earnest in the 18th century with a full-length figure of Shakespeare, but the sinner Oscar Wilde didn't get a memorial window until 1995.

The **Tomb of the Unknown Soldier** honors the fallen of World War I. The nameless man lies under Belgian stone in soil brought back from the battlefields of France. Above the West Door, on the outside, you'll see the tradition of commemoration still continues with the **statues of 20th-century martyrs** such as Martin Luther King and Maximilian Kolbe, the Catholic priest who died at Auschwitz.

Guided tours of the abbey, lead by the vergers, cost £3 ($4.80). These start at 10, 10:30, 11am, 2, 2:30, and 3pm during the week April through October; at 10, 11am, 2, and 3pm on winter weekdays; and at 10, 10:30, and 11am on Saturday year-round. It's best to reserve ahead. Audio guides are only £2 ($3.20). With both, you get discounted entry to the **Chapter House** (1245–55) in the east cloister, the nearby **Pyx Chamber,** and the **Abbey Museum,** all of which are now administered by the English Heritage organization. Call to find out if any concerts are scheduled; hearing music in this space is a memorable experience. *Note:* The Pyx Chamber and Abbey Museum were closed as of press time, but will hopefully reopen in 2004.

Dean's Yard, SW1. ✆ **020/7222-5152,** 020/7222-5897 Chapter House, or 020/7233-0019 Pyx Chamber and Abbey Museum. www.westminster-abbey.org. Admission £5 ($7.20) adults, £3 ($4.35) seniors and students, £2 ($2.90) under-16s, £10 ($14.50) family ticket. Chapter House, Pyx Chamber, and Abbey Museum £2.50 ($3.65) adults, £1.90 ($2.75) seniors and students, £1.30 ($1.90) under-16s; reduced with Abbey admission, free with guided and audio tour. Cloisters, College Garden, St. Margaret's Church free. Abbey Mon–Fri 9:30am–4:45pm; Sat 9:30am–2:45pm; last admission 1 hr. before closing, Sun for worship. Chapter House Apr–Sept 9:30am–5:30pm; Oct 10am–5pm; Nov–Mar 10am–4pm. Pyx Chamber and Abbey Museum daily 10:30am–4pm. Cloisters 8am–6pm. College Garden Apr–Sept 10am–6pm; Oct–Mar 10am–4pm. St. Margaret's Church Mon–Fri 9:30am–3:45pm; Sat 9:30am–1:45pm; Sun 2–5pm. Tube: Westminster.

3 More Museums, Galleries & Historic Buildings

Apsley House, The Wellington Museum ⍟   Once known as "No. 1 London" because it was the first house outside the tollgate, Apsley House has been the magnificent city residence of the dukes of Wellington since 1817. (The name comes from its first owner, the Earl of Bathurst, Baron Apsley.) Wellington moved in on his return from a triumphant military career in India, Spain, and Portugal, culminating in the victory at Waterloo. He entertained extravagantly, dining off the gorgeous Sèvres Egyptian Service that Napoléon had commissioned for Josephine, and a vast silver Portuguese service with a 26-foot-long centerpiece. Wellington's heroic military success earned him lavish gifts as well as royal respect. No wonder the original Robert Adam house (1771–78) had to be enlarged to house the duke's treasures. Today, it is crammed with silver, porcelain, sculpture (note the nude glamorized statue of Napoléon by Canova on the main staircase), furniture, medals, hundreds of paintings by Velázquez, Goya, Rubens, Brueghel, and other masters. It's one of the few great London town houses where such collections remain intact and the family is still in residence: The eighth Duke of Wellington and his son have private apartments.

149 Piccadilly, Hyde Park Corner, W1. © 020/7499-5676. www.apsleyhouse.org.uk. Admission (includes audio guide) £4.50 ($7) adults, free seniors and under-18s. Tues–Sun 11am–5pm. Closed Jan 1, Good Friday, May 1, and Dec 24–26. Tube: Hyde Park Corner (exit 3).

Cabinet War Rooms 🐝🐝 This warren of underground rooms served as Prime Minister Winston Churchill's nerve center and the secret HQ of the British government during World War II. It is preserved exactly as it was back then: the Cabinet Room, where the PM, his ministers, and military men made their crucial decisions; the Map Room, where they plotted out the progress of the war; the Telephone Room, where so many calls were placed to and received from FDR; even the PM's Emergency Bedroom. In 1995, the Heritage Lottery Fund bought the Churchill Papers for the nation. The core of the collection is held in Cambridge, but there are always pieces on display here. It is eerie and oddly exciting imagining the great man and his staff living their tense subterranean life.

Clive Steps, King Charles St., SW1. © 020/7760-0121. www.iwm.org.uk. Admission £5.80 ($9) adults, £4.20 ($7) students and seniors, free under-16s. Apr–Sept daily 9:30am–6pm, Oct–Mar daily 10–6pm; last admission 5:15pm. Closed Dec 24–26. Tube: Westminster, St. James's Park.

British Library 🐝🐝 If you love English literature, make it a point to visit the British Library, housed in a new building in St. Pancras designed by Colin St. John Wilson and opened in 1998. This is the national research library responsible for Britain's printed archive. Legally, publishers must send in one copy of everything they produce. The library has three exhibition spaces. The **John Ritblat Gallery** displays the permanent collection of treasures brought from the library's old home, the British Museum: the *Magna Carta,* Shakespeare's first folio, the handwritten manuscript of Charlotte Brontë's *Jane Eyre,* and dozens of others. Throughout, there are audio stations where visitors can listen to poets and writers reading from their works—James Joyce from *Finnegan's Wake,* for example, or Virginia Woolf giving a lecture on the BBC. Truly amazing, though, are the interactive exhibits that allow you to flip through an illuminated manuscript, such as Leonardo's *Notebooks.* A second gallery is used for temporary exhibitions, and the third, The Workshop of Words, Sounds & Images, traces the history of book production from the earliest written documents to the current digital revolution—and there are regular free book-craft demonstrations. Also in the busy events schedule are free Monday lunchtime talks, based on the collections, and Friday lunchtime author visits and discussions held in the excellent British Library shop. There's also a very pleasant and reasonably priced cafeteria, right next to a six-story glass tower that houses George III's library, given to the nation in 1823.

96 Euston Rd., NW1. (C) 020/7412-7332. www.bl.uk. Free admission. Galleries and public areas Mon and Wed–Fri 9:30am–6pm; Tues 9:30am–8pm; Sat 9:30am–5pm; Sun 11am–5pm. Tours of public areas: Mon, Wed, Fri 3pm, Sat 10:30am and 3pm; tickets £6 ($10) adults, £4.50 ($7) seniors and students. Tours including a reading room: Tues 6:30pm, Sun 11:30am and 3pm; tickets £7 ($11), £5.50 ($9) seniors and students. Tube: Euston, King's Cross.

The Dickens House Museum   This terraced house on the edge of Bloomsbury was home to Victorian London's quintessential chronicler for only 2 years (1837–39). In that time, though, the prolific Dickens produced some of his best-loved works, including a portion of *The Pickwick Papers, Nicholas Nickleby,* and *Oliver Twist.* His letters, furniture, and first editions are on display in rooms restored to their original appearance.

48 Doughty St., WC1. (C) 020/7405-2127. www.dickensmuseum.com. Admission £4 ($6) adults, £3 ($4.80) students and seniors, £2 ($3.20) children, £9 ($14) families. Mon–Sat 10am–5pm; Sun 11am–5pm. Tube: Russell Sq., Chancery Lane.

Imperial War Museum 🏛🏛 *Kids*   The IWM excels in explaining and re-creating 20th-century conflicts, to honor those who fought in them and to make sure they never happen again. A clock in the basement keeps a grim tally of the human cost of war—over 100 million people now. The Holocaust Exhibition, opened in 2000, continues that tradition. Four years in the making, it uses historical material—a funeral cart from the Warsaw Ghetto, victims' diaries and photograph albums, part of a deportation railcar—to tell the story of Nazi persecution. Eighteen survivors have given their testimony, while other exhibits explain the spread of anti-Semitism across Europe after the First World War. This exhibit is not recommended for under-14s. Life in the trenches during World War I is the subject of another exhibit, as is the Blitz of World War II, which dramatically re-enacts an air raid with special effects, sound, and scents—clinical disinfectant, dusty old buildings, burnt wood, and cooking at the tea stands serving the rescuers. The curators, who collect a lot of witness reminiscences, say that smells are often the strongest memories. So they often use them to heighten reality, like the cheesy feet and body odor in the simulated submarine, which kids will love. There are tales of espionage and dirty tricks in the Secret War section, plus a German Enigma machine, invisible ink, and a re-creation of the SAS operation to break the Iranian Embassy siege in 1980. Women and War is scheduled to open in Fall 2003 and run through Summer 2004. Call to find out about gallery talks, history evenings, and children's workshops.

Lambeth Rd., SE1. ✆ 020/7416-5320. www.iwm.org.uk. Free admission. Daily 10am–6pm. Closed Dec 24–26. Tube: Lambeth North, Waterloo.

London Transport Museum *Kids* This enjoyable museum, in the old Covent Garden flower market, traces the 200-year history of public transport in London, from the days when cabs were horse-drawn. Like a Noah's Ark for machinery, it has examples of just about everything Londoners have used to get around, from omnibuses to trams to Tube trains, as well as paintings, posters, working models, and interactive exhibits. Kids love it. Actors play characters like a 1906 tunnel miner and a World War II clippie (bus conductor). There's lots of stuff to pull and push. The museum even organizes guided London tours, with a transport bent, on the river, Tube, or bus (£10/$16). The shop is terrific, selling models, posters, and other original gifts.

The London Transport Museum can only display about 400 of the 370,000 items in its massive collection, so it has taken over a defunct Tube shed in West London for storage and as somewhere to work on conservation. On the last Friday of the month, there are guided tours of **The Depot.** Tickets cost £10 ($16), and you must book ahead. There are also a few open weekends each year, when you can explore the main shed and its vehicles, machinery, signs, and shelters, as well as enjoy the stalls and themed displays. Tickets cost £6.95 ($11). No need to book, just call for dates and take the Tube to Acton Town.

The Piazza, Covent Garden, WC2. ℂ **020/7565-7299** recorded info, or 020/7379-6344. www.ltmuseum.co.uk. Admission £5.95 ($10) adults, £3.95 ($6) seniors and students, free under-16s. Sat–Thurs 10am–6pm; Fri 11am–6pm (last admission 45 min. before closing). Closed Dec 24–26. Tube: Covent Garden, Charing Cross.

Museum of London 𝕽𝕽 *Kids*   The first phase of this museum's 5-year redevelopment plan was the opening of the new **World City Gallery,** which opened in 2001 and traces London's development between 1789 and 1914 into the first great metropolis of the industrial age. In 2002, **London Before London** opened and rewound history to look at life before the Romans, when hippos and elephants roamed Trafalgar Square.

Not only is this the biggest and most comprehensive city museum in the world, but it is genuinely engaging and creative. Among the highlights are a reconstruction of a Roman interior; a bedroom in a merchant's house from the Stuart period; the lord mayor's coach; a brilliant, audio-visual, dioramic presentation on the Great Fire with a voiceover reading diarist Samuel Pepys' account; a Victorian barber's shop; and the original elevators from Selfridges department store. The museum's archaeologists get called in at the start of most big building projects in London and their finds generally go on display once the study and conservation process is completed. Every year, there are three big temporary exhibitions, often looking at the social culture of the modern city. Many of the resident experts take part in the talks, museum tours, and workshops program (ranging in cost from free to £5/$8), as well as leading London walks and outside visits (£3–£10/$4.80–$16). In 2002, the "open-door" policy began at the museum's storage facility in East London. The huge former warehouse is like a 3-D reference library, with curators explaining their work and leading tours.

150 London Wall, EC2. ℂ **020/7600-3699.** www.museumoflondon.org.uk. Free admission. Mon–Sat 10am–5:50pm; Sun noon–5:50pm; last admission 5:30pm. Tube: St. Paul's, Moorgate, Barbican.

National Portrait Gallery 𝕽𝕽   Celebrity vanity and the paparazzo spirit are clearly nothing new, evidenced by this gallery of 10,000 paintings and 250,000 photographs. The portrait gallery charts the history of the nation through its famous faces. The curators have consigned Helmut Newton's portrait of Margaret Thatcher, among others, to the historical section, to make room for such nanosecond icons as David Beckham (Posh Spice's footballer husband) and mega-bucks celeb J. K. Rowling, author of *Harry Potter.* The flow through the gallery is much improved by the bright white

Ondaatje Wing, built in a courtyard pinched from the neighboring National Gallery. The permanent collection is displayed chronologically. You'll find Henry VII, Henry VIII, and Sir Thomas More, all painted by Holbein; the only extant portrait of Shakespeare; and T. S. Eliot by Sir Jacob Epstein. There are endearing amateur daubs, too, including one of Jane Austen by her sister, and the three talented Brontë sisters painted by their untalented brother Branwell. Temporary exhibitions take on big themes and single artists.

The NPG puts on free lectures and events, on a huge range of topics, on Tuesday and Thursday lunchtimes and weekend afternoons. Thursday evening lectures mostly start at 7pm (free–£3/$4.80). On Friday at 6:30pm, there are free musical events. As well as the cafe, there is the stunning **Portrait Restaurant & Bar** (*Ⓒ* 020/7312-2490), looking out across the rooftops from under the Ondaatje Wing's glass roof.

St. Martin's Place, WC2. *Ⓒ* 020/7306-0055. www.npg.org.uk. Free admission; Special exhibitions £5 ($8) adults, £3 ($4.80) seniors and students. Sat–Wed 10am–6pm; Thurs–Fri 10am–9pm. Closed Jan 1, Good Friday, Dec 24–26. Tube: Leicester Sq., Charing Cross.

Saatchi Gallery   Charles Saatchi certainly knows how to create a sensation. He was the force behind the ultra-controversial show of the same name (Sensation) that was shown at the Brooklyn Museum and caused city officials to wet their pants in fury. In our opinion a lot of the Saatchi collection is self-publicizing crap. But that doesn't mean you shouldn't have a look at the art trends of the second. The ex-adman Saatchi has amassed one of the largest independent collections of contemporary British and international art in the world. He is famous for launching new British artists and for creating brand trends (Neurotic Realism). In April 2003, after a predictable flurry of publicity, the Saatchi Gallery moved to County Hall (former home of the Greater London Council) on the south bank, right next to the British Airways London Eye observation wheel. It exhibits art from its own collections and also hosts exhibitions from other international collections and museums.

County Hall, Southbank, SE1. *Ⓒ* 020/7825-2363. www.saatchigallery.org.uk. Admission £8.50 ($14), £6.50 ($11) seniors and students. Sun–Thurs 10am–6pm; Fri–Sat 10am–10pm. Tube: Waterloo, Westminster.

St. Martin-in-the-Fields *Ⓡ*   This church is one of the best-loved in London. The current building dates from 1726. Designed by James Gibbs, the intricate plasterwork ceiling enhances the simple nave. Curiously, the parish boundary passes through the middle of

Buckingham Palace, and the names of many royal children appear on the baptismal registry. St. Martin's is famous for its music: Handel played the organ here, though not the current 3,637-pipe instrument, which was installed in 1990. There are free concerts at 1:05pm on Monday, Tuesday, and Friday. Evening recitals take place from Thursday to Saturday. Many are by candlelight, and the program leans heavily toward the baroque. The choral music during the three Sunday services is sublime. Evensong is the most quintessentially Anglican, usually at 5pm, but call ahead for specific times.

In the crypt of St. Martin's is the **London Brass Rubbing Centre,** which has replicas of about 100 medieval and Tudor church brasses as well as unusual Celtic patterns and early woodcuts of the zodiac. Materials and instruction are provided, and it's great fun. If you have time, take a break for tea or a delicious meal at the **Café in the Crypt** (p. 105).

Trafalgar Sq., WC2. ✆ **020/7766-1100** for church info, 020/7839-8362 for box office, or 020/7930-9306 London Brass Rubbing Centre. www.stmartin-in-the-fields. org. Free admission to church and lunchtime recitals; evening concerts £6–£17 ($10–$27). Brass rubbings £2–£15 ($3.20–$24), £1 ($1.60) discount under-12s. Church daily 9am–6pm (except during services); London Brass Rubbing Centre Mon–Sat 10am–6pm, Sun noon–6pm. Tube: Charing Cross, Leicester Sq.

Sir John Soane's Museum ⟨R⟩⟨R⟩ The son of a bricklayer, Sir John Soane (1753–1837) apprenticed himself to George Dance the Younger and Henry Holland before opening an architectural practice of his own. He married into great wealth and began collecting the objects displayed in this house, which he both designed and lived in. It's a marvelous hodgepodge, stuffed full of architectural fragments, casts, bronzes, sculpture, and cork models. The sarcophagus of Seti I (Pharaoh 1303–1290 B.C.) is also here. Soane used colored glass and mirrors to create reflections of architectural details and other dramatic effects—magical during evening opening when the rooms are candlelit. The collection includes works by Turner, three Canalettos, and two series of paintings by Hogarth, *An Election* and *The Rake's Progress*. Others, including a wonderful group of Piranesi drawings, are ingeniously hung behind movable panels in the Picture Room. Meanwhile, the gallery displays changing exhibitions from Soane's collection of over 30,000 architectural drawings, which includes works by Dance, Sir Christopher Wren, Sir William Chambers, and Robert and James Adam. There's a tour every Saturday at 2:30pm. Tickets cost £3 ($4.80) and go on sale half an hour before. Be early—there are only 22 spaces.

13 Lincoln's Inn Fields, WC2. ⓒ 020/7405-2107. www.soane.org. Free admission (£1 ($1.60) donation requested). Tues–Sat 10am–5pm; first Tues of each month also 6–9pm. Tube: Holborn.

Wallace Collection ⭐⭐ According to the terms of Lady Wallace's bequest, this collection must remain "unmixed with other objects of art." So the collection remains a perfect time capsule of 19th-century Anglo-French taste. Sir Richard Wallace was the illegitimate heir of the Marquis of Hertford, and the fifth generation to add to the acquisitions of exquisite furniture, armor, paintings, and decorative arts in the family's London home. There's much to delight the eye—Sèvres porcelain, Limoges enamels, 17th-century Dutch paintings, 18th-century French (Watteau, Fragonard, and Boucher) and British art, and Italian majolica. The new sculpture garden and cafe under a glass roof covering the internal courtyard is a real boon. For free tours, come at 1pm any weekday, 11:30am on Wednesday and Saturday, or 3pm on Sunday.

Hertford House, Manchester Sq., W1. ⓒ 020/7563-9500. www.the-wallace-collection.org.uk. Free admission. Mon–Sat 10am–5pm; Sun noon–5pm. Closed Dec 24–26, Jan 1, Good Fri, May Day. Tube: Bond St.

4 Especially for Kids

The top kid-picks are: touring the **Tower of London,** seeing the **Changing of the Guard** at Buckingham Palace, taking a "flight" in the **British Airways London Eye,** climbing aboard old Tube trains at the **London Transport Museum,** and quaking in front of the life-size animatronic T-Rex in the ever-popular Dinosaur exhibit at the **Museum of Natural History. Madame Tussaud's** is always a hit. You should also try the **London Brass Rubbing Centre** in the crypt at St. Martin-in-the-Fields.

Little Angel Theatre This magical theater is the only one like it in London. It puts on a huge variety of puppet shows from fairy tales to adaptations of children's books, by its own company and visiting masters of the art. Performances take place on weekends at 11am and 3pm, from late July through August, and during half-terms and school holidays. It's not for children under 3, and every show is designated for a specific age group.

14 Dagmar Passage, Islington, N1. ⓒ 020/7226-1787. www.littleangeltheatre.com. Tickets £5.50–£8 ($10–$13). Box office Sat–Mon 9am–5pm; Tues–Fri 9:30am–5:30pm. Tube: Angel, Highbury, Islington.

London Dungeon ⭐ This state-of-the-art horror chamber has huge appeal for kids with a taste for the gruesome and ghoulish, but it will frighten the little ones, so be careful. You have to deal with things like warty actors with wild hair leaping out at you in the dark. The dungeon re-enacts the goriest events from British history: one bloody night in the life of Jack the Ripper, the passing of a death sentence that sends you by barge through Traitors' Gate at the Tower of London, a medieval city ransacked by invaders, a roaring red tableau of the Great Fire of London, and so on. Rank smells and a smoke machine ratchet up the atmosphere. Much more fun than Madame Tussaud's.

28–34 Tooley St., SE1. ℂ 09001/600-0666. www.thedungeons.com. Admission £10.95 ($18) adults, £9.50 ($15) students, £6.95 ($11) under-15s (must be accompanied by an adult). Apr–Sept daily 10am–6:30pm; Oct–Mar daily 10am–5:30pm; late openings July–Aug. Closed Dec 25. Tube: London Bridge. River services: London Bridge City Pier.

London Zoo   Animal experts from the zoo went on safari in north London last year after a reported sighting of a Big Cat, which turned out to be an endangered European lynx. They rushed it back to hospital to recover from its adventure. London Zoo already looks after more than a hundred endangered species. It also takes part in 146 breeding programs, so there are always cute baby animals to see, as well as the perennial favorites: penguins, lions, tigers, hippos, chimps, and so on. There's something going on every hour of the day, from chow-time to the elephants' bath-time, so pick up a copy of the daily guide. The newest attraction is Web of Life, a state-of-the-art education center promoting conservation and biodiversity. The zoo opened in 1827 and is like a 36-acre architectural theme park.

Regent's Park, NW1. ℂ 020/7722-3333. www.londonzoo.co.uk. Admission £11 ($18) adults, £9 ($14) seniors and students, £8 ($13) children 3–15, £30 ($48) family. Daily Mar–Oct 10am–5:30pm, Nov–Feb 10am–4pm. Closed Dec 25. Tube: Camden Town. London Waterbus: From Camden Lock or Little Venice; for joint boat trip/zoo entry tickets, see "Boat Trips," below.

5 Parks & Gardens

Behind Kensington High Street, **Holland Park** is a pretty oasis of woods and gardens set around the ruins of Holland House. That's where the open-air theater and opera (ℂ 020/7602-7856; see chapter 7) take place in the summer. Take the Tube to High Street Kensington or Holland Park.

Hyde Park (ℂ 020/7298-2100) is the largest (350 acres) and most popular of all London's parks. The aptly named Serpentine Lake, created in the 1730s, is its most notable feature. On Sundays, the northeast corner near Marble Arch becomes **Speaker's Corner.**

Anyone can stand on a soapbox here and spout their opinions and grievances.

Kensington Gardens (℗ **020/7298-2117**) abuts the western perimeter of Hyde Park. Laid out in the early 18th century, the trees, lawns, and criss-crossed paths stretch over to Kensington Palace (p. 124) on the opposite side. There, you can wander around the sunken gardens, enjoy a bite at the Orangery, and wile away the time on a bench near the Round Pond, where enthusiasts make their model boats buzz between the ducks. Near the Long Water, you'll find the famous bronze statue of Peter Pan with his rabbits. And, on the south side of the park, near Queen's Gate, is the overpoweringly neo-gothic Albert Memorial.

Regent's Park (℗ **020/7486-7905**) was once Henry VIII's private hunting ground but it was formally laid out in 1811 by the Prince Regent and John Nash as part of an elaborate remodeling of London. Now, it's the people's playground. Besides the zoo, Regent's Park is famous for the boating lake, summer open-air theater (℗ **020/ 7486-2431,** brass band concerts on Holme Green, and Queen Mary's Rose Garden.

Opposite Buckingham Palace, **St. James's Park,** The Mall (℗ **020/ 7930-1793**), is perhaps the most beautiful of all of London's parks. It was landscaped by Le Notre and John Nash. The famous lake and Duck Island are a waterfowl sanctuary for lots of species, including pelicans, descendants of a feathered present given by a 17th-century Russian ambassador.

Named for its absence of flowers (except for a short time in spring), **Green Park** (℗ **020/7930-1793**) provides ample shade from tall trees that make it an ideal picnic bower.

6 Organized Tours

GUIDED WALKS

The **Original London Walks,** P.O. Box 1708, London NW6 4LW (℗ **020/7624-3978,** or 020/7625-9255; www.walks.com), has been going since 1965. It boasts an unrivalled schedule of themed tours, from spies to royalty to rock-'n'-roll legends, all led by experts, actors, and top Blue Badge guides. You can even go on a historic Thames-side pub crawl. The famous "Jack the Ripper" walk leaves daily at 7:30pm from Tower Hill Tube station. Tours cover up to 1½ miles and take around 2 hours: £5 ($8) adults, £4 ($6) seniors and students. No need to book.

BUS TOURS

The Big Bus Company (© 020/7233-9533; www.bigbus.co.uk) leaves from Green Park, Victoria, and Marble Arch daily, from 8:30am to 7pm (4:30pm in winter) on three different routes that take anything from 1½ to 2½ hours. Tickets include a river cruise and walking tours, and cost £16 ($26) for adults and £6 ($10) children. Valid for 24 hours, they let you hop on and off at 54 locations.

BOAT TRIPS

The fabulously loopy **London Frog Tours** ☆☆ (© 020/7928-3132; www.frogtours.com) has adapted several World War II amphibious troop carriers and now runs 80-minute road and river trips. Tours start behind County Hall (site of the British Airways London Eye giant observation wheel). You're picked up on Chicheley Street, then rumble through Westminster and up to Piccadilly before the vehicle splashes into the Thames at Vauxhall for a 30-minute cruise up as far as the Houses of Parliament. The high ticket price of £16.50 ($26) for adults, £13 ($21) seniors, £11 ($18) children, and £49 ($78) for families is worth it in vacation-snap value alone.

Crown River Cruises (© 020/7936-2033) run boats from Westminster to St. Katherine's Dock, stopping by the South Bank Centre and London Bridge, from 11am to 6:30pm in summer (until 3pm in winter). A return ticket costs £6.30 ($10) for adults, £5.30 ($8) seniors, and £3.15 ($5) under-16s. The round-trip takes 1 hour but the ticket is valid all day, so you can hop on and off to sightsee.

6

Shopping

The Brits still like to see, touch, scratch, and sniff what they're buying, so they're not into online shopping as much as Americans are. Shopping is a British buzz and, with around 30,000 stores, nowhere is buzzier or busier than London.

Stores are usually open from 10am to 6pm, and most add on an extra hour at least 1 night a week. There's "late-night shopping," as it's called, on Wednesday in Knightsbridge, Kensington, and Chelsea, and on Thursday in the West End. Around touristy Covent Garden, many doors don't close until 7 or 8pm every night. Shops can open for 6 hours on a Sunday, and many do, usually from 11am or noon.

TAXES & SHIPPING

In Britain, most goods and services, with the exception of books, newspapers, groceries, and children's clothing, carry 17.5% value-added tax (VAT), which is included in the price. Visitors from non-EC countries can reclaim the tax on some of the shopping they take home. In order to do so, you'll need to do your shopping at stores where you see the **Global Refund Tax-Free Shopping** sign. And although there is no official minimum purchase requirement, many stores set their own, usually around £50 ($80).

To make a claim, you must show identification at the store and fill out a VAT reclaim form then and there. Keep the receipt, form, and goods handy to show to the British Customs office at the airport (allowing ½ hour to stand in line). There are two ways to get the money. The easiest way is to go to the **Global Refunds** desk, where you will get an immediate cash refund (but lose money on the conversion rate if you take other than sterling). The second way is to mail the stamped form back to the store, choosing a credit card refund. For more info, call Customs' **Passenger Enquiry Point** (© **020/8910-3744**) or check out www.londontown.com/global refund.phtml.

1 The Shopping Scene

The **West End** is the heart of London shopping. Its main artery is **Oxford Street,** a mile of mass-market chains and department stores. At the eastern end, St. Giles High Street is the gateway into **Covent Garden,** a warren of narrow streets lined with stores selling quirky specialties and the hottest fashion trends. The old market is home to boutiques and craft stalls, while the piazza is a nonstop street festival of mime artists, singers, and entertainers.

Oxford Circus is the first big intersection walking west along Oxford Street, where it crosses the patchily elegant **Regent Street:** Turn south for Liberty, Aquascutum, Austin Reed, and Hamleys.

The next landmark westwards is **New Bond Street**, which changes to **Old Bond Street** as it heads south through **Mayfair.** It's wonderful for designer window-shopping and for fine art and antiques. Both Regent Street and Old Bond Street run into Piccadilly, to the south of which is **St James's** and some seriously upper-crust shopping. Here you'll find Hatchards for books; Swaine, Adeney Brigg & Sons for fine leather goods and riding equipment; and the fabulous food halls of Fortnum & Mason. **Jermyn Street** is famous for shirtmakers; other fine shops include Paxton & Whitfield, a specialist cheesemonger, Taylor of Old Bond Street, for men's shaving and toiletry articles, and Floris, which has been blending perfume and soaps since 1730.

Continue west from Piccadilly and Hyde Park Corner, to posh **Knightsbridge** and the world-famous Harrods department store on Brompton Road. Off Knightsbridge (it's a street as well as a neighborhood), is **Sloane Street**, lined with the most rarified names in haute couture. This runs down to Sloane Square and King's Road in **Chelsea**. King's Road was the center of Swinging London in the 1960s and of the punk revolution a decade later. Mainstream boutiques have invaded now, but there's still a healthy dose of streetwise avant-garde.

Young fashion and outdoor sports gear flourishes on **Kensington High Street.** Nearby **Notting Hill** is crammed with funky boutiques of every kind, especially around Portobello Market, though budget-busters are pushing out the neighborhood bargains—Westbourne Grove and Ledbury Road are *Vogue*'s idea of heaven. You have to travel east to find a hip shopping scene still on the way up: creative **Clerkenwell,** or **Brick Lane** in the City, where you'll find a market and Dray Walk, an enclave of quirky studio-shops and galleries.

2 Shopping A to Z

ANTIQUES

Alfie's Antique Market   With 150-plus dealers crammed into this old Edwardian department store, Alfie's would fox the most expert maze-builder. You name it, you'll find it here, from Art-Deco lighting to 20th-century ceramics, and at prices below the West End. Michael Jackson (known as "Wacko Jacko" in England) popped in to buy a bit of movie memorabilia during one of his visits to the U.K. Closed Sunday and Monday. 13–25 Church St., NW8. ℂ 020/7723-6066. www.ealfies.com. Tube: Edgware Rd., Marylebone.

Grays Antiques Market & Grays in the Mews   The main antiques market is home to 85 dealers and it is red hot on jewelry, but the Mews is a better bet for bargain hunters, especially if they're looking for something pocket-size, like a model car or music box. **Biblion** is an enormous hall especially for books, antiquarian and merely secondhand. Grays is closed on the weekends. Call for details on regular exhibitions. 58 and 1–7 Davies St., W1. ℂ 020/7629-7034. www. egrays.com. Tube: Bond St.

London Silver Vaults   This is a marvelous place to buy a wedding or christening present. Over 40 dealers trade in modern and antique silver, with prices starting at around £20 ($32). Closed Sundays. Chancery House, 53–64 Chancery Lane, WC2. ℂ 020/7242-3844. www.london silvervaults.co.uk. Tube: Chancery Lane.

ART

Will's Art Warehouse   Will Ramsay set up his warehouse in an old motorcycle garage in 1996 to debunk art-market snobbishness and offshore-bank-account prices. The 200 pictures on display change every 6 weeks. Customers can peruse the entire collection on a computer screen and choose which piece(s) they would like to see. Prices range from £50 ($80) to £2,500 ($4,000), and you can buy works on Will's website too. Unit 3, Heathmans Rd., SW6. ℂ 020/7371-8787. www. wills-art.com. Tube: Parson's Green.

BATH & BODY

Lush   You've probably never seen anything quite like Lush—it's a beauty shop that takes "organic" to a whole new level. Huge slabs of soap made with pineapple slices (good for the skin) or poppy seeds (a great exfoliator) sit on tables and counters like rounds of cheese at a deli. You can have the amount you want sliced off, or buy already cut bars. The store whips up fresh facial masks and keeps them on ice. Just scoop some into a take-home container and keep refrigerated. Lush is a fabulous source for gifts. The best-seller is the "bath bomb," which fizzes and scents the water. There are branches on King's Road, Chelsea, and Carnaby Street in Soho, as well as at Victoria railway station. Units 7 and 11, The Piazza, Covent Garden, WC2. ℂ 020/7240-4570. www.lush.co.uk. Tube: Covent Garden.

Neal's Yard Remedies Founded in 1981, this is still the best shop in London for herbal toiletries, homeopathic hair remedies, and alternative medicines. Most of the products come in cobalt-blue glass bottles, and make attractive and reasonably priced gifts. Try Remedies-to-Roll, roll-on essential oils to fit in your handbag, including one for sleep. Or create your own potions, choosing oils and extracts to add to base lotions and creams. They also have the best lip balm we've ever used. The store is at the end of a short cul-de-sac off Short's Gardens. There is a second one at Chelsea Farmers Market in Sydney Street, SW3. 15 Neal's Yard, WC2. ℂ 020/7379-7222. www.neals yardremedies.com. Tube: Covent Garden.

Taylor of Old Bond Street In business since 1854, this rather quaint emporium is devoted to the shaving and personal hygiene needs of men. Here's where you'll find the world's finest collection of shaving brushes, razors, and combs, plus soaps and hair lotions. 74 Jermyn St., SW1. ℂ 020/7930-5544. Tube: Piccadilly Circus.

BOOKS

Books for Cooks This store in Notting Hill stocks nearly 12,000 cookbooks, everything from the classics to hot manifestos from celebrity chefs and recipes from virtually every ethnic cuisine. BFC has also compiled a series of little books of recipes tried out in its test kitchen—a great bargain buy. That's also where the chefs rustle up the soups, salads, and puddings that make this such a great pit stop. 4 Blenheim Crescent, W11. ℂ 020/7221-1992. www.booksforcooks.com. Tube: Ladbroke Grove, Notting Hill Gate.

Children's Book Centre A brilliant place for baby bookworms and their parents. There are more than 15,000 titles for every age group up to 15, from fiction to fun factual stuff. The shop is crammed with toys, CD-ROMs, and audiotapes, too. Some Saturdays, it arranges "personal appearances" by popular cartoon characters. 237 Kensington High St., W8. ℂ 020/7937-7497. www.childrensbookcentre.co.uk. Tube: Kensington High St.

Gay's the Word   The amazingly comprehensive stock makes this Britain's biggest gay and lesbian bookshop. It has everything from literary fiction to detective novels and erotica, as well as issues-based titles, philosophy, and politics. 66 Marchmont St., WC1. © 020/7278-7654. www.gaystheword.co.uk. Tube: Russell Sq.

Hatchards   A holder of Royal Warrants from the Duke of Edinburgh and the Prince of Wales, Hatchards has been selling books since 1797. Oscar Wilde shopped here, and his wife Constance reputedly had an affair with the owner. It carries popular fiction and nonfiction titles, and all the latest releases. Just climbing the creaking stairs and browsing the venerable wooden stacks makes one feel frightfully upper crust. 187 Piccadilly, W1. © 020/7439-9921. www.hatchards.co.uk. Tube: Piccadilly Circus.

CHINA & GLASS

Reject China Shop   Most of the very wide range of English china sold here (including Portmeiron, Wedgwood, and Royal Doulton) is seconds or discontinued lines. This branch also stocks cutlery and Waterford crystal. Shoppers who know the going prices in the United States may pick up a bargain (sometimes up to 60% lower than U.S. prices). The other shops are in Brompton Road, Knightsbridge, and Covent Garden Piazza. 134 Regent St., W1. © 020/7734-2502. www.chinacraft.co.uk. Tube: Piccadilly Circus.

Royal Doulton   Founded over 200 years ago, Royal Doulton is one of the most famous names from the heart of English china production in Staffordshire. The company also produces Minton, Royal Albert, and Royal Crown Derby, all stocked here. 154 Regent St., W1. © 020/7734-3184. www.royal-doulton.com. Tube: Piccadilly Circus.

Waterford Wedgwood   Waterford crystal and Wedgwood china share the same table at this upscale shop. Fine cut-glass vases, platters, and objets d'art come in a wide range of prices. You'll find complete sets of the famous powder-blue and white Jasper china, and lots of other styles and patterns, too. There's a smaller branch on Piccadilly. 158 Regent St., W1. © 020/7734-7262. www.waterfordwedgwood.co.uk. Tube: Piccadilly Circus.

DEPARTMENT STORES

Debenhams   Once-dowdy Debenhams shocked the fashion pack when it became one of the first chain stores to persuade big name designers to descend to high street level. Now the list of hot-name collaborators includes **Pearce II Fionda, Maria Grachvogel, Edina**

Ronay, John Rocha, and undies queen **Janet Reger. Tristan Webber** is the latest addition. Chic chicks might be able to slip into a floaty satin dress by **Jasper Conran** for £80 ($128). The lads get tasty bargains, too, like black wool trousers designed by **Oswald Boateng** for £45 ($72). As well as her covetable womenswear, **Elspeth Gibson** has created the Sweet Pea range for girls aged 3 to 8. Debenhams is even roping some of these same designers into creating interiors. 334–348 Oxford St., W1. ⓒ 020/7580-3000. www.debenhams.co.uk. Tube: Bond St., Oxford Circus.

Harrods Opened in 1849, Harrods claims it's the most famous department store in the world, and that anything in the world can be bought (or ordered) here. The incredible ground-floor food halls are a feast for all the senses. And, for sheer theme-park excess, nothing beats the Egyptian escalator and the children's department with its cartoon cafe and specialty hairdresser. On the minus side, the store layout is frustrating and the fashions can be dowdy as opposed to cool. With around 35,000 visitors a day, Harrods can become a nightmare experience, like Disney World on the 4th of July. Harrods also has a snooty dress code: no dirty or unkempt clothing, ripped jeans, high-cut shorts, athletic tops, cycling shorts, or, horror of horrors, bare tummies or feet. Knightsbridge, SW1. ⓒ 020/7730-1234. www.harrods.com. Tube: Knightsbridge.

Harvey Nichols This elegant store is nicknamed Harvey Nics by its fashion-pack and It-Girl clientele, and it could hardly be more different from its brash Knightsbridge neighbor, Harrods. Whereas the latter is crammed to opulent bursting point with everything under the sun, and much of it in dubious taste, Harvey Nichols is a cool haven of chic. It pioneered the showcasing of designer collections from London, Paris, and Milan—from Chloe to Gaultier, Tocca to Joseph—and has a decent menswear department, too. And you won't go hungry here either: as well as the food hall and fifth-floor bar, cafe, and restaurant, Harvey Nics also has a YO! Sushi and a Wagamama (see chapter 5 for reviews). 109–125 Knightsbridge, SW1. ⓒ 020/7235-5000; www.harveynichols.com. Tube: Knightsbridge.

John Lewis This is one of the few remaining traditional department stores that really does stock everything, from fashions and fashion fabrics, to curtain fabrics and furniture, clothing, washing machines, and nice leather-bound daily planners. John Lewis makes a big promise—"Never Knowingly Undersold." If customers find the same goods locally at a better price, the store will refund the difference. (And it employs an army of undercover shoppers to check out the competition.) Sister store **Peter Jones,** Sloane Sq., SW1 (© 020/7730-3434; www.peterjones.co.uk; Tube: Sloane Sq.), is the Sloane Ranger's spiritual home. It is having an £80-million refurb, due to be complete in 2004. 278–306 Oxford St., W1. © 020/7629-7711. www.johnlewis.com. Tube: Oxford Circus.

Liberty   If Selfridges is all flash, cash, marble, and gold, then Liberty is baroque sensuality. London's prettiest department store may be olde worlde on the outside (neo-Tudor, in fact), but everything here is very, very stylish. As well as clothing with the famous Liberty imprint, it has a big array of women's fashions by well-known and up-and-coming designers. And don't miss the world-famous furnishing and dress fabrics. Liberty is far from cheap, but you're bound to find something to take home as a small gift on the bazaar-like first floor or among the housewares downstairs. 210–214 Regent St., W1. © 020/7734-1234. www.liberty-of-london.com. Tube: Oxford Circus.

Marks & Spencer   When the French protested against closures of Marks & Spencer in Paris, the Brits wondered why on earth they were so upset. That's because the home crowd has lost all respect for the venerable M&S. Neither the new vampy undies range, Salon Rose, nor the Autograph label, designed by Katherine Hamnett, Betty Jackson, and others, managed to reverse its plummeting fortunes. If it hasn't gone bankrupt by the time you arrive, at least stop in at the food hall, which does yummy lunchtime sandwiches and salads. 458 Oxford St., W1. © 020/7935-7954. www.marksandspencer.com. Tube: Marble Arch.

Selfridges   Chicago salesman Harry Selfridge opened this store in 1909, stunning Londoners with his marble halls and sheer variety of goods. An opulent revamp, just completed, is stunning them again. The ground-floor perfumery and cosmetics department is the biggest in Europe. Upstairs is crammed with covetable designer fashions and home accessories. And Miss Selfridge is several shops within a shop within a shop. It has its own teen-queen label—which you can also find in a chain of outlets around the country—and hosts high street names, including Oasis and Warehouse, alongside some funky young designers. Selfridges also boasts one of London's finest food halls, and the biggest choice of restaurants and cafes of all the department stores. 400 Oxford St., W1. © 020/7629-1234. www. selfridges.co.uk. Tube: Bond St., Marble Arch.

FASHION
CONTEMPORARY

Accessorize This fabulous shop can help you turn any old dress into a knock 'em dead dazzler, and prices are so reasonable you don't have to save up to buy its wares or save them just for special occasions. Flirty little bags cost £15 to £25 ($24–$40). It also has sumptuous scarves, hats, and girly jewelry, in all the season's prettiest colors. You'll find branches all over, including Covent Garden, King's Road, Kensington High Street, and Brompton Road. 386 Oxford St., W1. ② 020/7491-9424. www.accessorize.co.uk. Tube: Bond St.

H&M This Swedish chain has its flagship store on the other side of Oxford Circus from Top Shop. It's been around a long time yet always seems to be of the moment, constantly refreshing its image. Like ice-cream flavors, different H&M labels cater to different tastes, from frontline fashion trends to clubbing skimpies, slouching streetwear to classics for work. And three cheers for a store that recognizes women are not all Hollywood lollipop-heads, a la Ally McBeal: the Big is Beautiful range goes up to size 30 (26 U.S.). H&M also does funky maternity wear, tough stuff for kids, and menswear too; guys, if you're looking for a men's skirt, this is where you'll find it. All at very good value prices. 261–271 Regent St., W1. ② 020/7493-4004. www.hm.com. Tube: Oxford Circus.

Top Shop/Top Man The multi-floored, multi-everything Top Shop used to sell cheap togs for teenyboppers, but its funky styles have now become top wannabuys for would-be style junkies. Yet, it's still amazingly cheap. The TS Design label boasts an army of A-list names: **Clements Ribeiro, Hussein Chalayan, Tracey Boyd,** plus **Markus Lupfer.** Others who haven't quite become international names yet take guest spots at Bazaar, a section that apes the feel of Portobello or Camden market. Top Shop's Tall Girl label features women's jeans with a 36' leg! You can get your clothes customized, get a haircut, and get severe brain ache because this is the kind of noisy full-on place that turns even dedicated shopaholics into shopping-phobes. 214 Oxford St., W1. ② 020/7636-7700. www.tops.co.uk. Tube: Oxford Circus.

DISCOUNT

Browns Labels for Less Browns is the sort of name that wins star treatment from a designer when the buyer visits a collection. The main boutique at 23–27 Moulton Street showcase only the best names—from Chloe to Jill Sander—and can make a hot young newcomer. All unsold stock from last season is moved across to Browns Labels for Less, where it is discounted from 30% to 70%. You never know what you'll find: Issy Miyake, perhaps, or Comme des Garcons, Dries van Noten, and Prada accessories. 50 S. Molton St., W1. ☎ 020/7514-0052. www.brownsfashion.com. Tube: Bond St.

Burberry's Factory Outlet   Burberry is back from the dead. Not long ago only tourists actually wore the famous plaid, but now Britain's best-known luxury marque is also one of the hippest and best loved. And that plaid is on everything—from trench coats to trench dresses, and even undies, eye masks, and bikinis. You have to take a local train to get to the factory shop, but savings of up to a third on samples and ends of lines will more than cover the cost of your ticket. (Burberry also has a very swanky new store at 21–23 New Bond St., W1.) 29–53 Chatham Place, E9. ☎ 020/8328-4320. Train: Hackney Central BR station.

Paul Smith   There are three floors stocking this hot British designer, mens and kidswear only, and mostly last season's. Discounts range from 30% to 70%. 23 Avery Row, W1. ☎ 020/7493-1287. www.paulsmith.co.uk. Tube: Bond St.

SHOES

Clarks   British kids have been growing up in Clarks' sensible shoes for over 175 years. Now this staid brand has blossomed, selling a small collection of great-value fashion shoes. Most are for well-scrubbed eco-hippies. Some are simple but smart. But none of them will give you bunions. 260 Oxford St., W1 ☎ 020/7499-0305. www.clarks.co.uk. Tube: Oxford Circus.

Office   This store sells the sort of shoes you drool over in glossy magazines—for men as well as women—but for very reasonable prices. There's a branch of the sister sports shoe shop, **Offspring,** nearby at no. 60 Neal Street. The **Office Sale Shop** at 61 St. Martin's Lane, WC2, has ends of lines and last year's models at up to half price. 57 Neal St., WC2. ☎ 020/7379-1896. www.office.co.uk. Tube: Covent Garden.

VINTAGE & SECONDHAND

Blackout II   This fun emporium has hidden depths—below the small storefront is a basement crammed with old clothes. From the glamorous 1930s to the glam 1970s and 1980s, from crocodile handbags and feather boas to kitsch fake fur and bell bottoms, you'll find it here. You can rent for a wild London club night, as well as buy. 51 Endell St., WC2. ☎ 020/7240-5006. www.blackout2.com. Tube: Covent Garden.

Cornucopia The stock is so huge that there are definitely bargains to be found here, it just takes a bit of rummaging to find them. But that's actually fun with this treasure trove of costumes from the 1920s on, all arranged by era. Women off to the hottest parties in town come here for entrance-making eveningwear and the costume jewelry to go with it. 12 Upper Tachbrook St., SW1. ✆ 020/7828-5752. Tube: Victoria.

Pandora Ladies who lunch don't throw last season's haute fashions away: They sell them through this Knightsbridge dress agency. Pandora is the grande dame of the secondhand scene, claiming to hold every famous designer from Armani to Zilkha (Ronit, that is). The stock is seasonally correct, and there are even sales: from July to August, and December to January. 16–22 Cheval Place, SW7. ✆ 020/7589-5289. Tube: Knightsbridge.

FOOD
Fortnum & Mason This may be a department store but few shoppers penetrate beyond the food hall—unless it's to have afternoon tea (see p. 115). Mr. Fortnum and Mr. Mason opened their doors in 1707 and it is *the* place to find the aristocratic foods and empire-building delicacies you've only seen in period movies—traditional hams and pies, for instance, as well as cheeses, handmade chocolates, and preserves. Fortnum knows everything there is to know about tea: The house range is pricey but includes more than 50 blends and it's said that if you take along a sample of your tap water, they'll know which one to pair it with. 181 Piccadilly, W1. ✆ 020/7734-8040. www.fortnumandmason.com. Tube: Green Park, Piccadilly Circus.

MARKETS
Bermondsey Market Forget Portobello Road, charming though it is. This is where serious antiques collectors and dealers come—burglary victims, too, tracking down stolen possessions. It starts at dawn with the serious business done by 9am and stalls closing from noon. The market is a bit of a trek from the Tube but it's an adventure. Bermondsey Sq., SE1. Fri only 5am–2pm. Tube: Bermondsey, London Bridge.

Camden Market This vast market fills the streets, arcades, and courtyards. Hundreds of stalls sell crafts, bric-a-brac, clothes, and furniture, with a big hippy-trippy contingent. The Stables concentrates on clothing, almost-junk, and 20th-century collectibles. The best vintage clothing can be found on Buck Street, Camden High Street, and in Electric Market (good for cheap Doc Martens). In an old timber yard by the canal, Camden Lock is crammed with craft workshops, stores, and cafes. It hosts a Producers' (Farmers') Market on Saturday and Sunday. Come to Camden early, particularly on Sundays, as this is one of London's biggest tourist attractions. Camden High St. and Chalk Farm Rd., NW1. Camden Market Thurs–Sun 9am–5:30pm; Camden Lock daily 10am–6pm; Stables Market Sat–Sun 8am–6pm; Camden Canal Market Sat–Sun 10am–6pm; Electric Market Sun 9am–5:30pm. Tube: Camden Town, Chalk Farm.

Portobello Market   Portobello Market is a lot of fun, despite the seething masses. Saturday is the full-on armoires-to-lava-lamps day. More than 2,000 antiques dealers set out their stalls at the southern, uphill, end: Head for Notting Hill Gate Tube station. For retro, street-hip, and club-chic clothing, secondhand music, and junkabilia, go to Ladbroke Grove instead. Cross the road out of the station to the passage left of the bridge. Weekdays, Portobello is an old-fashioned fruit and veg market, with organic food on Thursdays. Portobello Rd., W10, W11. Antiques Market Sat 4am–6pm; General Market Mon–Wed 8am–6pm, Thurs 9am–1pm, Fri–Sat 7am–7pm; Organic Market Thurs 11am–6pm. Clothes & Bric-a-brac Market Fri 7am–4pm, Sat 8am–5pm, Sun 9am–4pm. Tube: Notting Hill Gate, Ladbroke Grove.

RECORDS, CDS & TAPES

HMV   This HMV is a mega-megastore, so whatever you want it's probably got it. Dance music is a real strength, and the ground floor has all the new rock, soul, reggae, and pop releases. The range of world music and spoken-word recordings is huge. Last year, HMV opened a new super hi-tech branch at 360 Oxford St., W1 (© 020/7514-3600; Tube: Bond St.). It's the first music store in the country where customers can create their own CDs with digital downloads. 150 Oxford St., W1. © 020/7631-3424. www.hmv.co.uk. Tube: Oxford Circus.

Tower Records   A warehouse of sound, Tower has four floors of records, tapes, and compact discs—pop, rock, classical, jazz, bluegrass, folk, country, soundtracks, and more, all in separate departments. Downstairs you'll find a fantastic selection of international music magazines. You can also buy tickets to gigs here, and there are in-store signings. This store is open until midnight every day except Sunday. 1 Piccadilly Circus, W1. © 020/7439-2500. www.towerrecords.co.uk. Tube: Piccadilly Circus.

Virgin Megastore   The Virgin Megastore is a microcosm of Richard Branson's ever-expanding Virgin empire. You can buy a mobile phone, an airline ticket, or an hour on the Internet, as well as hardware and software for computer games, MP3 players . . . oh, and the usual albums and singles. And it holds regular live performances and signings. 14–16 Oxford St., W1. © 020/7631-1234. www.virginmega.co.uk. Tube: Tottenham Court Rd.

TOYS

Hamleys William Hamley founded Noah's Ark, as it was called in 1760, and it became one of the largest toy stores in the world. There are seven floors stuffed with more than 26,000 toys, games, models, dolls, cuddly animals, and electronic cars—even executive toys at very adult prices. Recently refurbished, the store is easier to get around, but you still have to navigate through the crowds watching toy demonstrations. 188–196 Regent St., W1. © 020/7494-2000. www.hamleys.com. Tube: Oxford Circus, Piccadilly Circus.

7

London After Dark

London's cultural life could hardly be more vibrant. In recent years, millions of pounds raised by the National Lottery have gone into supporting new work and refurbishing existing venues.

The theater scene continues, as it will always continue, with some mega-hits that seem to run forever and new shows appearing all the time. The theater world, to be honest, has suffered somewhat from lack of American tourists. Some shows have had to close early, and right now there's not as much exciting new work as there are endless revivals and what producers hope will be sure-fire hits. That's not to say that you won't find something wonderfully enjoyable or provocative playing in the West End. For nearly every show you can buy tickets at the box office when you arrive.

The news coming out of the club scene is a weird mixed bag, as usual. On the one hand, intimate club bars are supposedly becoming more trendy than gargantuan superclubs. But on the other hand, gigantic raves are still in.

WHERE TO FIND OUT WHAT'S GOING ON

Even if you have zero intention of actually buying a ticket from them, surf the ticket agencies' websites for advance notice of what's going on: www.gloabaltickets.com and www.ticketmaster.co.uk are the largest agencies. Once you get to London, buy a copy of the listings bible *Time Out* (www.timeout.com), which comes out on Wednesdays. The *Evening Standard* (www.thisislondon.com) produces a supplement, *Hot Tickets,* on Thursdays.

1 Entertainment on a Shoestring: Nightlife Bargains

FREEBIES

- **Holland Park Theatre** (p. 162)   Don't buy a ticket; just sit on the grass outside and soak up the music for free.
- **Royal Festival Hall** (p. 163)   Come for hot **Commuter Jazz** in the foyer on Fridays from 5:15 to 6:45pm.

- **Lamb & Flag** (p. 169)   Fantastic free jazz at a fantastically traditional pub in Covent Garden every Sunday night.
- **Bar Rumba** (p. 165)   Between 5 and 9pm, Monday through Thursday, drinks are two for the price of one *and* there's no cover charge, so come early and stay late for free clubbing.
- **Heaven** (p. 167)   London's most famous gay club is free with a flyer before 11:30pm on a Friday. Other nights that'll get you in for £1 ($1.60).

CHEAPIES

- **Royal Festival Hall** (p. 163)   Top orchestras play at this concert hall, and seats in the balcony, where the sound is just as good, generally cost £10 ($16) or less.
- **Barbican Centre** (p. 163)   Same-day unsold seats for concerts (the London Symphony Orchestra, for instance) go for £6 ($10) at the concert hall box office an hour before the performance.
- **Royal Court Theatre** (p. 158)   The cutting edge of contemporary theater for £7.50 ($12) a ticket every Monday night. Last-minute standbys at the Theatre Downstairs cost a token 10p (16¢).
- **Shakespeare's Globe** (p. 159)   Just as the Bard did it, both the stage and production style. Stand in the raucous central yard for only £5 ($8).
- **Soho Theatre** (p. 160)   Monday nights, all tickets are £5 ($8) at this recently re-launched hotbed of new writing and community theater.
- **The English National Opera** (p. 161)   Get here early for £3 ($4.80) day-of-performance balcony tickets to see one of Britain's finest opera companies.
- **G.A.Y. at the Astoria** (p. 167)   Pick up a flyer to have fabulous fun at this club for just £1 ($1.60).

2 London's Theater Scene

MAJOR COMPANIES

Royal Court Theatre   The 10p standby is a spectacular deal, so naturally there's a catch: You have to rely on a less-than-full house, and the deal doesn't apply to every show. But the £7.50 Mondays are a regular feature, and a real steal. The 400-seat proscenium arch theater and upstairs studio of the Royal Court are home to the English Stage Company. Since premiering the plays of the Angry Young Men of the 1950s, it has built a world-class reputation as a forum for challenging (and sometimes boring and ridiculously bad) new writing.

Sloane Sq., SW1. ☎ 020/7565-5000. www.royalcourttheatre.com. Jerwood Theatre Downstairs tickets £7.50–£26 ($12–$42), £7.50 ($12) on day of performance; tickets unsold 1 hr. before performance 10p (16¢). Jerwood Theatre Upstairs tickets £12.50–£15 ($20–$24). Mon evening, all seats in both theaters are £7.50 ($12): prebookable for Downstairs, in person at the box office from 10am for Upstairs (limit of 2 tickets per buyer). Tube: Sloane Sq.

Royal National Theatre   The core repertory company and ever-changing guest stars perform in three auditoria in this huge theatre complex on the South Bank. The box office is open Monday through Saturday 10am to 8pm. South Bank, SE1. ☎ 020/7452-3400, 020/7452-3000 box office. www.nt-online.org. Tickets £10–£32 ($16–$51); all tickets unsold 2 hr. before performance in the Olivier and Lyttleton theaters £15 ($24); student standby may also be available for £8 ($13) 45 min. before curtain at all 3 theaters. Tube: Waterloo, Embankment (cross over Hungerford Bridge). River services: Festival Pier.

Royal Shakespeare Company   To see this illustrious company perform you'll need to peruse the various theatre listings when you arrive in London, or, better yet, surf the RSC website **www.rsc.org.uk**. The ticket situation has been decentralized, so you'll have to get tickets at the various theatres, just as you would for any other West End show; ticket prices vary according to the show, the theatre, and the stars performing. For more information you can call the Ticket Hotline in Stratford (☎ 0870/609-1110), but remember: it's a long-distance call. Barbican Centre, Silk St., EC2; ☎ 020/7638-8891 for box office; Tube: Barbican, Moorgate; tickets £15–£32.50 ($24–$52). Gielgud Theatre, Shaftesbury Ave, W1; ☎ 020/7494-5065 for box office; Tube: Leicester Sq.; tickets £15–£37.50 ($24–$60), same-day tickets £15 ($24), standby ½ hr. before performance £15 ($24) seniors and students. Theatre Royal Haymarket, Haymarket, W1; ☎ 0870/609-1110 (Stratford box office) or go in person to theater box office; Tube: Piccadilly Circus; tickets £12–£40 ($19–$64).

Shakespeare's Globe Theatre   A night out at the Globe is a really fun experience. The replica theater stands on the site of Shakespeare's original amphitheater, which burned down in 1613. Constructed from the same materials as the original, four tiers of banked benches encircle the stage where the company performs the Bard's great works as their predecessors would have done in his day. The Elizabethan set shuns lighting and scenery. There are no little luxuries like cushions on the wooden bench seats, many of which are backless, or protection from the elements, hence the summer-only season. Hawkers selling food and drink roam through the audience standing in the central yard. The box office is open Monday through Saturday from 10am to 6pm.

The excellent **Shakespeare's Globe Exhibition** ☞ (℡ **020/ 7902-1500**), in the undercroft below the Globe, is open daily, May to September 9am to noon and October to April 10am to 5pm. 21 New Globe Walk, Bankside, SE1. ℡ **020/7401-9919**. www.shakespeares-globe.org. Tickets £8–£30 ($13–$48); £5 ($8) yard-standing tickets. Season runs end April–Sept; booking from mid-Feb. Tube: Mansion House and St. Paul's (cross over Millennium Bridge), Southwark. River services: Bankside Pier.

OFF–WEST END & FRINGE THEATER

Listings magazine *Time Out* carries details for around 60 off–West End theaters and fringe venues, where you'll see some of the most original drama in London—and also some of the worst.

Almeida Theatre   The theatre's mission has always been to provoke, and over the decades it has built such a hot reputation that A-list actors gladly play leading roles for £300 ($480) a week. The annual Festival of Contemporary Music, a.k.a. Almeida Opera, takes place in June and July. The box office is open Monday to Friday 10am to 7pm, and from 1pm on Saturday. Almeida St., N1. ℡ **020/ 7359-4404**. www.almeida.co.uk. Tickets £6–£27.50 ($10–$44). Tube: Angel.

Donmar Warehouse   The Donmar, now one of the hippest and most highly rated theaters in London, produces a huge range of old and new shows, including performances by visiting companies and a cabaret season. The box office is open from 10am to 8pm, but phone booking is round the clock. The 20 standing tickets go on sale once there's a full house. 41 Earlham St., WC2. ℡ **020/7369-1732**. www.donmar-warehouse.com. Tickets usually £15–£25 ($24–$40), but vary for each show; standing tickets £5 ($8). Tube: Covent Garden.

Soho Theatre   The evangelistic mission at this newly built theater and smaller studio is to foster new writing and new talent. It has been very successful at both, winning a reputation for high-quality drama. Downstairs there is also a Café Lazeez (p. 86): a two-course meal in the bar costs £7.50 ($12). The box office is open from 10am to curtain-up. 21 Dean St., W1. ℡ **020/7478-0100**. www.sohotheatre.com. Tickets £7.50–£14 ($12–$22); Mon all tickets £5 ($8). Tube: Tottenham Court Rd.

Young Vic   The Young Vic has a large main auditorium and a smaller studio, where tickets are no pricier than going to the movies. It not only puts on its own productions, with guest stars for banka-bi' ʰut hosts touring companies too. The faded decor and inad-
ʸ are somewhat redeemed by the delicious brasserie menu

at its Bright Light Cafe (p. 112). The box office is open Monday to Saturday 10am to 7pm. 66 The Cut, SE1. ℂ **020/7928-6363**. www. youngvic.org. Main House tickets £9–18 ($14–$29). Studio £5–£9 ($8–$14). Tube: Waterloo, Southwark.

3 The Performing Arts

OPERA & BALLET

The English National Opera The ENO thrills enthusiasts and rocks traditionalists with newly commissioned works and lively, theatrical reinterpretations of the classics. At Christmas and during the summer, the English National Ballet takes over the auditorium. If you're prepared to put in a bit of effort (hang around for standbys and so forth), tickets here are an incredible deal. The box office is open 10am to 8pm (9:30am–8:30pm, by phone), Monday through Saturday. London Coliseum, St. Martin's Lane, WC2. ℂ **020/7632-8300**. www.eno.org. Tickets £6–£60 ($10–$96). Discounted day-of-performance tickets Mon–Fri, Sat matinee: £29 ($42.05) in Dress Circle, £3 ($4.80) in the Balcony; on sale at the box office at 10am or by telephone from noon for matinees and 2:30pm for evening performances. Tickets unsold 3 hr. before performance: £28 ($45) in Dress/Upper Circle, Sat evening; £18 ($29) seniors and £12.50 ($20) students any day. £3 ($4.35) standing tickets may also be available. Each adult buying a full-price ticket can buy one half-price seat for a child under 18. No under-5s. Tube: Charing Cross, Leicester Sq.

The Royal Ballet Britain's leading ballet company is now firmly ensconced back at the Royal Opera House. The company's repertoire is extremely varied but veers toward the classics and works by its earlier choreographer-directors, Sir Frederick Ashton *(A Month in the Country)* and Kenneth Macmillan *(Romeo and Juliet)*. Royal Opera House, Bow St., WC2. ℂ **020/7304-4000**. www.royalballet.org. Tickets evening £3–£66 ($4.80–$106); 67 discounted seats for each show sold from 10am on day of performance. Tube: Covent Garden.

The Royal Opera The combined talents of the Orchestra of the Royal Opera House, the Chorus of the Royal Opera, and the dozens of guest artists and conductors make the Royal Opera one of the world's premiere operatic venues. Operas are sung in the original language with projected supertitles that translate the libretto for the audience. Royal Opera House, Bow St., WC2. ℂ **020/7304-4000**. www.royal opera.org. Tickets £3–£155 ($4.80–$248); 67 discounted seats for each show sold from 10am on day of performance. Tube: Covent Garden.

Performers in the Park

The **Open Air Theatre**, Inner Circle, Regent's Park, NW1 (℡ **020/7486-2431**; www.open-air-theatre.org.uk; Tube: Baker St., Regent's Park), has been staging summer drama, from June to early September, since 1932. Tickets cost £8.50 to £25 ($14–$40). **Holland Park Theatre**, Holland Park, W11 (℡ **020/7602-7856**; www.operahollandpark.com; Tube: Holland Park), has opera, and a week of ballet, to the accompaniment of the Royal Philharmonic Orchestra, from June to August under a temporary canopy in the ruins of the Jacobean Holland House. Tickets cost £28 ($45). Perhaps the most famous open-air concerts are during July and August at the outdoor amphitheatre near the Robert Adam–designed mansion, **Kenwood House.** Hampstead Lane, NW3 (℡ **020/7413-1443**; www.picnicconcerts.com). This is a magical scene, on Hampstead Heath, by a lake that reflects the spectacular firework finales—a favorite with unstuffy types enjoying popular classics. Tickets are £17 to £20 ($27–$32) for a deckchair, or £14.50 to £16.50 ($23–$26) to sit on the lawn. Take the Tube to East Finchley, and catch the courtesy bus.

CLASSICAL MUSIC

London Symphony Orchestra   London's top orchestra is a major international force under the direction of principal conductor Sir Colin Davis. It stages 85 concerts a year at the Barbican Hall. The sound in the Barbican is much better since the hall's big refurbishment and acoustical tune-up. Reduced-price standby tickets for £6 ($10) go on sale an hour before a performance. Barbican Centre, Silk St., EC2. ℡ **020/7638-8891.** www.lso.co.uk. Tickets £6.50–£35 ($10–$56); £3 ($4.80) under-16s. Tube: Barbican, Moorgate.

RECITAL VENUES

Don't forget to check out the magical candlelit concerts at **St. Martin-in-the-Fields** (p. 139).

Wigmore Hall   This venerable, vaulted auditorium celebrated its centenary in 2001 and is London's foremost venue for lieder and chamber music. The box office is open Monday to Saturday from

10am to 8:30pm, Sunday 10:30am to 8pm (5pm from Nov to mid-Mar). 36 Wigmore St., W1. ✆ 020/7935-2141. www.wigmore-hall.org.uk. Tickets £7–£20 ($11–$32). Tube: Bond St., Oxford Circus.

4 Major Arts Venues

Barbican Centre   The Barbican opened in 1982. Reputedly the largest arts complex in Europe, it is so badly laid out that yellow lines have been painted across its brick-paved walkways and piazzas to help visitors find their way from the Underground. As well as the Barbican Theatre and The Pit, it has two art galleries, three cinemas, and several restaurants, bars, and cafes. The newly refurbished concert hall is home to the London Symphony Orchestra (see "Classical Music," above), and hosts other festivals and large-scale events between LSO performances. Call the box office, open daily from 9am to 8pm, for tickets and to find out what's on. Silk St., EC2. ✆ 020/7638-8891. www.barbican.org.uk. Tube: Barbican or Moorgate.

Royal Albert Hall   A £4 ($6) standing ticket to one of the Sir Henry Wood Promenade Concerts at the Royal Albert Hall has to be one of the best buys of the summer cultural season (www.bbc.co.uk/proms). Every year, from mid-July to mid-September, the daily changing performances cover every conceivable spot on the classical music spectrum. The rest of the year, this circular hall serves as a venue for a huge range of entertainment, not all of it musical. Sheryl Crow, Burt Bacharach, Tony Bennett, B. B. King, Cirque du Soleil, and the world's top stand-up comedians, tennis players, sumo wrestlers, and amateur choirs—they've all appeared here. The box office opens daily from 9am to 9pm. Kensington Gore, SW7. ✆ 020/7589-8212. www.royalalberthall.com. Tube: South Kensington, Kensington High St.

Sadler's Wells Theatre   Recently rebuilt, this is one of the busiest stages in London and also one of the best, with superb sight lines. It hosts top visiting opera and dance companies from around the world. There are always some seats within reach of the budget traveler (£8.50–£35/$14–$56). Students, kids, and seniors can sometimes get standbys 1 hour before a performance. The ticket office is open Monday to Saturday 9am to 8:30pm. Rosebery Ave., EC1. ✆ 020/7863-8000. www.sadlers-wells.com. Tube: Angel.

South Bank Centre   This South Bank arts complex is home to the **Royal Festival Hall,** which comprises three music and dance venues. Come here for symphony concerts, chamber recitals, and dance programs. On Friday evenings, you can enjoy free Commuter Jazz from 5:15 to 6:45pm in the foyer. The box office is open daily from 9am to 9pm. Belvedere Rd., SE1. ℂ 020/7960-4242. www.sbc.org.uk. Tube: Waterloo, Southwark, Embankment (cross over Hungerford Bridge). River services: Festival Pier.

5 The Club & Music Scene

ROCK & POP

London has hundreds of live music venues hosting rock legends, pre-fab boy and girl bands, and the sharpest indie sounds. For big name gigs, you'll need to book well ahead—sometimes several months. The website **www.aloud.com** is an excellent source of advance info, as are the ticket agencies mentioned at the start of this chapter. But contact the box office directly to avoid the booking fee.

The ever-expanding Mean Fiddler Group owns three of London's premier venues: **Astoria** and next door **Mean Fiddler W1,** 157–165 Charing Cross Rd., WC2 (ℂ 020/7434-9592; Tube: Tottenham Court Rd.); and **Forum,** 9–17 Highgate Rd., NW5 (ℂ 020/7344-0044; Tube: Kentish Town). Find out what's on where at www.meanfiddler.com; tickets cost £8 to £20 ($13–$32). Two more venues to keep in mind are **Brixton Academy,** 211 Stockwell Rd., SW9 (ℂ 020/7771-2000; Tube: Brixton); and **Shepherds Bush Empire,** Shepherds Bush Green, W12 (ℂ 020/7771-2000; Tube: Shepherds Bush). Tickets to both are £10 to £25 ($16–$40).

JAZZ

PizzaExpress Jazz Club   Unlikely though it sounds, the basement of this chain restaurant is one of the city's most popular jazz venues. The house band, the PizzaExpress All-Stars, shares the stage with leading traditional and contemporary names. Doors open at 7:45pm, with the first set at 9pm. Also check out the more expensive Pizza on the Park (p. 81). 10 Dean St., W1. ℂ 020/7437-9595. www.pizza express.co.uk. Cover £10–£20 ($16–$32), plus food. Tube: Tottenham Court Rd.

Ronnie Scott's   Since it opened in 1959, London's best-known jazz room has featured all the greats, from Ella Fitzgerald and Dizzy Gillespie to Hugh Masekela and Charlie Watts. Book a week ahead for a Saturday show. On Sunday, an independent promoter puts on contemporary and world music. Ronnie Scott's is open Monday to Saturday 8:30pm to 3am, Sunday 7:30 to 11pm. There's a separate entrance for clubbers to get to Upstairs@Ronnies. On Wednesdays and Sundays, the Ratt Club spins some R&B, soul, and hip hop;

1970s jazz, funk, and soul takes over on Thursday at Starsky & Hutch (no sneakers); on Friday and Saturday, it's Club Latino and the first hour is a salsa lesson. Upstairs opens 10pm to 3am except on Sunday, when it opens 6pm to midnight. 47 Frith St., W1. © 020/ 7439-0747. www.ronniescotts.co.uk. Cover £15–£25 ($24–$40), includes admission to Upstairs@Ronnies, £10 ($16) students Mon–Wed; Upstairs@Ronnies alone £3–£7 ($4.80–$111). Tube: Leicester Sq., Tottenham Court Rd.

DANCE CLUBS & DISCOS

The hot spots change from week to week, so it's crucial to consult *Time Out* for the latest roster. Always check the dress code because many clubs ban sneakers.

GREAT VENUES

Bar Rumba   This club is a classy favorite. It travels through the whole musical spectrum every week—from Latin sounds to cosmic disco house and garage. And get this: Drinks are two-for-one during weeknight happy hour, *and* there's no cover charge, so come before 9pm and you can club it up later for free. On Tuesdays, a night of Latin mayhem starts with a salsa class (6:30–8:30pm). Open Monday to Thursday 5pm to 3:30am, Friday 5pm to 4am, Saturday 7pm to 6am, Sunday 8pm to 1am. 36 Shaftesbury Ave., W1. © 020/7287-2715. www.barrumba.co.uk. Happy hour Mon–Thurs 5–9pm. Cover £3–£12 ($4.80–$19). Tube: Piccadilly Circus.

The End   At this beautifully designed, cutting-edge club, the main sounds are techno, house, garage, and drum 'n' bass. Monday is Trash: dress code is "make an effort," music is anything excessive from 1980s electronica to hi-NRG, cover is a super-cheap £4 ($6), and drinks are cheap too! Be prepared for long lines any night. Open Monday 10pm to 3am, Thursday 7pm to 1am, Friday 11pm to 5am, Saturday 10pm to 6am, and Sunday 8pm to 3am. 18 West Central St., WC1. © 020/7419-9199. www.the-end-co.uk. Cover £4–£15 ($6–$24). Tube: Holborn, Tottenham Court Rd.

Fabric   The 15 Victorian brick arches of this minimalist superclub (capacity 2,500) used to be the old cold-storage area for Smithfield meat market. There are three rooms, various bars, a roof terrace, and chill-out rooms. A hi-tech sound system pumps the beat from some of the city's best house, garage, techno, and drum 'n' bass up through the main dance floor. One grumble: Fabric is notorious for its mile-long lines, both to get in and for the unisex bathrooms. Open Friday 10pm to 5am and Saturday 10pm to 7am. 77a Charterhouse St., EC1.

C 020/7336-8898. www.fabriclondon.com. Cover £12–£15 ($19–$24). Tube: Barbican, Farringdon.

Hanover Grand Here's the scene: A dress-conscious crowd cavorts around a renovated theater to a maelstrom of musical styles. It's the home of youth, glitter, and glam. Wednesday's Fresh 'n' Funky is a great cheap mid-weeker, £5 ($8) to get in before 11pm, then £7 ($11). Open Wednesday and Thursday 10pm to 4am, Friday 11pm to 4am, and Saturday 10:30pm to 4:30am. 6 Hanover St., W1. *C* 020/7499-7977. www.hanovergrand.com. Cover £5–£15 ($8–$24). Tube: Oxford Circus.

Scala This is the smallest of the so-called superclubs (capacity 800) and it is certainly the quirkiest. The shabby old cinema reopened in March 1999 as a live music venue, gallery, sometime film-house, and nightclub. Surf the website because the schedule of DJs, promoters, and special events is very eclectic. It's the gay Popstarz on Fridays. Open Thursday 9pm to 3am, Friday 10pm to 5am, and Saturday 9pm to 5am. 278 Pentonville Rd., N1. *C* 020/7833-2022. www.scala-london.co.uk. Cover £6–£12 ($10–$19). Tube: King's Cross.

CLUB BARS

For every action there is a reaction. And the reaction to superclubs has been the rise of the club bar. These are more intimate spaces, but with live music and specialist DJs. Nights tend to end earlier and the cover charge is much less.

Cargo Cargo is billed as a bar, not a club, but it has the feel of a nightclub in the decades up to the 1950s when venues were smaller and dancing, drinks, and food were part of an evening's entertainment. Cargo has updated that concept. Friday's Barrio, which is Latin house, funk, nu-jazz, and soul, is the only weekly fixture. Otherwise the schedule spans every kind of music style. Cocktails are £5 ($8). That's also the highest price for any nosh on the international street food menu. Cargo is open Monday to Friday from noon to 1am, Saturday 6pm to 1am, and Sunday noon to midnight. Kingsland Viaduct, 83 Rivington St., EC2. *C* 020/7739-3440. www.cargo-london.co.uk. Cover £3–£7 ($4.35–$10.15). Tube: Old St.

Notting Hill Arts Club Come before 8pm (6pm on Sun) and it's free to get in. Come early anyway or you'll have no chance at all of getting in to this cupboard-sized basement bar that hosts a mix of DJ and live music nights. Wednesday night is Deathdisco, a mix of punk, funk, indie, and glam for indie celebs and punk veterans. Bands take the sort-of stage on Saturday too, at RoTa. But the hottest spot on the dial is Sunday's hard dancing at Lazy Dog. NHAC is open Tuesday to Friday 6pm to 1am, Saturday 4pm to 1am, Sunday 4 to 11pm. The "art," by the way, is minimal and doubtful! 21 Notting Hill Gate, W11. ☎ 020/7460-4459. www.nottinghillarts club.com. Cover £5 ($8). Tube: Notting Hill Gate.

6 Gay & Lesbian London

Old Compton Street in Soho is the epicenter of gay London life. But there are plenty of bars and clubs elsewhere. To find out what's going on and where, pick up one of the free newspapers you'll find at most of the places listed below: the *Pink Paper* and *Boyz,* for instance. *QX* magazine is another top guide, and there are gay listings in *Time Out.* Lastly, for purely online help, check out the comprehensive **www.gaytoz.com** or **www.rainbownetwork.com.** Otherwise, the **Lesbian & Gay Switchboard** (☎ 020/7837-7324; www.llgs.org.uk) is a round-the-clock information source on absolutely everything.

   Note: Clubbers should check out the gay bars (see below) for discount flyers and jump-the-queue tickets.

GREAT VENUES

G.A.Y.   This colossal club is less about posing and more about a young unpretentious crowd having fun. The biggest night is strictly gay-only Saturday, when there are always some special surprises—big-name personal appearances, for instance. Five hundred queue-jump tickets go on sale at the Astoria box office from the Monday before, with some available on Saturday afternoon at Ku Bar (see below). G.A.Y. is open Monday 10:30pm to 3am, Thursday 11pm to 4am, Friday 11pm to 4am, and Saturday 10:30pm to 5am. Astoria and Mean Fiddler, 157–165 Charing Cross Rd., WC2. ☎ 0906/100-0160. www. g-a-y.co.uk. Cover £3 ($4.80) or £1 ($1.60) with a flyer, Sat £10 ($16) or £8 ($13) with a flyer. Tube: Tottenham Court Rd.

Heaven   The 2,000-capacity Heaven is London's most famous gay club, though its popularity has drawn a lot of heteros, too. It's like a self-supporting space colony, with three floors of separate bars and dance floors. Big name DJs power up the volume across the full musical spectrum. On a Monday, you'll get cheap drinks, with happy pop, disco trash, and dance downstairs, and indie upstairs. Wednesday is soul and heavy funk, Friday techno and hard house. Saturday is the one strictly gay-only night. Surf the website, and you can print "flyers" to save pounds getting in. Open Monday and Wednesday 10:30pm to 3am, Friday 10:30pm to 6am, and Saturday 10pm to 5am. The Arches, Craven St., WC2. © 020/7930-2020. www.heaven-london.com. Cover £4–£12 ($6–$19), free with a flyer before 11:30pm on Friday and £1–£6 ($1.60–$10) other nights; £1 ($1.60) with printable Web voucher. Tube: Embankment, Charing Cross.

PUBS, BARS & CAFES

Candy Bar Britain's first-ever 7-night lesbian bar has great beer, great cocktails, and great club nights. Gay men are welcome as guests. Open Monday to Thursday noon to 1pm, Friday and Saturday noon to 3am, and Sunday noon to 11pm. 23–24 Bateman St., W1. © 020/7437-1977. Cover Fri–Sat £5 ($8) after 9pm. No credit cards. Tube: Tottenham Court Rd.

Ku Bar Great place to start a night on the town as you'll find lots of discount flyers for clubs at this hip West End bar. You can also buy advance tickets on Saturday afternoon for that night's G.A.Y. (see above). All the beer is bottled, so no cheap pints. But there's another hot seller, schnapps shots. On Sundays, Ku Bar doesn't open until 1pm. 75 Charing Cross Rd., WC2. © 020/7437-4303. Happy hour daily noon–9pm. Tube: Leicester Sq.

Kudos A well-groomed pampered party crowd gather at what many think is the best boys' bar in London. Kudos certainly tries hard, with big video screens downstairs for semi-real music nights, and DJs on Wednesday and Saturday (no cover). It's also a good place to pick up club flyers and advance tickets. 10 Adelaide St., WC2. © 020/7379-4573. Happy hour Mon–Fri 4–6pm, Sat–Sun 6–8pm. Tube: Embankment, Charing Cross.

The Yard This is a friendly spot, attracting a laid-back mixed clientele and a big after-work crowd. There's a blissfully secluded courtyard, behind a set of iron gates, and two bars inside. The Yard opens at noon and is closed on Sundays. 57 Rupert St., W1. © 020/7437-2652. Tube: Piccadilly Circus.

7 The Pub Scene

Cittie of Yorke This soaring high-gabled room must have the longest bar in England. You can still see the huge vats originally used to dispense wine and liquors. All along one wall are private wood-carved cubicles, supposedly designed for lawyers from the dozens of chambers in the neighborhood to meet discreetly with clients. The pub dates from 1430, though it was rebuilt in 1923. 22–23 High Holborn, WC1. ✆ 020/7242-7670. Tube: Chancery Lane, Holborn.

French House   This Soho institution became the center of French life in London during World War II when de Gaulle and his circle gathered here. It still attracts a lot of French-speaking visitors. Beer is only sold in half pints—myths abound but no one really knows why. 49 Dean St., W1. ✆ 020/7437-2799. Tube: Tottenham Court Rd.

Grenadier   This cozy mews pub is always crowded. It was an officers' mess in the Duke of Wellington's time. Come to see the military memorabilia and maybe the resident ghost of a soldier flogged to death for cheating at cards. 18 Wilton Row, SW1. ✆ 020/7235-3074. Tube: Hyde Park Corner.

Jerusalem Tavern   This pub pulls a mean pint, supplied by the St. Peter's Brewery in Suffolk. So it's no surprise that the tiny Georgian-style bar, with its open fire, is always packed and getting more so as Clerkenwell zooms up the list of London's coolest neighborhoods. 55 Britton St., EC1. ✆ 020/7490-4281. Tube: Farringdon.

The Lamb   The etched and hinged glass screens stretching round the bar are called snob screens; they were put in so that customers didn't have to see the bartender. Apparently, they were the cat's pajamas at the turn of the last century when such snobby Victorian attitudes really mattered. 94 Lamb's Conduit St., WC1. ✆ 020/7405-0713. Tube: Oxford Circus.

Lamb & Flag   This old timber-framed pub is in a short cul-de-sac off Garrick Street, Covent Garden. The poet Dryden dubbed it the "Bucket of Blood" after he was almost beaten to death here. The Lamb & Flag can be hard to find, but the friendly atmosphere and list of 30 whiskies are ample reward for the effort. The food is good traditional pub grub, and there's free live jazz from 7:30pm on Sunday evenings. 33 Rose St., WC2. ✆ 020/7497-9504. Tube: Leicester Sq.

Punch Tavern   Charles Dickens and a bunch of his friends founded the satirical magazine *Punch* at this pub next to St. Bride's Church. It's known for its brilliant plush Victorian gin-palace interior and Punch & Judy memorabilia. 99 Fleet St., EC4. ✆ 020/7353-6658. Tube: Blackfriars.

8 Wine Bars

Wine lovers will thank their lucky stars for an alternative to the pub, where belch predominates over bouquet. A bottle of house red or white generally costs £10 to £15 ($16–$24), a great deal to share between two or three people, and most wine bars sell a selection by the glass (from £2.50/$4). You can almost always eat there, too. For great wine lists at more than manageable prices, try: **Bleeding Heart,** Bleeding Heart Yard, off Greville St., EC1 (© **020/7242-8238;** Tube: Chancery Lane, Farringdon); and **Cork & Bottle,** 44–46 Cranbourn St., WC2 (© **020/7734-7807;** Tube: Leicester Sq.).

Index

See also Accommodations, Restaurants, and Afternoon Tea indexes below.

RESTAURANTS

FROMMER'S® COMPLETE TRAVEL GUIDES

Alaska
Alaska Cruises & Ports of Call
Amsterdam
Argentina & Chile
Arizona
Atlanta
Australia
Austria
Bahamas
Barcelona, Madrid & Seville
Beijing
Belgium, Holland & Luxembourg
Bermuda
Boston
Brazil
British Columbia & the Canadian
  Rockies
Brussels & Bruges
Budapest & the Best of Hungary
California
Canada
Cancún, Cozumel & the Yucatán
Cape Cod, Nantucket & Martha's
  Vineyard
Caribbean
Caribbean Cruises & Ports of Call
Caribbean Ports of Call
Carolinas & Georgia
Chicago
China
Colorado
Costa Rica
Cuba
Denmark
Denver, Boulder & Colorado Springs
England
Europe
European Cruises & Ports of Call

Florida
France
Germany
Great Britain
Greece
Greek Islands
Hawaii
Hong Kong
Honolulu, Waikiki & Oahu
Ireland
Israel
Italy
Jamaica
Japan
Las Vegas
London
Los Angeles
Maryland & Delaware
Maui
Mexico
Montana & Wyoming
Montréal & Québec City
Munich & the Bavarian Alps
Nashville & Memphis
New England
New Mexico
New Orleans
New York City
New Zealand
Northern Italy
Norway
Nova Scotia, New Brunswick &
  Prince Edward Island
Oregon
Paris
Peru
Philadelphia & the Amish Country
Portugal

Prague & the Best of the Czech
  Republic
Provence & the Riviera
Puerto Rico
Rome
San Antonio & Austin
San Diego
San Francisco
Santa Fe, Taos & Albuquerque
Scandinavia
Scotland
Seattle & Portland
Shanghai
Sicily
Singapore & Malaysia
South Africa
South America
South Florida
South Pacific
Southeast Asia
Spain
Sweden
Switzerland
Texas
Thailand
Tokyo
Toronto
Tuscany & Umbria
USA
Utah
Vancouver & Victoria
Vermont, New Hampshire & Maine
Vienna & the Danube Valley
Virgin Islands
Virginia
Walt Disney World® & Orlando
Washington, D.C.
Washington State

FROMMER'S® DOLLAR-A-DAY GUIDES

Australia from $50 a Day
California from $70 a Day
England from $75 a Day
Europe from $70 a Day
Florida from $70 a Day
Hawaii from $80 a Day

Ireland from $60 a Day
Italy from $70 a Day
London from $85 a Day
New York from $90 a Day
Paris from $80 a Day

San Francisco from $70 a Day
Washington, D.C. from $80 a Day
Portable London from $85 a Day
Portable New York City from $90
  a Day

FROMMER'S® PORTABLE GUIDES

Acapulco, Ixtapa & Zihuatanejo
Amsterdam
Aruba
Australia's Great Barrier Reef
Bahamas
Berlin
Big Island of Hawaii
Boston
California Wine Country
Cancún
Cayman Islands
Charleston
Chicago
Disneyland®
Dublin
Florence

Frankfurt
Hong Kong
Houston
Las Vegas
Las Vegas for Non-Gamblers
London
Los Angeles
Los Cabos & Baja
Maine Coast
Maui
Miami
Nantucket & Martha's Vineyard
New Orleans
New York City
Paris
Phoenix & Scottsdale

Portland
Puerto Rico
Puerto Vallarta, Manzanillo &
  Guadalajara
Rio de Janeiro
San Diego
San Francisco
Savannah
Seattle
Sydney
Tampa & St. Petersburg
Vancouver
Venice
Virgin Islands
Washington, D.C.

FROMMER'S® NATIONAL PARK GUIDES

Banff & Jasper
Family Vacations in the National
  Parks

Grand Canyon
National Parks of the American West
Rocky Mountain

Yellowstone & Grand Teton
Yosemite & Sequoia/Kings Canyon
Zion & Bryce Canyon

FROMMER'S® MEMORABLE WALKS

Chicago
London

New York
Paris

San Francisco

FROMMER'S® WITH KIDS GUIDES

Chicago
Las Vegas
New York City

Ottawa
San Francisco
Toronto

Vancouver
Washington, D.C.

SUZY GERSHMAN'S BORN TO SHOP GUIDES

Born to Shop: France
Born to Shop: Hong Kong,
 Shanghai & Beijing

Born to Shop: Italy
Born to Shop: London

Born to Shop: New York
Born to Shop: Paris

FROMMER'S® IRREVERENT GUIDES

Amsterdam
Boston
Chicago
Las Vegas
London

Los Angeles
Manhattan
New Orleans
Paris
Rome

San Francisco
Seattle & Portland
Vancouver
Walt Disney World®
Washington, D.C.

FROMMER'S® BEST-LOVED DRIVING TOURS

Britain
California
Florida
France

Germany
Ireland
Italy
New England

Northern Italy
Scotland
Spain
Tuscany & Umbria

HANGING OUT™ GUIDES

Hanging Out in England
Hanging Out in Europe

Hanging Out in France
Hanging Out in Ireland

Hanging Out in Italy
Hanging Out in Spain

THE UNOFFICIAL GUIDES®

Bed & Breakfasts and Country
 Inns in:
 California
 Great Lakes States
 Mid-Atlantic
 New England
 Northwest
 Rockies
 Southeast
 Southwest
Best RV & Tent Campgrounds in:
 California & the West
 Florida & the Southeast
 Great Lakes States
 Mid-Atlantic
 Northeast
 Northwest & Central Plains

Southwest & South Central
 Plains
 U.S.A.
Beyond Disney
Branson, Missouri
California with Kids
Central Italy
Chicago
Cruises
Disneyland®
Florida with Kids
Golf Vacations in the Eastern U.S.
Great Smoky & Blue Ridge Region
Inside Disney
Hawaii
Las Vegas
London
Maui

Mexio's Best Beach Resorts
Mid-Atlantic with Kids
Mini Las Vegas
Mini-Mickey
New England & New York with
 Kids
New Orleans
New York City
Paris
San Francisco
Skiing & Snowboarding in the West
Southeast with Kids
Walt Disney World®
Walt Disney World® for
 Grown-ups
Walt Disney World® with Kids
Washington, D.C.
World's Best Diving Vacations

SPECIAL-INTEREST TITLES

Frommer's Adventure Guide to Australia &
 New Zealand
Frommer's Adventure Guide to Central America
Frommer's Adventure Guide to India & Pakistan
Frommer's Adventure Guide to South America
Frommer's Adventure Guide to Southeast Asia
Frommer's Adventure Guide to Southern Africa
Frommer's Britain's Best Bed & Breakfasts and
 Country Inns
Frommer's Caribbean Hideaways
Frommer's Exploring America by RV
Frommer's Fly Safe, Fly Smart

Frommer's France's Best Bed & Breakfasts and
 Country Inns
Frommer's Gay & Lesbian Europe
Frommer's Italy's Best Bed & Breakfasts and
 Country Inns
Frommer's Road Atlas Britain
Frommer's Road Atlas Europe
Frommer's Road Atlas France
The New York Times' Guide to Unforgettable
 Weekends
Places Rated Almanac
Retirement Places Rated
Rome Past & Present

Lastminute.com

Booked aisle seat.

Internet Cafe

Reserved room with a view.

With a queen – no, make that a king-size bed.

With Travelocity, you can book your flights and hotels together, so you can get even better deals than if you booked them separately. You'll save time and money without compromising the quality of your trip. Choose your airline seat, search for alternate airports, pick your hotel room type, even choose the neighborhood you'd like to stay in.

Travelocity

Visit www.travelocity.com or call 1-888-TRAVELOCITY